Days Of Our Lives

Hinguar and Shoeburyness High School 1898-2001

Mary Bright

I dedicate this book to Sue Murphy, (1955-2009) an inspirational and much loved Head Teacher of Shoeburyness High School

and

to all our scholars, pupils and students, the children of Shoebury, past and present.

These are the days of our lives

Sometimes I get to feeling
I was back in the old days – long ago
When we were kids, when we were young
Things seemed so perfect – you know?
The days were endless, we were crazy – we were young
The sun was always shining – we just lived for fun
Sometimes it seems like likely – I just don't know
The rest of my life's been – just a show.
Those were the days of our lives
The bad things in life were so few
Those days are all gone now but one thing is true –
When I look and I find I still love you.
QUEEN

I trust some effort may be made to give the Shoeburyness children an equal chance with those in other parts of the country. In eagerness and ability they are unmatched but they demand one who can control them.
Nicholas Hillyer 1921

Acknowledgements

I would like to thank all the people who have given their time, expertise, knowledge and support. It very much reflects the community spirit that this book depicts and without their help it would have been impossible to complete.

✎

In particular I would like to thank Lee Pankhurst and Russell Bradshaw who rescued the book at its darkest hour. Phil Stibbards, Henry Mercer, Sheila Askew and Sue Robinson all offered their support and generously lent me many resources. Tony Hill, Tom King and Judith Williams have advised me and again generously allowed me to use photographs from their own publications.

✎

Ken Crowe and his staff at Southend Museum have offered resources which have been invaluable in the preparation of this book.

✎

Andy Pay and Martin Edwards have provided an excellent Roll of Honour web-site, based on the men from Great Wakering who fought in the First World War.

✎

Andrew Cook offered additional information and sources linked to Viking influences on Shoeburynesss.

✎

The following people gave freely of their time so that the section on the evacuation of children 1940 could be completed: Maureen Andrews, Marian Whiting (nee Osborne), Edward Osborne, Alf Hallums, Don Pacey, June and Pamela Edmunds and Ruth Dawson.

✎

Poppy Byford provided excellent materials from Shoeburyness High School archives.

✎

If I have inadvertently failed to acknowledge any written or photographic sources I apologise for any unintentional omissions.

Proceeds from this book will be donated to the Cardiomyopathy Association in memory of my son Stuart Bright. He was a former pupil of Hinguar Primary School and Shoeburyness High School. Every week in the UK at least 12 young people die suddenly from undiagnosed hereditary heart disease. The Cardiomyopathy Association supports families and medical research into these conditions.

First published 2010

© Mary Bright, 2010

Published by Harknett Heritage Publishing.

The right of Mary Bright to be identified as the Author
of this work has been asserted in accordance with the
Copyrights, Designs and Patents Act 1988.

British Library Cataloguing in Publication Data.

A catalogue record for this book is available from the British Library.

ISBN 978-0-9566589-0-6

Typesetting and origination by Lee Pankhurst
Printed in England by DB Print & Design Ltd, Southend, Essex

Days Of Our Lives

Hinguar and
Shoeburyness High School
1898-2001

Mary Bright

Contents

Hinguar Primary School and Shoeburyness High School 1898-2001

This is a record based on the log books of these two schools. It begins with Hinguar in 1898 during the last 4 years of the Head teacher's forty year career. During this time the school leaving age rose from ten to twelve, although boys continued to work in the local brick fields during the summer months. Attendance showed that a fifth of all pupils were absent throughout the country and Hinguar was no exception. There were frequent holidays for Garrison events, regattas and Sunday school outings. The end of the Boer War is celebrated.

A common theme unites all Head teachers, they write about their struggles with class size, difficult governors, staffing problems, the health of the children, discipline and the curriculum. They also celebrate national events, monarchs, Empire Day and World Wars. The impact on the community is clearly shown, whether its Zeppelin raids and bombing in 1917 or building shelters, fitting gas masks and more bombing in 1942. Advances in education and health care that began before 1914 clearly falter in the devastation following the war.

Boys and girls are treated very differently and the curriculum makes no attempt to offer equality. Slowly courses are offered that encourage children to stay on an extra year and the first type writer is acquired in the 1930s after a difficult struggle with the LEA. In 1938 the pupils from Hinguar move to Shoeburyness High School carrying boxes and furniture in wheel

barrows. A year later the Second World War forces school closure and evacuation until 1942. The experiences, good and bad are recorded by past pupils.

During the 1950's the school reflects post-war conditions, the area is flooded in 1953, but is able to celebrate the Coronation and ascent of Everest. By the 60s boys are recording the loss of fields where they previously ran wild and Winston Churchill's death symbolises the end of an era.

During the 1970s, the school records that national industrial unrest is reflected by pupil strikes, Margaret Thatcher is elected and girls are allowed to wear trousers for the first time. Industrial unrest increases in the 80s, the school receives training about HIV/Aids, and there is a hurricane and the introduction of computers.

In 1991 during the First Gulf War the Head teacher is surprised that a trip to a London museum is cancelled as "I cannot imagine that a museum full of children would be a target for terrorists". Thinking the unthinkable had not yet become common place. Vandalism and break-ins

frustrate the school community, the funeral of Lady Diana takes place and the school achieves technology college status.

The school in 1900 shows an England that is aware of its place in the world, a local

community that celebrates a common heritage and culture and that despite hardships and a defined class structure has a sense of what it is to English. The century that follows unravels such certainties, until the school community sometimes seems to define the only thread to the past and the future.

Mary Bright.

Education in the Nineteenth and early Twentieth Centuries

As I write this history about Hinguar Primary School and Shoeburyness High School, it is difficult to remember that universal education was a new concept at the start of the records and that children, parents and teachers were pioneers. Statistics show that although 7000 voluntary schools were established by the 1860s, half the children of Britain did not attend day school and those that did had to pay. The Education Act of 1870 established the election of school boards with the power to build and manage schools and to replace inadequate voluntary schools.

In Hinguar's case, the school, which was established by Dale Knapping continued as a Church of England National School until 1903 when the school reopened as a board school. Following the 1870 Act all schools were subject to government inspection to ensure adequate standards. Although there was greater access to education, many children continued to work, so in 1880 education became compulsory with the school leaving age set at ten. In 1893 the leaving age was raised to eleven and in 1899 to twelve, except for those employed in agriculture. Sir John Gorst informed Parliament in the mid 1890s that although a quarter of a century had passed since the 1870 Act, nearly three quarters of a million children did not attend elementary school. Of the children who did attend, nearly a fifth were continually absent. In 1897 the national average attendance was 81.5% and this statistic is reflected by attendance at Hinguar Street. Many children, both boys and girls were working, but the frequent holidays recorded by Mr Cox also contributed to absence.

In 1891 the government abolished fee-paying in all voluntary and board schools. The Free Schooling Act gave parents the right to free elementary education for their children. The government gave a grant of not more than 10/- for each pupil and these grants are shown by Mr Hillyer in the Log Book.

Throughout the Nineteenth Century elementary education was dominated by pupil teachers. A pupil teacher could begin training at the age of thirteen, was taught by the Head before school and then taught the children during school. The minimum age for a pupil teacher was not raised to fourteen until 1877 and the system continued into the Twentieth Century. Most Head Teachers were ex-pupil teachers who had secured a certificate through part-time study. Few adult assistant teachers or Heads were college trained and Mr Hillyer recorded those teachers who were certificated and those who had remained unqualified by a C or U in his staff lists.

In 1902 the responsibility for providing elementary, secondary and technical education was given to 330 local education authorities under a central Board of Education. The Elementary School Code 1904 provided for council rather than board schools. In 1906 the LEAs began the system of school dinners and in 1907 set up a school medical service. Mr Hillyer mentions the dental clinics set up in Hinguar, the school nurse and doctor and inoculations. The First World War severely affected progress at Hinguar as the two masters joined up.

Entry by Mr Hillier:

In Nov. 1915 two men teachers left for the Army and one Mistress was appointed to the vacancies, since that date the school has never been fully staffed. It is questionable whether the parents of scholars of any school in any part of the County would have quietly submitted to such neglect of their children.

Five cert. teachers are required and so far one only is promised & he has scarcely any experience. Miss Howard leaves us in August.

I feel the added strain is severely injuring my health and that of the competent staff for these latter share the extra work. Today I had no teacher for 3 classes and a fourth I had to maintain contact with — making 221 in all.

Everything has been done to maintain the tone of the school by means of sports &c but there is a limit to human ~~endurance~~ endeavour.

The teachers sent by the County are practically worthless & I trust some effort may be made to give the Shoeburyness chn. an equal chance with those in other parts of the Country. In eagerness & ability they are unmatchable but they demand one who can control them.

There was bomb damage and a shortage of competent staff. Class numbers rose and the impact on health, living conditions and education was felt for a long time. The Second World War meant that all schools in Shoeburyness closed abruptly shortly after secondary education was established in 1938. Shoeburyness High School became part of the country's civil defence efforts, an emergency centre and temporary mortuary in the event of invasion and remained closed until 1942. The 1944 Education Act established a three tier system of secondary education: grammar, technical and secondary modern. The school leaving age was raised to fifteen in 1947 and sixteen in 1965.

Most of the text in this history is taken verbatim from the School Log Books. It begins with Hinguar in 1898 during the last 4 years of the Head teacher's forty year career.

Entry by Mr Cox:

1

1898

Shoeburyness C. E. School.

Aug. 29. Re-opened School after Summer Holiday.

Aug. 31. Holiday in the afternoon. Garden Fête at the Rectory.

Sept 5th Southend Regatta - Attendance thin P.M. Began Drawal Fr. with St. VI.

Sep 14 Shoebury Fête - Holiday in Afternoon

" 21 Garrison Sports in Afternoon. Attendance thin.

Sep. 30 Holiday in Afternoon that the Room may be prepared for a Harvest Thanksgiving Service in the Evening.

Oct. 3rd Several children who have been away in Kent hop-picking returned to School.

" 10 Gave the Attendance Officer the names of several very irregular children to inquire about and look up -

Each head teacher kept a written account in the log book and these records are dated and take the form of a school diary. They were open to inspection by the school managers or governors, as these became, and to school inspectors.

For such official records however, they are surprisingly personal. As each Head teacher takes up his post, (during this period they were all men) as they commit their thoughts to paper, their personality, hopes and frustrations are illuminated. Perhaps the most fascinating aspect of the entries is that they reflect the small everyday events, thoughts and the accepted norms of each era.

Common theme unites all Head teachers, they write about their struggles with class sizes, difficult governors, staffing problems, teachers who can't control their classes, the health of the children, discipline, the curriculum, academic successes and failures.

They also celebrate national events, monarchs, Empire Day and life in Shoeburyness. The impact on the community of the two World Wars is clearly recorded, whether its Zeppelin raids and bombing in 1917 or building shelters, fitting gas masks and more bombing in 1942.

Entry by Mr Dale:

Boys and girls were treated very differently and the curriculum makes no attempt to offer equality. Slowly courses were offered that encouraged children to stay on an extra year and the first typewriter was acquired in the 1930s after a difficult struggle with the LEA.

In 1938 the pupils from Hinguar moved to Shoeburyness High School carrying boxes and furniture in wheel barrows. A year later the Second World War forces school closure and evacuation until 1942.

Entry by Mr Poutney:

During the 1950's the school reflected post-war conditions and slowly recovered from another period when education had been severely disjointed. Although parts of

Shoeburyness and surrounding areas were severely flooded in 1953, the Coronation and ascent of Everest raised spirits.

Entry by Mr Mills:

The attendance reached the low level of 400 owing not only to the severity of the weather and influenza epidemic but also to the floods which struck this part of the coast over the weekend. Foulness and Canvey Islands were flooded. Canvey was evacuated but contact with Foulness was not made until this morning by the Southend lifeboat. Floods reached up to the Cambridge Hotel area and also to Greenways in Lifstan Way – Southchurch Park being inundated last night. Boats were being used for deliveries along Shaftesbury Avenue.

By the 1960s boys are recording the loss of fields where they previously ran wild and Winston Churchill's death symbolises the end of an era.

The school records that in the next decade national industrial unrest is reflected by pupil strikes, triggered by the loss of Christmas shopping days, Margaret Thatcher is elected and girls allowed to wear trousers for the first time.

Entry by Mr Shaw:

Fri 3 Oct	Received petition from 5th form girls re wearing trousers.
Fri 10 Oct	Fire Drill 11.50 am
Wed 15 Oct	Mr. Shuttcliff HMI visited the school.
Fri 24 Oct	School closed for half term
Mon 3 Nov	School reopened. 5th form girls now may wear trousers until Easter. 2.60

Industrial unrest increased in the 80s, the school received training about HIV/Aids, there is a hurricane and the introduction of computers.

Entry by Mr Arkell:

16/11/87. Hurricane Conditions occurred! School lost half the swimming pool Roof. Much destruction caused by the 100.2 mph winds i local area although school (except for swimming Pool) only marginally affected. Only 100 pupils turned up. School closed at lunchtime.

In 1991 during the First Gulf War the Head teacher was surprised that terrorists might target children, 'thinking the unthinkable', was just becoming part of the culture. Vandalism and break-ins frustrate the school community, the funeral of Lady Diana took place and the school achieved technology college status.

Entries by Mr Gardiner:

25 The war in the Gulf caused 2 or 3 parents to wonder about the Year 7 visit to the Science Museum. We telephoned and Museum staff explained the checks they make. I cannot imagine that a museum full of children would be a target for terrorists.

Received a telephone call from the DfEE that our Technology College Initiative bid had been successful. However, I was told that I should tell no-one until it had been made public on Tuesday 15th June

The school in 1900 shows an England that was aware of its place in the world, a local community that celebrates a common heritage and culture and that despite hardships and a defined class structure has a sense of its Engilsh identity. The century that follows unravels such certainties, until the school community sometimes seems to define the only thread to the past and the future.

I have kept the format, dates, abbreviations, spelling and terms exactly as written by the head teachers in the school log books. Occasionally spelling is incorrect but I have reflected individual styles as a true record of the individuals who wrote about their experiences. Although so much has changed, the continuity of the educational struggle has not been broken.

Just as the smell of school is vivid and immediate when you return, so are the words recorded here.

Head Teachers and School Names

WILLIAM COX (1898 – May 28th 1903)

1898　　　　　　　　The school is listed as Shoeburyness C.E. School (Church of England).

NICHOLAS HILLYER (1903 – 1929)

1903　　　　　　　　Senior South Shoebury School Board.

May 1904　　　　　　The Junior and Senior Departments of the school were amalgamated as the Hinguar Street Mixed School.

November 1922　　　The school is named by H.M.I as Shoeburyness Council School.

1923　　　　　　　　Hinguar Street Council School, Shoeburyness Mixed Department.

1927　　　　　　　　Shoeburyness Hinguar St. Senior School

MR S. TILSON　(April 8th 1929 to August 31st 1931)

FRANK CYRIL DALE　(Nov 2nd 1931 – August 30th 1943)

May 19th 1939　　　School cupboards removed to Caulfield Road today.

May 26th 1939　　　Pupils and Staff walked to the new buildings in Caulfield Rd. during the latter portion of the afternoon.

Sept　5th 1939　　　School occupied by A.R.P. casualty post. School work carried on in houses lent by parents.

Dec. 31st 1939　　　R.E. Strong and R. Hogsflesh transferred to Hinguar St. as the Seniors living near Hinguar St. will be permitted to attend there.

May 28th 1940　　　The Head Master attended a meeting at the Education Office yesterday at 4.30 P.M. in connection with evacuation preparations.

May 31st　1940　　　Log Book, Admission Book and Summary Book taken to Southend Education Office. Registers of Classes to go with Party. (School to be evacuated).

R.F. POUNTNEY (August 31st 1943 to July 26th 1946)

R.W.J. NAPIER (Sept 10th 1946 to 31st May 1954)

E.FRANCIS MILLS (1954 to July 1973)

HAROLD F. SHAW B.Sc (Sept 1st 1973 to 31st August 1983)

KEVIN ARKELL (January 1st 1984 to July 19th 1990)

June 16th 1986   Public Meeting – Drama Hall over 300 parents attended with County Councillors and pressed for:
- A fully comprehensive system
- Retention of the Sixth Form.

Considerable debate within Southend since two of options would mean the closing of at least two of the existing Grammar Schools. All but six of my staff voted in favour of a fully comprehensive 11-18 school.

March 13th 1988   Architects in school to discuss sighting of 2 temporary mobile classrooms. Everyone still positive for permanent accommodation including new Sports Hall!

JKW GARDINER (January 1st 1991 to 31st August 2001)

Dec 15th 1994   The recommendation that Southend becomes a Unitary Authority was announced.

April 2nd 1996   Informed that the National Lottery bid for Sports Hall funding has been successful: £648,680 the highest award made in Essex to date.

June 11th 1999   Received a telephone call from DFEE that our Technology College Initiative bid had been successful.

National School 1862

William Cox (Master) and Mrs Eleanor Cox (Mistress) – 175 children

Mr William Cox

1898 – May 28th 1903 Shoeburyness C.E. School (Church of England)

This part of the School's history covers the last four years of the first school master's career. Also ending was the Victorian era, which had embraced Empire, industry and trade.

Mr William Cox had been appointed as Head Teacher of the Church School referred to as Ingard Street National School, in the Kelly's Directory of 1901. (See Appendix 1, page 282).

It was established by Dale Knapping, the last Lord of the Manor and originally it offered some education to the children of the workers in his brickfields – although it was understood that the older boys would work in the brickfields during the summer months. Every building in Shoeburyness from this era used his stock bricks and there were hundreds of barges taking bricks up the Thames to London (see Appendix 2, page 284).

The barge is the Cheshire, capacity 38-44 thousand bricks. The skipper was Alf Harknett, my uncle (pictured on the right). Eastwood's Brick Makers took over the Shoebury brickworks previously belonging to J.Jackson around 1850 – 1860. This was by the beach and known as Shore Field and at its peak produced 14 -15 million bricks a year. The other brickfield was further inland and called Model Field. Forty seven Eastwood skippers are listed pre 1912, taking bricks up river to London and across the Thames to Kent. Skippers aimed to make each leg of the journey count by loading other cargoes, my Granddad told the family he had orchards in Kent! When King George V visited Southend in 1921, the skippers provided the public with views from their barges.

Shoebury beach showing brickworks, barges and Mr Cundy's boathouse.

It was the purchase of land for a firing range in 1849 which led to the garrison being built over the next two decades. Before this development and the opening of Dale Knapping's Brickfield Shoeburyness was entirely rural, without even a village. The following population figures illustrate this.

Campfield Road, Shoeburyness.

Population of South Shoebury	
1801	101
1851	158
1881	1274
1891	1986
1901	2990

North Shoebury in contrast, continued as a distinctly agricultural community as the following statistics show:

North Shoebury Population in 1801: 202.

North Shoebury Population in 1901: 205.

The name of the school is particularly interesting as it links to the Saxon Viking warfare for dominance of this part of the coast (see Appendix 3, page 286).

Milton Hall Brickworks c. 19th.

Shoebury's first school built in 1862.

Sadly we do not have the first School Log Book which would have recorded the opening of the School in 1862 and the introduction of compulsory elementary education in 1870.

Once elementary education was introduced (1870) most children stayed on to Standard 5 - to about ten and a half years of age.

The school at this time seemed to be a family affair as it employed both Mr and Mrs Cox but also two teachers who may have been their daughters.

Anyone familiar with school life will recognise that the recorded issues, struggles, trials and triumphs have changed very little.

The past is palpably present in this record.

Shoeburyness C.E. School (Church of England).

1898

Aug 29th	Re-opened school after Summer Holiday.
Aug 31st	Holiday in the afternoon. Garden Fete at the Rectory.
Sept 5th	Southend Regatta. Attendance this p.m.
Sept 14th	Shoebury Fete – Holiday in Afternoon
Sept 21st	Garrison Sports in Afternoon, attended there.
Sept 30th	Holiday in Afternoon that the room may be prepared for a Harvest Thanksgiving Service in the evening.
Oct 3rd	Several children who have been away in Kent hop-picking returned to school.
Oct 10th	Gave the attendance Officer the names of several very irregular children to enquire about and look up.
Nov14th	Mr Millbank (Attendance Officer) reported that Minnie and Arthur Wood had been sent by the Guardian to the Workhouse at Rochford –
Dec 2nd	Saw Mrs Harp about her daughter Annie who is staying at Leigh with her aunt who is very ill –
Dec 16th	Holiday P.M. I had to attend a Meeting of the Union Assessment Committee at Southend.

1899

Feb. 9th	Holiday – I had to attend the Audit of the Overseers' Accounts at Rochford.
Feb. 13th	Moved all the children that I possibly could with any chance of success to Senior division of Standard 111 from Standard 11.
Feb 20th	Mr. Pricter called to say that Ruby was going to a Ladies School in Southend.
Feb 27th	Mrs Cook saw me and told me that Bertha would leave school as she was required at home to assist in the home and shop. She is at present unwell and I kept her name on the register thinking it possible she might come for a few weeks longer.
April 21st	Work for Summer begun in the Brickfields – Senior boys will be working half time and those who are qualified Full time.

Report of the Inspector of Schools for week ended May 31st 1899

Good progress has been made in the instruction and the tone and order continues to be very good. The elementary work of the higher standards indicates careful and successful teaching, with a marked advance in Arithmetic: in the second and part of the third standard this subject is not yet strong, and the Reading lacks clearness and fluency: - Both girls and boys answer well in Geography and fairly well in Grammar: a good beginning has also been made with singing from note – Drawing and Needlework are well taught.

Staff		
	William Cox	Cert Teacher 1st - C
	Eleanor Cox	Cert Teacher 1st - C
	L.J. Beaty	Asst – Cert 50
	E.M. Cox	P.T. 10 4th Year. Extd.
	L.M. Cox	P.T. 4th Year Extd.
	E.M. Causton	M.A. Rector

July 4th	Holiday – I went for a trip on the water to the Barge Match of Messer Eastwood Thames Barges.
July 19th	Attendance thin today. Excursion of Sons of Phoenix Lodge to Earls Court Exhibition- Prittlewell Fete today –
July 20th	Salvation Army Excursion to Hadleigh Farm Colony. Several cases of measles have occurred and some children are away on that account.
July 21st	Very small attendance – Some children are away owing to measles in the house, and others have gone to Barnum's Show at Southend with friends or relations.

Barnum's Circus 1901, probably on its way to perform in the recently opened Kursaal, making its way down Southend High Street, with Thomas Dowsett's shop on the right, on the corner of Alexander Street.

Oct. 14th	Mr Garnham saw me about his boy: He has a situation at Mr Cockburn's offered him, and thinks it will be a good opening for the lad.
Oct 27th	Miss Beaty left this day:- I am advertising for another Assistant each week, but have not yet received a reply of any kind.
Nov. 14th	Attendance thin this P.M. – A good number of packages and some loose nuts washed up on shore from a wrecked vessel, and the children were picking them up.

Salvage from wrecked boats in the Thames was a regular feature of the 19th and early 20th Centuries, ship shown at Shoeburyness.

Dec 14th	Miss J. M. Hawke, Asst. under Cert.50 late Asst. at St. Andrews C.E. School Romford, Commenced duties here.
Dec 15th	Eva M. Cox P.T. has been away this week attending the Scholarship Exam at Colchester.

1900

Jan 12th	Attendance this week has not been good: Bad colds are very prevalent both among parents and children – the Reverend E. A. Causton called this afternoon.
March 13th	Attendance Officer reported that Daisy Mortlock has very bad eyes and unable to attend School.
March 26th	Received Dr. Cert. to say that Daisy Mortlock's eyes would not be well enough to attend School for another week.
April 5th	A huge storm at Dinner Time – Very wet at School time P.M. Attendance thin.
April 11th	Attendance Officer reported on Joseph Bamish. He is assisting his father in the business as he is a man short.
April 26th	Mrs. Amos called about her boy Arthur, who is a very delicate lad, and is ill again.
April 30th	Attendance Officer reported on James Barnett: He is assisting his father in his business as he is a man short.
May 4th	Enquired about A. Standing. She is required at home to do the work of the house as her mother is obliged to assist her husband in the Brickfield as he is unable to get a barrow-loader.
May 14th	Asked the Attendance Officer to enquire about V. Benson, a big boy and considerable help to his father.
May 21st	Attendance Officer reports that Mr Benson proposes to keep his son at home as he cannot do very well without his help.
May 24th	Holiday – Tea for the children. Queen's Birthday.
May 28th	Holiday P.M. Took the children to the Common in the Afternoon to give them some races it being wet on the 24th.
May 30th	Holiday in afternoon – I had to attend the Archdeacon's Visitation at Southend as Churchwarden.
July 11th	Wesleyan Chapel Choir Excursion to Crystal Palace; Attendance not good in consequence.
July 25th	Closed School for the Summer Holidays – to August 25th.
August 29th	Holiday in afternoon – Sunday School Treat at Rectory.
Sept. 5th	Attendance thin P.M. – Presbyterian Sunday School Tea Party and Treat in Mr Clark's Meadow.

1901

Jan 11th   The weather has been very wintry this week and the attendance has been very poor.

Congregational Band of Hope outing c.1911 Great Wakering.

Queen Victoria died on the 22nd January 1901. This shows 'Buffs' walking along Prittlewell Avenue on their way to a service at St. Mary's Church following wreath laying at the statue of Queen Victoria.

July 26th	Closed School at Dinner Time for the Summer Holiday – One Month.
Aug. 26th	Commenced School after Summer Holiday. Attendance as good as I expected. A few have gone into Kent for hop picking, and some are away – A few have left Shoebury.
Aug 28th	Holiday – Shoeburyness Fete.
Aug 29th	Holiday P.M. Children's Afternoon in Fete Field.
Oct 12th	Took E. Tattershall's name of the Register. She is unwell and very nervous and the Dr has recommended complete rest from school for a time.
Nov. 18th	Mrs Harknett called to say that her little girl was very unwell, and the Doctor had ordered her to be kept from school – she is a very nervous excitable child and has a tendency to St Vitas Dance.
Nov 27th	Attendance Officer reported several cases where children have been away for a long time – Jos. Pizzey Bad Hands – Mary Wildish and F. Hubbard bad heads. And A.M. Mc Gregor Bad Hand.

1902

Feb 7th	The attendance this week has been poor. A good number of children have bad colds and sore throats.
Feb 14th	Holiday P.M. The two Assistants wanted to get away for a Little Change (for a week end). Closed School at Dinner Time. Attendance very poor this week.
April 7th	Re-opened School after Easter Holiday – Brick making has commenced, and a good number of boys are working halftime.
May 2nd	A short shower just at School Time P.M. Attendance poor.
May 2nd	Mabel (Eva) Harknett returned to school having been ill for nearly 6 months.
May 31st	Close of School Year.

Report for Year ended May 31st 1902   Dated July 8th 1902

The tone and order in this School continue to be thoroughly good; the supervision and teaching of the upper school division are able and well directed; the younger scholars are taught with conscientious care and much success. The instruction in elementary subjects – Recitation and Geography is uniformly good, the Singing and Needlework are very good.

Some of the oral answering in English and History requires to be further strengthened, but generally there is evidence of careful sustained work.

....H.M. Inspector reports that less than one hour's Physical Training per week has been given. I am to request attention to Paragraph 3 of Schedule 111 of the Code which must be carefully complied with in future..

Staff

William Cox- Cert: Head Teacher

Eleanor Cox – Cert Mistress

Eva M. Cox – Assistant Cert . 50

Linda M. Cox – Asst. Cert. 50

June 2nd	Took over children from Junior Mixed School.
June 2nd	Closed School at 3P.M. Peace Proclaimed – Cancelled Attendance. (End of the Boer War).
June 3rd	Commenced new work in all the Standards.
June 23 – 27th	Holiday – Proposed Coronation Week. Children had tea in Camp Field on the 26th.
July 25th	Attendance not good this week: there have been three Sunday School Treats -22. 23. 24 .

Royal Terrace Southend celebrating Mafeking Relief Day, May 18th 1900.

July 31st	Closed School to Summer Holiday to Sept. 1st.
Sept 10th	Holiday P.M. – Tea and Sports to finish up the Coronation Festivities and Funds –
Sept 12th	No School in afternoon. I had to attend the Revising Barrister's Court.
Sept 18th	Holiday in Afternoon for School Sports as it turned out wet on the 10th and Sports were not finished –
Oct 6th	Began fractions with Standard V.
Nov 10th	Began Simple Proportions with Std. V.

Received Notice of Voluntary Aid Grant. £25

For painting and colouring inside £10

For Maps £3

For Geography and History Reading Books £12

Dec 5th	A very cold snowy and wintry morning: Attendance thin
Dec 16th	The two Assistants are away from School attending the Scholarship Exam.
Dec 19th	Closed school at Dinner Time for the Christmas Holiday –

1903

Jan 13th	A cold snowy morning – very wintry, attendance thin.
Jan 17th	Several children away with bad colds –
Jan 23rd	Some cases of Influenza among the children – several have been visited by the Attendance Officer.
Feb 7th	Linda M. Cox Pupil Teacher, away from school, unwell.
Feb12	Mr Petty called to say his boy Harry has St. Vitas Dance and the Dr has ordered him to be away from school and run about as much as possible in the open air. He has suffered in the same way before and will probably be away for some time.
Feb 27th	Holiday in Afternoon – I had to attend at Rochford with the Parish accounts for Audit
Mar 1st	Very wet at Dinner Time. Attendance thin P.M.
Mar 13th	Attendance among girls in Std. V very poor indeed - have asked Attendance Officer to look them up particularly Edward Wildish.
March 13th	Attendance amongst girls in School very poor. Have asked Attendance Officer to look them up particularly -.
April 6th	Brick making commenced. Several boys who are qualified for full time employment have left: others will now be Half Timers.

May 6th	Holiday in Afternoon – Being Churchwarden I had to attend the Archdeacon's Visitation in Southend.
May 8th	Very wet at Dinner Time. Attendance bad P.M.
May 22nd	Holiday in Afternoon.
May 27th	Examination in Religious Knowledge –
May 28th	Closed School for Whitsun Holidays.
	Mrs Cox and myself retire from School today.

H.M.I. Report 1902 -1903

Average Attendance	Boys	Girls	Total
1902-3	70.12	92.59	162.71

The order and tone in this School are particularly good, and the teaching is conscientious and successful. The elementary subjects receive special attention. Arithmetic is well taught, and the written exercises are neat & accurate. Good use is made of the reading books in giving class lessons, and the answering is bright in general. Needlework continues to be well taught.

Mr & Mrs Cox are retiring after 40 years diligent and conscientious service in this school. They leave it in an efficient state and carry with them the respect of the Managers and the love and esteem of the scholars.

Mary Barren recalls her father's experience of Mr Cox and the Board School:

My Father went to the Board School which had been opened by Dale Knapping the Lord of the Manor and which is now St. Peter's Church. It was one big room, with the two sisters and Mr Cox, sitting on a high desk with the older boys and girls at one end. They paid a penny a week. The teaching was Parrot Fashion. My father was six when he first went & got the cane the first day. The teacher said Verbs are part of speech. She asked him to repeat what she had said & Dad said – because it didn't makes any sense to him anyhow & he hadn't heard properly verbs are hearts of speech. He got the cane for insolence the first day.

Nicholas Hillyer 1903 -1929

Senior School South Shoebury School Board

Nicholas Hillyer was appointed Head Teacher of the Senior South Shoebury School Board in 1903. In May 1904 the Junior and Senior Departments of the school were amalgamated as the Hinguar Street Mixed School. Mr Hillyer had vision and was ambitious for the pupils and the school but he found the standards when he arrived a considerable challenge.

"The written work of the children is neatly done, but the children are greatly lacking in intelligence".

He embarked on a new curriculum and scholarships, offered trips to London and established sporting activities together with swimming and cookery lessons for girls.

Staff often failed to keep control and he chronicles this, together with their need to seek his permission to leave their lodgings in Shoeburyness to return to their homes during the school week. Class sizes however, remained huge, parents at times threatening and the buildings inadequate. During the winter months there were epidemics of measles, mumps and diphtheria and one pupil died from "spotted fever". Nevertheless, great strides were being taken to improve health and the doctor was a regular visitor to the school, dental surgeries were held there together with the inoculation of 'Army children'.

The close knit community celebrated Empire Day every year; the school closed for a week in June 1911 for the Coronation of George V and raised £3. 18.6d for the Titanic Disaster fund in 1912. Mr Hillyer recorded the effect of the First World War on the school with ongoing staff and fuel shortages. He lost his two male staff when they both join up in the same week. In order to help wounded soldiers he took a course on "Remedial Gymnastics" and he also recorded how he visited his wounded son in a London hospital. There was ongoing rivalry between Hinguar and the Garrison school and clashes with Garrison staff about the use of choir boys for war time funerals. He refused the transfer of boys from his school to the Garrison School, perhaps preventing the recruitment of two boy soldiers. Another closely recorded theme is the long term struggle with Miss Banning a school manager.

In 1917 there were frequent bombing raids on Shoebury and Mr Hillyer records that the children "were perfectly quiet and unalarmed".

Conditions after the War were harsh and earlier gains in social improvements were set back but Mr Hillyer continued his educational plans introducing a "Special Class" for children which with voluntary agreement with parents extended education to the age of 14 and gave opportunities to children for individual research which was far in advance of educational practice at that time.

Mr Hillyer retired in 1929. He was unremitting in his efforts to improve his school and the lot of the children. In 1921 he wrote, "I trust some effort may be made to give the Shoeburyness children an equal chance with those in other parts of the country. In eagerness and ability they are unmatched but they demand one who can control them". Nicholas Hillyer made an extraordinary impact on the school. To my parents, and their generation he was a legend that they compared all other teachers to. He was never forgotten by his community.

1903

June 8th   This school, now under the authority of the South Shoebury School Board, was opened this morning by the following staff.

Head Master   Nicholas Hillyer, trained Certificate Master

Assistant Mistress   Mary Cox Certificate 50 born 12/8/1879

Assistant Mistress   Linda Mary Cox Certificate 50 born 20/12/1880

Assistant Mistress   Ellen Elizabeth Fean Cert. 50 born 21/9/1880

                    Last school Crossness L.C.C. School

The Time Table of the late Master will be used till I am able to find out what the children can do.

June 20th   The written work of the children is on the whole neatly done, but the children are greatly lacking in intelligence.

Owing to the overcrowded state of the school and the closeness of the desks the children are unable to change their position after entering the school till they are dismissed. This is most detrimental to childrens' health and efficient working.

Mr Hillyer and Miss Cox with Hinguar pupils. My Aunt Eva is third row from the top, 7th from the right in the white apron.

June 27th   The following is a copy of a report sent to the South Shoebury School Board.

I regret having to inform you the exceptionally bad attendance throughout the dept. It is the worst I have ever known during my 20 years experience. There are 265 children on the Registers and of this number at times less than 60 percent are present, but at all times about 60 children are absent.

I beg to apply for an Additional Assistant on the staff. As you are aware the general work and intelligence of the school is of an indifferent character and the discipline weak and there is no chance of improvement under the present conditions. At present with one Assistant Ex. Pupil Teacher I am confined to a class of 148 scholars and am unable to get to the other classes without these children being neglected, thus I am quite ignorant of the work of Standards, 111 + 1V, consisting of 140 children under the charge of two Ex. P.T.s.

I desire to draw your attention to the frequency of threats from complaining parents in the event of any punishment whatsoever to their children and to notes written in most objectionable language to the teachers. This of course cannot be continued as a good tone could never be obtained and I personally greatly object to my authority being questioned whilst I am in charge of the school. I therefore ask for your co-operation in this respect.

Aug 31st   Miss Fean Cert 50, reports that she was married during the holidays and asks for an early release from her present appointment.

Three parents have been fined 5/- each for bad attendance.

Sept 7th   The first bi-monthly Exam was held before the Summer Holidays and the results generally are poor throughout. The Mental Arith. And those subjects requiring intellectual reasoning are scarcely satisfactory but the written work is good and the essay writing introduced to all the Standards is most satisfactory.

Sept 17th   Visit of Inspection

The attendance is most unsatisfactory & calls for prompt measures on the part of the authorities. The work alas is carried on under the most uncomfortable conditions. The question of staff requires attention. I. Watkins.

Oct 12th   I am suffering from Lumbago & am in so much pain that I must go home 10.15 AM.

Oct 14th   Attended school today for a few minutes.

Oct 15th   Stayed a short time during each session.

The E.C. (Evening Class) School was not opened on Tuesday night notices being sent previously to the students.

Oct 16th Was able to remain at school the whole day. E.C. School taken last night.

Oct 22nd I have just severely punished Robert Johnson of Stand. 111. This boy was guilty of gross disobedience and impudence and when told to come out of his class at once shouted at his loudest that he would tell his mother. There is no doubt that this boy took advantage of my apparent helplessness for I can scarcely walk even with sticks and thought he would get off free, as he did a fortnight ago. In this instance he was sent in by the Assist. Master from the playground because he was not paying attention to the Drill. Instead of coming into he went out of the playground saying what his mother would do. His punishment was delayed for 3 or 4 days as I was still too ill and I had heard in the meantime that he had told his mother that he was going to run out again if punished. I thought the punishment ought to rest equally on the parents for encouraging him. I put him down to Stand. 3.

Oct 27th The attendance has been raised to 213, the accommodation is therefore quite insufficient for our needs. On occasions when there are 225 children present, 8 children are often seated in desks only 8 feet long, it may thus be seen how powerless the teachers are to produce any good work.

Old Red House, Shoeburyness.

Often during needlework lessons, books have to be taken from the cupboards to provide seats for the girls. Since a better staff has been provided I have been able to give attention to the lower Division of the school. Stand. 111, which came up from the Junior Dept. In June is in a very bad condition so that I have been compelled to form a Lower Division and begin Standard 11 work. Many of these children are over 11 years of age and some are 13. There are about 40 children, the greater number have only the slightest idea of Simple Addition & Subtraction, and cannot multiply or divide by numbers greater than seven.

Nov 19th Miss J. Eynon has been transferred to the Infant Dept. And commenced duties there today, this leaves me with the Lower portion of Std 111, and the selected children from V1 & V11 to teach.

Nov 30th Was absent from school the whole of last week, being confined to bed with an attack of Rheumatism.

Dec 8th Robert Johnson who was punished on Oct. 10th for impudence has again been grossly impudent to his mistress. The parents are in league with the boy and as I have no intention of taking upon myself the parents' duties again I have dismissed him from the school.

The Rev. B.G.Popham has interceded on behalf of the boy Johnson & as the parents appear to be sorry I have consented to allow him to return on the condition that his mother brings him.

Adverts are constantly inserted in the different Educational papers, and applicants are appointed but as soon as they receive notification of appointment they refuse to come.

1904

Jan 18th The school reopened last Monday. The average attendance for the week was 210. We have no ink and some of the chn. cannot therefore write with it. The Requisition for it has been sent in thrice. Sept, Easter & December.

Jan 25th Miss Frost commenced work this morning. Gertrude Frost, born Oct. 13th 1881. Cert No. 04/753. Trained Norwich, 1902 -3, P.T. Snape National School.

Mar 28th School closed for Election purposes.

Apr 11th School reopened (Easter Holiday). Some children have commences work as Half –timers without necessary Qualifications. Matter reported this morning.

The Brickfields Stables. Shoeburyness.

Apr 22nd Miss Wood, Ex. P.T. in Junior Dept. Has been reported to Managers by parents of a child Nelly Wallace for punishing it irregularly. It appears the child had a mark on its arm after the morning session but as the matter was not reported to me by the Teacher till the morning of the next day I did not see the child's mark. I saw the child who stated that the mark has entirely disappeared & upon examining the arm I found it was so.

Apr 25th It has since transpired that the case given above was quite an accident, & should not have been considered by the Managers in my absence.

May 16th H.M.I. dissatisfied with Miss Wood's teaching.

May 30th The Junior & Senior Depts were amalgamated in this the Hinguar Street (new) Mixed School, which was opened this morning.

The Staff consists of:

Head Teacher	Mr Hillyer .
Cert Assist.	L.T. Cooper
(Trained) Cert Assist.	Gertrude Frost
Cert 50	Miss E. Brooks
Cert 50	Miss E. Cox
Cert 50	Miss L. Cox
Cert 50	Miss M.A. Woods
Cert 50	Mrs Helen Robinson

Mr R.O Hughes, Normal College, Bangor, has been appointed an Assistant in the school.

Miss Bessie Castle of Swansea T. College has been appointed an Assistant at this school.

June 7th Some members of the Sub- Advisors Committee think the School too large for one Head Teacher and desire to divide it. All attempts to organise the school have been stopped by me until their decision has been received.

July 11th Have transferred Mrs Robinson, Cert.50 from Std. 1V (Lower Division) to Stand. 1 her work there being unsatisfactory.

Sep 5th The School has had to be closed an extra week owing to the decorations not being finished.

Sep 18th Miss Eva Gooderham, Range House, High St. born Feb 27. 1886. Commenced work Sept 13th. She will be apprenticed in Oct for 2 years.

Sep 27th Evening Classes commenced tonight. 33 Admitted.

Oct 19th About 30 cases of measles have been reported to me during the last week.

My child shewed symptoms of the complaint yesterday noon. I at once left home & procured lodgings in this district. The matter has been reported to the Managers.

Nov 3rd   About 8% of the children are absent through measles. An order has been received closing the school. A protest has been made to the Medical Officer of Health and to the Managers.

Dec 11th   Report sent to Managers concerning Mrs Robinson, Cert. 50.

Dec 19th   Mrs Robinson resigns her appointment.

Managers asked to shorten time of closure. Date altered from Jan 9th to Jan 2nd.

On Dec 2nd at my request, a large number of children met me in the school playground to ascertain how many children were still infected. Not a single case of Measles was found out of the whole number of children on registers. Some of the children met the teachers and me here each morning for Home-work during the remaining part of the time.

The High Street, South Shoebury.

Reports for 1903-1904

This Junior School was for the latter part of the school year amalgamated with the Senior Mixed Dept. Whilst it formed a separate Dept. the teaching was earnest and painstaking but it did not induce in the children the power of thinking for themselves or of applying such information as they had acquired. Grant £224-8-0.

Senior Dept: The work of the older scholars has been carried on under great difficulty owing to the overcrowded state of the school. Order is good, but the children's power of attention is not.

The more mechanical exercises have been carefully practised, but the teaching has been rather wanting in vitality and confined in range and opportunities for improvement. In all these points however, there is good prospect for improvement under the new conditions. Grant £207 -18/-

1905

Jan 2nd   School re-opened Attendance low.

Feb 1st   Miss Emily Colby Commenced work today as a Supplementary Teacher. Born 1883 June 22nd 5 years as a Pupil Teacher in Garrison.

Mar 3rd   Friday absent this afternoon. Mr R.O. Hughes has resigned his appointment.

Mar 13   Miss E. Cox has been advised to leave Shoebury for a few weeks to benefit her health. Standard 1 is now without a teacher.
Miss Castle (C.A.) was absent from School on 7th, 8th, & 9th inst.

Mar 31st   Mr R. O. Hughes terminated his services today.

Apr 3rd   Holiday given U.D.C. Election.3

Apr 4th   Standard 1V will be taken by Mr Cooper with Stands V, V1, & V11. No applications have been received for the post.

June 2nd   Mr Cooper has received instructions from Mr Ingram to take temporary Headship at Hawkwell School.
Knowing the difficulty of procuring a suitable man I have asked Mr Cooper to take the temporary post for a time, though we are already 2 Cert. Assists. Short & the C. Committee do not require ordinary Assists. to go "on Supply".

Jun 13th   I have written to Mr Ingram asking that Mr Cooper be returned at once.

Jun 19th   Mr Cooper returned to School.

School Report for 1904-1905

"Mixed" The children are in good order, and careful with their work which is improving and may be expected to improve still further in a year of less difficulty than that which has just elapsed.   *N. Hillyer. June 22nd.*

Staff for 1905-1906

Nicholas Hillyer	Head T.
Gertrude Frost	T.C.
L.T.Cooper	C.
Nora Frost	T.C. From July 10
Mr Ernest Gascoigne	T.C. From July 10
Miss E. Brooks	U
Miss Eva Cox	U
Miss Linda Cox	U
Miss A. Woods	U
Miss Emily Colby	U
Miss Eva Gooderham	Pupil Teacher

Mr Hillyer, centre and pupils c. 1905.

July 10th Have had to remove Miss Woods from Standard 1.

Aug 3rd Summer Holidays commenced.

Sep 29th Miss Woods's services terminated today. During the last 3 weeks she has served as a transfer teacher in another school under the County.

Oct 1st Teachers held examinations.

Nov 6th Term Exams of all classes taken.

Nov 20th The County Comm. have supplied the Board of Education "Suggestions to Teachers". In order that the Teachers may become acquainted with its contents and as the book would take some months to get round the Staff (for private reading) we are taking a subject together each afternoon after the session. In order to lessen any inconvenience we shall close at 4 o'clock each day until such time as the "Suggestions" be finished.

Nov 25th   The Exam held by me gives very hopeful results. Standard 1 has much improved in intelligence. In all, 13 children were promoted to a higher class.

Dec 11th   P.I. Gooderham and Miss E. Colby are absent from School this week attending the Scholarship Exam.

Dec 14th   Results of Free Scholarships received. Report sent to S.A.C. that report incorrect and misleading and asking that "Results" may be revised and reprinted for the credit of this school. The errors and omissions are as follows:-

Two girls – Elsie Cowley and Annie Brooks – have been left off entirely though the former was selected for a scholarship. Both these children would have occupied a position close to their classmate Gladys Rowe – the top child – had they been inserted. Annie Brooks held a higher position than Gladys Rowe in County Minor Exam Results.

b) Thomas Wright, the lowest child on the list, is presented as belonging to Shoebury School. He never was a scholar here, but for twelve months preceding Exam, was a scholar at Southend Technical School.

Muriel Rowe is represented as having 'Failed' in History – she did not take this subject.

She is represented as not having taken Algebra and English – she would secure at least 70% of marks in both.

The Total Marks for 2nd 4th 5th 6th & 7th child were incorrect. The Sixth child should occupy the Fifth place to be in order of merit.

Dec 21st   School closes today.

Rampart Street, showing Shoebury Hotel.

1906

Jan 8th   School re-opens today.

Jan 12th   Attendance for week is fairly good. 91.8% Av. 388.

Jan 12th   Previous to holidays at the request of the Correspondent I forward the following
            suggestions to Managers.
            The advisability of tarring the playground.
            The advisability of heating the school with hot water in preference to the expensive
            system of grates.

Jan 24th   Reported to Managers the unfit state of school after meetings in the Cent. Hall and
            asked that a rule be made that in future the school be only let on condition that there
            be no smoking or expectoration.

Feb 17th   Wrote to Advis. Committee asking that the revised list of Scholarship Exam children
            might be published in the interests of the Shoebury Children (p.61)

Mar 17th   Entry re Feb 17th – wrote to Clerk asking what steps the Ad. C. had taken.

Mar 21st   Received request from S.A.C. for the the name of a scholar to be erased from the
            Register. This child Daisy Hubbard is absent through Eczema.
            I have written to say that the action is illegal and according to the Code no child can
            be crossed off unless it be:
            • Dead
            • Left the district
            • In another school
            • And to ask for further instructions.

Apr 10th   Letter to Clerk asking what steps, if any had been taken in reference to my entries
            of March and Feb 17th.
            Miss E. Brooks absent. Suspicious case of Scarlet Fever in house.

Apr 12th   Miss E. Brooks returned today.

June 15th   Mr Hudson H.M.I. of Art visited the School this A.M. & inspected the Drawing.

July 10th   Wrote to Clerk suggesting that the Scripture Exam should be held at an early date as possible as the syllabus of work which was quite covered was not commenced till Sept. Last and as the classes have now been changed about 2 months the results may be somewhat hazy.

July 11th   Today 26 children of the First class were taken on a trip to London by two teachers and me. During the morning we did Tower Hill, Tower Bridge, Monument and London Bridge. At noon we went to Westminster where we were joined by the remainder of the staff – 8 teachers and under the escort of Mr Rowland Whithead M.P. visited the Houses of Parliament and Westminster Hall. After dinner we did Westminster Abbey, Whitehall, and Trafalgar Square and then wended our way through the Strand, Newspaper land and Cheapside to the Bank and Mansion House and after tea caught the 7.20 train home. The expenses of half the children were defrayed by the staff.

Shoeburyness Station 1907.

Sept 3rd   Wm. Ferguson born 17th May, 1890 has been appointed here as Pupil Teacher for 2 years as from August 1st.
            Mary Francis Hodgkins born 9th August 1889 has been appointed here as P.T. for a 2 year course as from Aug 1st.

Sept 3rd   Muriel Rowe has secured a Local Scholarship. Annie Brooks & Norah Gooderham have secured Pupil Teacher Scholarships, the latter heading the list of the Rochford

Hundred competition.

School re-opened today – a large number of children have not returned from their holiday.

Sept 17th   The 3 best papers in the last Exam of the 1st Class relating to the trip to London were sent to the M.P. for district as he was instrumental in adding to the children's pleasure on that day. In asking permission to give each of the children a book in recognition of their work he writes "I have been very much interested in reading them (the essays). I think they have remembered what they saw with remarkable accuracy and very fully, whilst the writing and composition are I think a great credit to them, yourself and the School Authorities.

Oct 10th   An 'Attendance Holiday' was given this afternoon.

Oct 18th   The Registers were not marked this afternoon as an Examination in Religious Knowledge was held the Examiners being the Rev. G. Padfield of Hawkwell & Rev. W. Gibson of Raleigh.

The terminal Exam has been held the Reports are now complete. Arith. And English are weakest. The Examination was a searching one, 20 sums being given in Classes 1, 2, 3&4 and 12 sums in the lower classes. Lower Standard 1V is very much behind the other classes. On the whole the results are very satisfactory; the intelligence is of a high order.

Oct 20th   Miss Eva Gooderham has been transferred to Raleigh School & left today.

Nov 1st   Miss Colby's services terminated yesterday. She has been transferred to Wakering School & will be a distinct loss to ours.

Nov 10th   Received wire from Secretary to close school for Scarlet Fever which I did at 11.30 AM. There is practically none in the school. Two cases occurred 3 weeks ago and our attendance is now almost as high as during any time in the last 3 years. No enquiries were made by the Sanitary Authority or Medical Officer the latter person issuing the order arbitrarily without conforming with the L.G. Board's instructions to confer with the Councillors.

I am sending a letter to protest to the U.D.C. meeting this evening.

Dec 10th   School re-opened this morning.

Dec 14th   Suggest to Mr Ingram and the Managers that we have one week only for Christmas Holidays this year.

Dec 18th   School closed for Xmas Holiday from Dec 21st to Dec 30th.

The Garrison School, 1904. School Master Mr Bolsover.

1907

Jan 30/31   Concert on behalf of Sports Fund held for these two evenings. Present the 1st evening were Mr Rowland Whitehead M.P., Mrs Whitehead and Mr A.E. Wedd. Mrs Whitehead presented 3 books to children who had supplied him with the best essays on their visit to London on July 11th when about 30 were shown the Houses of Parliament by him.

    Mr and Mrs Steel and Mr Millbank were present the second evening when Mrs Steel presented prizes to the best swimmers in the school.

School Report for 1906-1907

Mar 4th   The discipline is good and the oral work has continued to improve. Most of it is now of a very satisfactory quality. Throughout the middle and lower parts of the school the progress is particularly hopeful. The first class contains some of the older children who received their early education under less favourable circumstances, and it is moreover too large for the teacher. It, therefore, is relatively not so far advanced as the junior classes. The boys in it are readier in their answering than the girls.

    Now that the foundations are being well laid, it will be wise to throw the children more on their own resources. Still more time can be devoted to oral and written composition.

May 1st   Drew Secretary's attention to shortness of staff of 2 teachers & to the fact that work & tone are suffering in consequence.

Sept 2nd   Miss Annie Clouting commenced work today.

Born	Aug 13th 1886
Apprenticed	Aldeburgh Girls C.
Trained	Norwich
Scholarship	1904 Class 2
Certificate	1907. Pass. Dist. In Music
Registered No.	

Sept 7th   Miss Clouting absent with Influenza on the 4th, 5th & 6th.

Sept 9th   Absent today with Influenza.

Copy of Schedule of Grants September 4th 1907

Boys	343 @ 22/-	£377 - 06 - 0
Infants	108 @ 17/-	£91 - 16 - 0
Total payable		**£469 - 2 - 0**
Fee Grant	449@ 10/-	£224 - 10 - 0
		£693 - 12 - 0
Superannuation contribution		£ 14 - 01 - 6

The following Return and Report have been sent to R (?). S.A.C at their request

Average of class class for year	Average number on register	Average for last week	Teacher per class
30	26	24	Mr E.Gascoigne
48	48	45	Mr E.Gascoigne
32	55	48	Miss E. Colby
49	48	45	Miss E.Cox
53	53	48	Miss E .Brooks
55	54	50	Miss N. Frost
52	52	49	Miss L. Cox
60	64	60	Miss A. Clouting

A Cert. 50 Uncertificated Teacher is required in addition to present permanent staff... The large size of Standard V1 & V11 combined were adversely commented on by H.M.I in his report of last year. Standard 11 of 68 children is too large for the teacher. Though a very good trained Cert. Teacher has been with them since they came to this Dept they are still more backward in discipline and attainments than the children of the same age of any previous year since 1903. The Cert 50, preferably a man, is required to help with both these large Divisions. Owing to W.D. pensioners increasing we have admitted 84 new children since June 1st. Thus the usual autumnal decrease has not taken place with us.

Oct 4th	**Present Staff**	
	Mr. Nicholas Hillyer HeadMaster	C T.
	Mr Ernest Gasoigne	C.T.
	Mr C.L.Evans	C.T.
	Miss A. Clouting	C.T.
	Miss E. Brooks	U
	Miss E Cox	U
	Miss L. Cox	U

Oct 4th   Mr. Liddle terminated his duties here today.

Oct 15th   Miss Clouting has been cautioned about unsatisfactory work.

Oct 17th   Mr Evans has been told that his work and manner are unsatisfactory.

Oct 28th   Shall leave at 3 o'clock to attend the opening of the Working Lads Institute in which I am interested. Returned at 4 -5.13

Nov 1st   Mr. Arthur Herbert Hurrell commenced duties today. Last School Southminster C. Born 12th Sept, 1887. Apprenticed July 1903 -6.

Nov 6th   Mr Hurrell absent this afternoon without reason or note.

Entrance to Garrison via Ness Road with Sentry Post and Guard.

Nov 8th   Mr Hurrell returned this A.M.

Mr Hurrell went home yesterday but as his father refused to receive him he asked to be allowed to recommence work. I sent for the Chairman and together we advised him to be stronger with and make greater efforts to overcome his imaginary fears of being unable to control his class.

He promised that nothing should induce him to leave without notice again.

Hinguar Street pupils standing outsidethe Garrison main entrance in the High Street, c. 1905.

Nov13th   Mr Hurrell absent without permission. I have received the following note.
"Dear Sir,
I shall not be able to attend school today owing to caeroration"

Nov15th   Detailed report re-above sent to County Offices and to L.G.L.A.S.C.

Nov 28th   Political Meeting held in school last evening by Mr Newman at which smoking was allowed. The room was quite unfit for children to occupy this morning owing to the taint of smoke and the spitting upon the floor. I was compelled to thoroughly sprinkle the floor with strong carbolic twice before I would allow the children to sit in the room.

Dec 19th   There was a concert this afternoon given by some children from each room; afterwards the prizes were distributed by myself
In future our 'school years' will be only of 6 months duration. This change has been necessitated by the advent of 55 girls after the holidays.

1908

Jan 6th   School opened. Attendance very satisfactory. There are a few cases of infectious diseases. 14

We admitted 58 fresh children this morning.

We have finally abolished the "Standard" system of classification and the twelve month school year. On the results of the December examinations the whole school has been reorganised and 8 classes have been formed from 7, so that it will be possible for a child to pass through the school in three or four years. G. Ellis Jones 5/2/08

An examination of the Garrison School girls was held in their own school before transfer to this school and the work chosen by Mr. Garenty, their Headmaster was that of the last Monthly examination given to our own children.

The following are the results in Arithmetic.

Stand V11   3.6 out of a max of 20

Stand V1   1 out of a max of 20

Stand V   1.12 out of a max of 20

Stand 1V   3.6 out of a max of 20

Stand 111   2.05 out of a max of 8

Stand 11   3.3 out of a max of 6

Stand 1   3.3 out of a max of 6

The girls being unused to free composition the results in this subject are not given.

Jan 25th   The Managers gave the teachers the free use of the school last evening for a social gathering.

Feb 4th   About 2 dozen boys and girls went with me for a ramble this afternoon from 2 to 3.20.

Feb 24th   Was late attending school this A.M.

Officers Shoeburyness Garrison c. 19th.

Mar 5th   Mr I.G. Saltmarsh, from the Board of Education called this afternoon respecting the needs of Technical Classes for Shoeburyness.

19.3.08 The Attendance of the children from the garrison is not up to War Office requirements and in regard to this matter I called upon the Adjutant this A.M. This gentleman showed, or pretended to show, a real ignorance of Army regulations affecting children attending civil schools until it was pointed out to him that negotiations would be made direct to the War Office if something were not done directly. He promised to furnish me with the following:-

1) Course with reference to the attendance of irregulars and sick.

11) Roll showing all girls over 5 and all boys 5 to 7 (Half yearly)

111) Notice of withdrawal of children.

1V) Copy of regimental garrison orders for a) purpose of Quarantine b) Military public.

The Garrison Army Schoolmaster with his pupils c. 1901.

Mar 24th   Visited Garrison Offices with Mr Cooper but both the Adjutant & Staff Capt. Were absent.

Mar 26th   Reported above matter to the Commandant.

Mar 27th   School closes tomorrow for Stock-Taking (Friday instead of Wednesday).

May 18th   Reply received from Capt. Blount respecting attendance, rolls, vacations and orders. All the requests in my letter of March 25th have been fully granted and notification has been made to the Garrison Orders dates 14-5-08.

May 25th   Empire kept today Monday – a day's holiday being given.

May 26th   Managers held their meeting in my room today for the first time.

June 4th   William Ferguson Pupil Teacher away this week for Metric Exam.

June 30th   William Ferguson has asked to be absent on Wednesday next to go to London.

July 30th   No. Of Scholars at end of each school year

	Boys	Girls	Total
May 1905	168	231	399
May 1907	174	219	393
May 1908	168	229	397
And at the end of			
August 1905	196	254	450
August 1906	177	222	399
August 1907	190	209	399

July 6th   A family, living in Wakering, applied for admission but were told to go back to their own school.

We commenced swimming lessons with the girls last Friday. Mr Gascoigne takes the boys but as we have no mistress who can swim I have been obliged to hire the services of Mr Carreck,17 a retired Naval non-commissioned officer. The funds have been guaranteed by the Staff but I shall apply to the Advisory Committee for help.

William Ferguson P.T. was absent today & yesterday on account of a wound on the head caused by a cricket ball.

Coastguard's Station, Shoeburyness.

July 14th   William Ferguson passed Probation with two distinctions
Mary Hodgkins passed Probation with one distinction.

July 17th   Mary Hodgkins will be absent this afternoon to go to the Military Hospital for an operation – throat.

July 28th   Mary Hodgkins will not now return to school having had a relapse after her operation.

The Military Hospital was built in 1856 with a detached 'Itch Ward and the 'Dead House' at the rear. There were 6 wards, Surgery and Store Room with Kitchen and Washhouse at the rear. Urinals and Privvies formed part of the 'Dead House'. Florence Nightingale visited the hospital and recommended it as a model for other military hospitals.

Sept 9th   18 girls commenced Cookery Instruction at the Parish Hall under Miss Forrest this day. They will attend alternate Wednesdays and Fridays

Dec 5th   The school will close at 4 o'clock this week till Xmas no recreation time will be taken. This alteration has been made on account of the dark afternoons preceding Xmas.

1909

Jan 13th   Cookery Class altered to Jan14. (this week).

On returning from Xmas Holiday I noted:-

1. Gallery in each room had not been washed.

2. Windows had not been cleaned

3. W.Cs and urinals had not been swilled

4. Desks were not clean.

Contrary to E.E.C Bye-Laws. N. Hillyer.

Jan 18th   Returned to duties today. I have not yet recovered from my relapse but as Dr Roper has ordered me to go to Bath for a term I feel I must get the half yearly Exams & the classes re-organised before I leave.

Jan 22nd   The Managers at a special meeting have granted me leave of absence for a month! I am leaving for Bath.

Jan 27th   Drill not taken this A.M. owing to slippery conditions of playground.

Feb 10th   Snowing heavily just before 9 a.m. attendance thin.

Apr 6th   H.M.I. (Mr Waumsley) visited school & held Labour Certificate Examination.

Apr 26th   School closed for Annual Stocktaking.

May 10th Recommenced duties today. N. Hillyer.

May 17-19 Medical Inspection by Dr Corbett.

The High Street, Shoeburyness.

Report on Scripture Examination 1909

Received July 1st 1909

"The lower Standards 1 to V passed a most satisfactory examination, special commendation should be given to Class 11 for the knowledge of Commandments etc. and accuracy in repeating the hymns. Class 111 has been excellently well taught in both Old and New Testament subjects. Class 1V did remarkably well in Old Testament history and their knowledge of the New Testament subjects was very good. Class V deserve special mention for the accuracy of the answers given to questions upon "the life of Elijah and Elisha".

The three highest Standards in this school have passed a very creditable examination. With very few exceptions all the children shewed that they had been carefully and prayerfully instructed in religious truths, which must beneficially influence their entrance upon and conduct through life's work, which lies before them.

The singing of the massed Classes was very effective."

Herbert Bell

July 18th   When we return after the Summer Holidays the Staff and subjects will be re-organised and some of the subjects will be taken throughout by Special Teachers. Each member of the staff will be responsible for the subjects embraced under the 3RS' but the following subjects are specialities and the teachers' whose names appear against them are responsible for the results.

In many cases under the present class system teachers take subjects which they not only dislike but are most unfitted to teach and consequently the scholars suffer. Others are perhaps only qualified to teach the 3Rs in the lower classes but are more fitted than a teacher of higher school qualification to teach some subject such as needlework or singing in the Upper Division of school.

Our new system must raise the quality of the work though the special teachers are only the ordinary staff and had previously had no idea of taking special subjects – for a teacher who takes a subject for 3 or 4 hours per week must become more expert than the one who takes it unwillingly for half an hour.

Again the beneficial effects of the change of teacher and method upon a class and of the change of faces to a teacher cannot be overestimated.

Singing	Upper	Miss Smith
Lower	Miss Cox	
Drawing	Upper	Mr Gascoigne
Lower		Mr Jones
Needlework	Upper	Miss Brooks
Lower		Miss Cox
Drill	Boys Classes V111, V11	Mr Jones
	Girls Classes V111, V11	Miss Colby
	Mixed Classes V1, V, 1V	Miss Colby
	111, 11	
Games	Miss Wootton	
	The Masters	

Campfield Shoeburyness leading to Barge Pier.

Aug 30th   School re-opened this A. M. Cleaning not in conformity with E.E.P. rules.

Nov 22nd   A fortnight ago I discovered that a defective child has developed tendencies which I thought should be reported to the Medical Officer (or the County). The matter was reported to the Secretary who advised me to write at once.
The Med. Officer acknowledged my letter on 18th inst.

Ages of the children admitted from the Infant School in August 1909

	Girls	Boys	Total
Over 8 years 6 months	9	13	22
Over 9 years	12	16	28
Average age of children on admission		Richmond Avenue School 8.3	
		Hinguar Street School 8.1	

1910

Jan 10th   School re-opened this A.M. Attendance good.

The Caretaker reports that the school was left in a horribly disgusting condition after the Political Meeting of Jan 4th. The floors and desks were covered with expectoration & mud & both had to be completely sprinkled with disinfectant before the cleaners could attempt the work of cleaning. She states that had the scholars been attending the room could not have been occupied for at least two days. I have again reported this unsatisfactory condition of things. PS nothing was broken but considerable damage was done to furniture.

Mar 9th   The Army Medical Officer this morning inspected the children of all the Army men for vaccination marks.

Mar 16th   Mr Walmsley H.M.I. held Latin Exam here this afternoon.

May 4th   The Commandant, Colonel Nichols, has promised to address the children on Empire Day.

Hinguar Street boys dancing a Horn Pipe at Empire Day celebrations.
Thanks to Henry Mercer former pupil for this copy of a family photo.

May 24th   This being Empire Day the school met this A.M. and lessons were given suitable to the occasion by the teachers. Afterwards I spoke to the whole school on the "Ideals of Empire".

Owing to the death of our late sovereign the celebration was very quiet and Cols. Gardiner and Nichols R.A. were asked to postpone their visit.

June 10th   About 60 children of those marked 'Left' during the last school year migrated to other towns.

Whent Grocer and Butcher, Seaview Road Cambridge Town.

June 15th   The Managers met on Tuesday to consider the applications for the post of Assistant. Two applications had previously been submitted to Messrs Cox, Bacon & Glasscock for their perusal. Mr Bacon in returning the forms suggested a meeting & called personally on Messrs Cox & Bacon suggested with the approval of the other two members, that Mr Warren and Mr Cardwell be appointed. The remaining two members were not consulted as both lived so far away and it was important that no time be lost as there were but two men eligible to take the Chief Assistantship.

Nov 8th   Mr Warren was absent from school from October 24 to Nov 7th having been transferred to Barling C.S. to take charge during Mr Davis' absence.

Nov 15th   The School Year has now been altered to May 31st – the old date.

Dec 20th   Both oral and written work are now finished but the Term Reports will not be issued to the children until after the Holidays. I think that in the excitement of preparing for Xmas the full value of the School Reports are lost. They will be given out after we return.

Dec 23rd   The school closes this morning. Mr Cox distributed the prizes. The Rector was present. 70 prizes were given.

1911

Jan 9th   School re-opened today – the weather is wet & close & some children are still absent owing to infections by Mumps, Measles & Diptheria.

Feb 16th   Mr Hitchcock visited the school today this A.M. to report on the Student Teacher – Lucy Leaney.

Copy of H.M.I's Report Oct 11th 1910

The schools are overcrowded for part of the year. Children have been refused admission in the Summer months.
The Girls' Cloakroom is too small for the number on the books. The pegs are in three rows The rooms are cold in winter. The end classroom of the mixed school is dark and so is the corresponding room in the Infants' Dept.

June 26th   School closed for Coronation Week – July 19th to 24th by order of the County Committee.

June 30th An "open afternoon" will be given today from 3 o'clock when Managers, Councillors, parents and friends will be allowed to visit the school and see the work of the children.

At 4 o'clock the school will be dismissed and at 4.15 teas will be served in the garden.

At 6.30 the fathers have a special invitation to be present to inspect the school gardens. Two Gardiners will be present to judge each plot and award marks for the gardening prize. The Time Table will not be adhered to in the afternoon session.

July 1st More than 200 were present at tea.

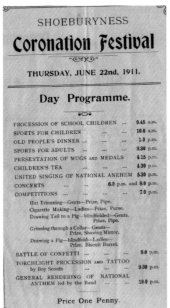

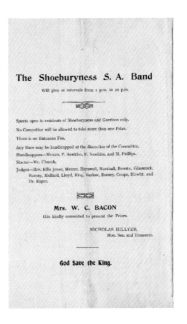

Shoeburyness Beach early 20C.

July 24th   Mr Legge terminated his duties here today. Discipline & work have suffered rather considerably during the three weeks Mr Legge has had charge.

Sept 27th   The Swimming Competition for the School Challenge Cups was held this afternoon.

SHOEBURYNESS COUNCIL SCHOOL SWIMMING CLUB

The second annual races for this year's cup holders, boys and girls, were held on Tuesday with the following results: - Girls, 60 yards speed: - 1st, Evelyn Rutter; 2nd, Izie Hillyer; 3rd, Eva Scholes. The first two girls swam a distance of 240 yards and Eva Scholes 80 yards. Distance, stroke and speed are the three qualifications for the cup and Evelyn Rutter who is three years the senior of the other two girls, succeeded in winning the cup for the second time. Boys, 60 yards speed: - 1st Howarth; 2nd, Cook; 3rd, Webb; 4th, Parkins. Howarth, Cook and Webb swam a quarter of a mile along the coast and Howarth, who is only eleven years old, holds the cup this year for the first time.

*The final heat race for this year's novices (Girls) was also held: - 1st, Eva Scholes; 2nd, Florence Horswell; 3rd, Ellen Metherall and Hilda Rumsey; and 4th, Dorothy Higgleton. The silver challenge cup for the girls was presented last year by Miss Marie Willis, medical gymnast of Cambridge. Mr. Elliott Davidson presented the boys'. There was a large gathering of parents and older scholars on the beach to witness the event. ***

* (NEWSPAPER REPORT PASTED INTO LOG BOOK).

Oct 17th   Harold Pomfritt, a scholar, fractured his leg yesterday morning immediately after liberation for morning recreation. On the Doctor's advice he was sent to Southend Hospital.

Oct 20th   Dr. Wyche examined the sight of some Wakering children & also five of our own scholars today.

Nov 10th   Dr Wyche here 11 to 3.20 testing sight of 8 children.

Nov 21st   Bought school prizes.

Dec 1st   Owing to the absence of the Head Mistress of the Infant Dept Miss Wootton will visit there each morning and afternoon to take one of the classes in Needlework, Reading and Arithmetic. A girl from our top class will also be sent to help.

1912

Feb 19th   Miss Wootton re-commenced work here today on Miss Howslip taking up the new Head T. Duties in the Infant Dept.

Miss Howslip has asked me to take into the school about 20 children who are considerably over age for her Dept. Duplicate registers have had to be made & the bottom classes re-organised. I find the children are unable to read & have no idea of number. The majority are over 8 some are 9 years of age.

Apr 15th   Titanic Disaster Fund raised £3-18-6.

Apr 30th   Mr H.E. Cardwell terminated his services here today.

May 2nd   Miss E. Colby absent with an abscess on the lower jaw.

May 3rd   Mr Cardwell's salary sent to him as he has not called for it.

May 9th   Miss Wootton has asked permission to go home to Westcliff occasionally during the week instead of remaining at her lodgings each night. I have given her my consent owing to her extremely nervy condition.

Miss Colby returned today – she is still unfit to do much and I have sent an upper Standard girl to help her.

May 17th   Miss Emily Colby terminated her services here today. On behalf of the children I presented her with a silver cruet, a silver toast rack and a cake dish.

May 24th   Owing to the loss of a teacher, the absence of two mistresses and the Term Examinations the Time Table has not been strictly adhered to during the last 3 weeks.

During the first week of the month I took charge of Class V1 which Mr Cardwell had left. The children were diffident and the work slipshod and careless and consequently the Exam gave very poor results – Arith 18.5%.

It was not that the work set was too difficult but that the children were not trained to concentrate their attention upon their work. Subsequently I gave the class the Exam paper of a class lower when V were examined & the results were still very poor. Only 38% of marks were obtained & much of this was very indifferent work. One child had been in the class three terms + 23 children had been in it for two terms so it was not that they did not know their work.

The other class that did badly was No 2. In December when the new term commenced the children were placed in classes according to merit but when a temporary school was being discussed for the Cambridge Scholars the children were re-distributed into classes accordingly as they lived in the village or Cambridge end of Shoebury. As Miss Golding's children were always better prepared than those of the village it may be assumed that the village gave the least satisfactory results. Such was not the case. In Arithmetic Miss Goodfellow's scored 24% & Miss Wooton's 62%. There was a great difference also in the other subjects of the Examination. Before taking the Examination Miss Goodfellow complained that she had been unable to cover the work of the syllabus, so the Arithmetic was altered & the sums set covered only that portion of the syllabus taken.

- I found the children had not been taught
- Mult & Divis by numbers less than 100
- 1st lessons on Fractions and Dec.
- Simple little bills.

Every term there is the same difficulty with this mistress – the syllabus is never covered in whatever class she teaches and the results of her Examinations are most unsatisfactory. Owing to the bad results in the classes taught by Mr Cardwell & Miss Goodfellow I have deemed it wisest not to send out to the parents the usual terminal reports & the staff have been informed that owing to changes I am too busy to attend to them.

June 25th   Miss Smith and Miss Goodfellow terminated their services here today having been transferred to the Temporary Dept in Richmond Av.

July 12th   The playground is so hot now in the afternoon that I think it is best to discontinue
            "Playtime" & close 15 minutes earlier.24

July 25th   As the Garrison Sports and Flower Show are held today we will return to school at 1.30
            instead of 2 o'clock dismiss at 3.30 in the afternoon. Our girls give a Maypole Dance.

*The Garrison Clock Tower
and Guardroom built
between 1860 – 62. The
Parade Ground lies behind
the Clock Tower, Cricket
Pitch in front.*

Sep 2nd   Miss D.E. Wootton has been transferred to Leigh C.S. as I could not consent to her
            living away from Shoebury.
            Her place is taken by: - Miss Mildred Dora Cross

Sept 6th   1912 Miss Cross is quite unable to control her class.

Sept 16th   Absent from 2.30 – 3.35 Station Master's funeral. By request.

Sept 16th   At the Bell's request I met Mr Burrows at the Office on Saturday, the 14th visit. He
            wished me to give Miss Cross a month's tuition in class management. I readily

agreed for the sake of Miss Cross' future though I pointed out to the Chairman that the general work of the school would suffer.

Mr Bell called to see Miss Cross at the Chairman's request – to urge her to place herself entirely in my hands.

I spent the whole morning with Miss Cross the Student Teacher and gave them demonstrations on bright impelling methods of class management. I was absent from school for an hour and Miss Cross told me on my return that the class would not allow her to take the geography lesson in my absence.

Sept18th   I think Miss Cross is improving. She now moves about in front of the class and gives other signs of animation whilst teaching.

Sept 20th   During the last two days I have left the class during each lesson for a few minutes to see if Miss Cross has really improved in control. On Thursday she did pretty well with the S.T. to help her and on Friday morning without him there evident signs of improvement but in the afternoon I had to remain most of the time with her
I am satisfied however that there is not improvement in teaching and discipline and I believe she is afflicted with deafness.

Oct 2nd   Mr Elford and Mr Hitchard came down to see Miss Cross.

Oct 3rd   Miss Cross has received a letter from Dr Sinclair to present herself for med. exam. this morning.

Oct 9th   Miss Cross terminated her services here today. She is transferred to Wakering Infant School.

Oct 19th   Medical Inspection by Dr Wyche on Tues & Wed 15th. 91 children were examined.

Nov 7th   Dr Wyche examined eyes today. 20 children.

Nov 26th   A dental clinic was held here today. The fee was 1/6d and included all extractions but no stoppings or other treatment. Mr Weakly of Valkyrie Rd., Westcliff, the dentist was assisted by his son and also by Dr Wyche, County M.O. and a Nurse Newby of the County Staff.

School	Applications		Treated		Untreated	
	Boys	Girls	Boys	Girls	Boys	Girls
Hinguar St. Mixed	19	34	8	27	11	7
Hinguar St. Infants	1		1			
Richmond Ave.	8	7			8	7
Wakering C S	1			1		
Barling C S	2			2		
	28	44	8	30	20	14

Two refused treatment and the remainder were postponed till Dec 5th.
All of our children who were present today who were treated have been individually inspected by me and in some cases a boracic mouth wash has been advised. Of those who were absent enquiries have been made and one case of excessive bleeding was reported to Dr Roper who visited her at her home.

Nov 28th   Another case of intermittent bleeding and swellings of the lower jaw has been reported to me. I suggested a mouthwash.

Nov 29th   Every case treated is so far very satisfactory.

Dec 5th   Dental Clinic
9.25 to 4.10 Extractions completed. 74 children treated – 93 teeth extracted. 56 children from this Dept to18 from Richmond Avenue, Wakering and Barling.

Dec 6th   Inspected all children treated by Dentist yesterday.

Dec 2nd   A child Nelly Morris was sent home today Monday as she seemed very feverish.

Dec 5th   As the child has returned I asked Dr Wyche to examine her at once did. He advised me to send her home.

Dec7th   Nelly Morris sent to infirmary today (Scarlet) fever

1913

Jan 4th   Telegram received from Dr Sinclair to close school for additional week.

Jan 13th   School reopened attendance good 313. Dr Wyche visited the school and spent the afternoon examining the scholars:

3 found with Scabies

1 Conjunctivitis (opthalmic)

Apr 8th   Mr Warmesley visited the school for Labour Exam.

Apr 14th   Results of Exam received.
- 4 boys passed 7 failed
- 11girls passed 2 failed.

Apr 21st   Copy of letter sent to Mr Bell.

In submitting Form Sm157 I began to draw attention to my Trained Certif. Staff. Not one of the three is competent to take the Number of children required by Code of County Rules. At Present Miss Heron's number in books is 40 but not more than 1 dozen receive instruction unless I am present.

The result of the boys' recent Labour Exam when compared to that of the girls shows the utterly poor standard of work obtained by the Chief Assistant. A similar result was obtained by him last year & for the two years since Mr Warren has had charge of the Upper Boys no single boy has arrived at the Pass stage of the County Exams. The first year Mr W. Took boys and girls & neither was successful.

I give below the results of the last Labour Exam.

	No. Presented	No. Passed
Mr Warren	11 boys	4
Miss Brook	13 girls	11

May 23rd   As tomorrow Saturday is Empire Day it was celebrated in school today.

The Commandant of the Shoebury School of Gunnery attended by Major Massie and Mrs Gardiner spoke to the children (assembled in a semicircle in the playground) on the virtues of the great men who have helped to build the Empire. Previous to the address the children sang an Empire Song and 36 girls danced a Minuet. The children then sang the National Anthem after three cheers had been given for the King and for the King's representative, Col. Gardiner. (and Mrs Gardiner) The children were given half of an hour in the afternoon.

June 3rd   Owing to shortness of staff and also to there only being 3 teachers capable of taking special subjects I have had to discontinue specialising Needlework, Singing, Drawing and Geography. For the next few months each Teacher will be responsible for all the subjects of her own class when a teacher is weak in one convenient arrangements will be made.

June 3rd   The King's birthday celebrated by the singing of the National Anthem this AM, a slight mention of the fact and going home AM and PM a half hour early.

June 6th   I called upon Major Massie this morning respecting Miss Banning's statement yesterday about the Army Chaplain being dissatisfied with my protest to the Commandant concerning children at funerals & services.

The Staff Captain expressed his regret that anything had been said or done by the Chaplain since the former's letter to me last month.

He said he would see the Chaplain & thought the matter could be amicably settled without obtaining a decision from the War Office.

Children have been requested to be present at Church on the occasion of the funeral of a soldier, fresh here & practically unknown a boy – Dickinson – about 10 years old & a baby. These choir boys are not paid for funerals but they receive something for ordinary services & it was pointed out to the Commandant in my previous letter the danger of breaking the law against illegal employment.

July 23rd   Miss Banning visited school this afternoon. In course of a conversation on the lack of a sewing machine she said "You told us (referring to a report to Managers) you had sent a report to some cheap paper "Home Chat" or something of the sort & had got a very good report." As she repeated it in a most satirical and irritating manner I conclude she did it to indicate my efforts to obtain an unbiased report. No further report on this subject will in future be submitted to the Managers. The work was not sent to "Home Chat" but to a Needlework Expert.

July 31st   Mr Warren terminated his duties here today.

Scripture Examination Report 1913

Upper Girls - Classes 1&11 and Upper Boys – Classes V1 & V11

I think that class 11 and the Upper Girls have suffered a little from working with two different teachers for the New and Old Testament. This seems necessary owing to one teacher being a Jewess. Certainly two classes were not quite up to last year's work.

The upper girls knew the advanced subject of the captivity well, as did the Upper Boys the earlier part of the Acts of the Apostles. The singing I heard in the school was excellent.

Class 111

Nothing could be better. The examination of the class gave me great pleasure.

Class 1V

Singing repetition, Old Testament questions excellently done. The New Testament portion not quite so good.

Class V

The children seemed nervous but recovered later and answered well. The repetition was intelligently given and the singing very good.

Infants Class 1

The singing was very good. Repetition accurate. A Bible story told in the words of the scholars was really wonderful. The teaching has been carefully done.

Infants Class 11

Here also great praise is due to intelligent teaching. All my questions were satisfactorily answered.

Infants Class 111

The singing, repetition were all well done. For such small children the result was surprisingly good.

ANNUAL GRANTS 1913

Oct 20th   Average Attendance Mixed   324

                 Infants   166

                 490 at 21/4 = £522 – 13 -4 – Annual Grant

                 490 at 10/- = £245 - 0 -0 - Fee Grant

                 Total   = £767 – 13 -4

                 Superannuation Contribution £ 17 -15-8

Dec 7th   To defray the expenses of our Sports' Club a class collection was made for funds – this realized about 10/- and was insufficient.

An outside collection was made of friends and parents of scholars a £ has been realised and it is expected will cover debts for ground man, mowing grass, marker, etc as well as leaving enough to cover fares to outside football matches.

A complaint was made to Mr Bell (verbally) that the children in one case called three times for a subscription. This is quite untrue only in one case did boy collectors overlap and this was at the corner of Ness and Church Rd; both were anxious to claim the subscription but each called but once.

In answer to the request to Mr Bell to give name of complainant he says he is unable to give name without permission.

The boys assure me they did not call at the house more than once and then only on Thursday.

1914

Feb 10th   The following is a copy of a report re Miss Cox sent to Managers on Friday last for consideration by them.

"I have recently received three complaints from parents regarding the incident of Miss L.Cox in addition to an unfortunate tongue Miss Cox at times punishes the children contrary to school rules. I deeply regret having to report the matter for I had hoped that she had overcome a bad recurring habit until three cases were brought to my notice."

At the interview with the managers I suggested that a letter to Miss C. Would be sufficient & that the question, "What other cases of complaint have you received against Miss Cox?" from Miss Banning might not be pressed.

Feb 17th   No letter was sent re-above & nothing further was done.

Feb 17th   Miss L. Cox left at 10AM to see Dr – and did not return.

Feb 19th   Medical Certif re Miss L.Cox.

Mar 9th   Chairman called respecting Fryar family who are supposed to have diphtheria throat.

Mar 16th   Dr Wyche called to swab the throats of the Fryar girls. He said that representation has been made by Miss Banning that they were suffering from Diptheria.

April 1st   Eye Clinic for Wakering and Barling

April 7th   Dental Clinic for Shoeburyness, Wakering & Barling. Treated by Mr Wilson of Leigh. 51 cases. 46 by gas. 114 teeth extracted. 30 cases from this Dept and 29 from Richmond Avenue, Wakering & Barling.

May 8   Dr Wyche says that the Fryar swabs gave negative results.

May 31st   Mrs Hood brought her child Gwen for inspection of the head. It was found not clean and the Nurse cut off some of the infected hair.

Shoeburyness Hinguar St. Mixed
HMI Reports (23rd. Oct, 1913 & 23rd. Jan. 1914

1. This is a school with high aims. Changes in the assistant staff have for the time checked progress, but a good standard is reached. In particular the children in the upper classes are accurate working in Arithmetic, sums, and understand what they are doing, but it is suggested that the syllabus in this subject might be simplified by the omission of the less useful rules.

2. The other subjects of the curriculum are being successfully handled with the exception of composition which does not quite reach the same high order. The essays are rather too short and are not striking in quality. A more extensive and definite study of literature would greatly help in improving the children's command of language.

3. Special praise is due to the instruction in Gardening which is practical. Full advantage is taken on this instruction to make the boys reason on what they are doing.

4. It was suggested to the master that it might be possible to let Standard V11 work apart from Standard V1 more than they do at present.

5. The woman inspector of Domestic Subjects reports that the needlework is taught on good lines and that the work generally is good. There is a tendency to give the younger girls too difficult garments to make. The classes are large.

    It is important that close touch should be kept with the cookery centre. Girls qualified by age ought to attend the centre even though they may not be high up in the school.

Empire Day was kept on the 22nd of June as the 24th fell on a Sunday.

I gave children a talk on Empire.

- Growth of Empire during Queen Victoria's reign.
- Why the day was chosen.
- Why the day was celebrated.
- Magnitude and responsibility of our Empire.
- How boys and girls can help to maintain the Empire.

July 15th   Rain – Sunday School Treat postponed – Holiday postponed

July 17th   Mr Bacon called this morning with Mrs Panton. Mrs P accused Mr Few of bruising her son on the head. I promised to attend to matter on Monday. The boy has a large bruise on the forehead.

Mr few admits striking the boy. Mr Few to call on parents.

Mrs P wants to prosecute.

Mr Sawkins called respecting treatment of Mr Few to his son: case reported to Mr Bell.

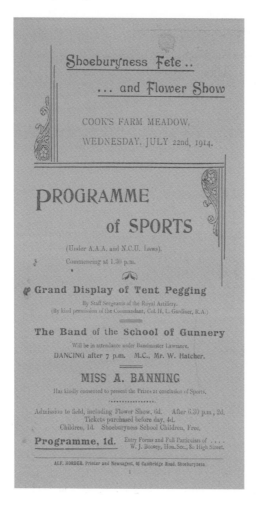

Aug 4th   **Britain declares War on Germany.**

Oct 14th   Visit this P.M. at 6 o'clock from Lieut. & the Sarg. of the Police inspecting the lighting of the school for cleaning purposes. It was pointed out that the windows presented such a large lighted area that it was positively dangerous under the present conditions.

Letter from Col, Earnest Harrison acting Staff Capt. Respecting accommodation of the boys of the Garrison School – about 40. Called on Mr Bell concerning both matters. Called upon Colonel Harrison and told him that under the circumstances we would take the boys.

Asked Mrs Crombie to get her cleaning done morning, noon and early afternoon to avoid evening lighting.

Oct 26th   We open at he afternoon session at 1.30 and close at 4 o'clock to help Mrs Crombie. Time Table is advanced a half hour but the periods are not altered.

Nov. 2nd   Mr Bell visited school children. Interview with Staff Capt. 43 boys as withdrawn from Garrison

Nov 3rd   Mr Metcalfe visited the School, Major Harrison, Staff Capt, called respecting recreation room.

Dec 9th   Went to London to buy prizes, returned 2 – 6 P.M.

Dec 22nd   Prizes given – 2 presented for general improvement.

Join up! Your country needs you! Southend Mayor Alderman Joseph Francis addresses a recruitment parade on Dec 3rd 1914. The Council aimed to recruit 1000 men for Kitchener's British Expeditionary Force. See Appendix 4: Wakering Roll of Honour, Sidney Morris Smith killed in action 26th September 1915. (See Appendix 4, Wakering Roll Of Honour, pages 287-288)

1915

During the early hours of Monday 10th May 1915 a Zeppelin LZ38 dropped over 100 incendiary bombs on Southend. The Zeppelin was commanded by Erich Linnarz and the first bomb dropped near the Royal Edward Prison Ship moored alongside the Pier.

Linnarz, returned to attack Ramsgate, Shoeburyness and Southend on the 17th May. Despite anti-aircraft fire from Shoeburyness 70 bombs were dropped. Two women were killed .Again; on the 31st May Linarz attacked London, dropping 120 bombs, skirting Shoeburyness and Southend en route. There were seven deaths. Flight Lieutenant A.W. Robertson took off from Rochford in his Bleriot, but engine failure forced his return. On June 7th 1915 the LZ38 was bombed and destroyed.

Aug 30th   Mr Bell called this afternoon. Spoke to him of my leaving school 2 or 3 afternoons each week at 4.5 – I am desirous of completing a course of Remedial Gymnastics for the benefit of wounded troops.

13th Sept   Mrs A.I.Bridges commenced duties this afternoon. Army Schoolmistress.

With kind permission of Ken Crowe from Zeppelins over Southend 2008

Sept 30th   Mrs Joliffe terminated her duties here today. The Staff presented her with a handbag.

Oct 5th   3 boys (of the Garrison School) left here & applied for admission at Royal Artillery School. They were admitted contrary to Garrison Orders.
I wrote to parents this A.M. and they were sent back.

Nov 1st   22 Boys and 25 Girls transferred from Royal Artillery School. Another 10 Boys are in Standard V.

The two Assistant masters Swanworth and Tew, discontinued work here on Friday afternoon having enlisted in the R.G.A. I notified Mr Bell on Tuesday as soon as I heard from the men, and informed him I could carry on.

1916

April 6th   His Majesty's visit to Shoebury.
Children taken to Mrs Mott's meadow at 10.30 returned 10.55. Afternoon session closed at 3.35 to enable the scholars to see him return.

Mount Farm, North Shoebury.

July 6th   Mrs Harris complained that Miss L.Cox excessively punished her child. There was a bruise on the spine of the scapula. Miss Cox apologised.

Oct 24th   Miss Hicks reports that on Friday afternoon nearly the whole class rebelled, one boy T. Crowhurst struck at her.
I separated the greater part of the class and am taking them in the Hall. Parents of the boy were sent for – they were grieved and punished him. The work has much deteriorated.

Oct 31st   Miss Forrest did not give Bessie Eves her attendance mark though the child was at the Cookery Kitchen. Miss F. Says she could not recognise her as the child was suffering from a septic finger. The finger had been bad for 2 weeks but it is now dry and whole. In the first week she was allowed to attend though she had a poultice on the finger. She worked at the oven. In the second week there was ointment on the finger & the child greased the tins. Mr D. has been asked to sanction the child's mark in the registers.

1917

March 5th Absent this P.M. Funeral of father in law.

Dr Truman and Dr Roper inspected all children this morning owing to one of the scholars having died on Friday of Spotted Fever.

May 2nd Staff Capt .wrote asking that boys might attend military funerals of 2 men. Referred to Mr Bell.

May 3rd Chaplain called this P.M. says permission received.

May 3rd Acting on instructions received from Mr Bell this morning Form DR17 sent in to Recruiting Officer. Form N.S.V.I. has also been forwarded. I was under the impression that teachers were exempt.

Request from Army Chaplain that Choir boys be excused for attending Military Funerals referred to Mr Bell.

May 4th Chaplain present at 1.15 and peremptorily ordered me to deliver the boys as he had obtained permission: No notice of this has been sent me.

May 5th Letter from Mr Bell requesting that Choir boys be absent from school to attend another Military Funeral.

"It is hoped that the services of the boys will not be required very often, but should they be wanted it is felt that no serious objection ought to be taken."

Church Parade in Horseshoe Barracks, Shoeburyness

May 10th Request today from Army Chaplain, G.W. Bates for my boys (10) to attend Military Funeral. The attendance of children at funerals is evidently of no importance to this

Chaplain for this is the third in a fortnight. The Officer to be buried is not on the staff, was engaged on a temporary work and died of disease contacted before he came here.

The Chaplain's method of procedure is contrary to War Office Regulations for such application can only be made through the Staff Capt. or Adjutant and permission can only be given by the father to the Officer Commanding the unit. Children of soldiers attending Civil Schools are bound by the rules governing Army Scholars.

May 11th   Wrote to Mr Bell that the privileges granted to Miss Bacon – re Choir boy's funerals, might be given to Miss Franks of Parish Church. This permission would prevent boys breaking a rule which has always been observed.

A Zeppelin shot down in the Thames Estuary, 1916.

June 13th   1917 Air Raid 10.55. Return Raid 12.5.
Visited rooms. Children perfectly quiet and unalarmed. Many did not know though the extraordinary din of firing caused some to flinch.
The Upper children were filing into school after recreation when the guns drew their attention to the visitors. One class took voice exercises in the Hall during the worst phase.

June 13th   Cooking Demonstration – Public.
Repeated on the 20th inst.
The class did not meet on both these days but the only intimation I got that the girls

were to visit the centre was from the scholars themselves.

6 girls on the first day & 8 on the second day were at the Cookery Centre and were not marked on the Register.

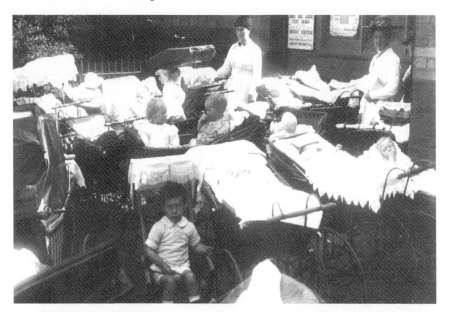

The baby clinic. Probably at Argyll Road Westcliff during the First World War.

July 7th   To aid in Baby week celebrations the scholars gave a concert in the playground from 2.45 – 3.45. Capt & Mrs Raith and the Chairman of the U.D.C. were present together with about 200 mothers and friends.

Sept 3rd   School re-opened. Attendance fairly good.
              R.J.Horner absent – illness.

Sept 4th   Cycled to Barling to pay Mr Horner his salary.

Sept 5th   Air Raids on Monday night and again last night. Many children this morning show signs of loss of sleep.
              Conferred with Infant Mistress Miss Lewis and decided to send the children home at 11.30 this morning and to give them this afternoon from 30 to 50 minutes for complete rest in their rooms.
              Night Raids: Sept 2nd, 3rd, 4th, 23rd, 24th, 25th, 28th, 29th, 30th, Oct 1st.
              Midday Raid: Oct 2nd, 24 children returned in Afternoon. School closed for P.M.

Oct 4th   False Alarm 11.45 A.M.

Oct 10th   Air Raid 8P.M – 2P.M.   Oct 26. 27. 28. Attempted Raid.

Oct 27th   Air Raid

Oct 29th   Request by Head Teachers Barling, Wakering & Shoebury for holiday refused.

Oct 31st   A.M. Estuary Raid
           P.M. Raid 11 P.M to 3 A.M.

Nov 26th   Offer of invalid couch and weighing machine free for school use. Went to inspect them at Wakering this morning.

Bomb damage in Southend during the First World War. A boarding house in Cromwell Road, Southend is gutted by a bomb.

Nov 26th   16 boys left for Garrison School which re-opened today.

Dec 6th   Air Raids this AM, 4.20 & 7.30. 50 children absent this AM, 5 teachers. Mr Bacon checked register.

Dec 12th   Open Day & Sale of Work
           Halls and rooms crowded. Classes 111, 1V, V1, V11 each gave songs (2). There was no room for the Dance. Total received £47 – 1 – 0, 5 sacks of potatoes and some bags of vegetables.
           Whole for the sick and wounded in Overcliff Hospital. Miss Banning came in at 2 o'clock, visited each room & asked to see work done by children of school telling teachers that she was a Manager & also that she wanted to see the material as she had several complaints about its quality.

Dec 21st   Closed for Xmas
           Air Raids Dec 22 Jan 3rd.

*Excited crowds packed Pier Hill and wounded soldiers cheered from
the balconies as Princess Mary visited the hospital in 1917.*

1918

Jan 10th   Information requested by Mr Bell & forwarded today.

           No. depositors in Post Office   116

           No. depositors in War Savings Certs. 143

           Amt. Subs. Since Feb 1917 in War Saving Certs. £528.6.0.

Jan 28th   Air Raid 8 P.M. to 1.15 A.M.

Jan 29th   Air Raid 9.30 PM to 1.30 AM.

Mar 8th   Air Raid last night 11 to 1.30.

Apr 10th   Went to London to visit wounded son this afternoon. Wrote to Mr Bell concerning absence.

Apr 12th   Attending Capt Massey's funeral Absent 2.15 to 3 o'clock.

May 19th Air Raid 11/ - 2.30 (B) Sun – Mon.

May 24th   Empire Day: Rector Rev. G. Ellis Jones supported by Mr Boosey, Chairman of U.D.C. addressed the assembled children. Miss Banning came in after the proceedings had commenced & stayed at the end of the Hall until after dismissal. She then came to the Hall where I greeted her & after some casual remarks to Rector & Mr Boosey she turned to go and said in passing, "I have not questioned your teachers, Mr Hillyer", and the following dialogue ensued between Miss B. and myself. I write it down as it occurred that the facts may not in future be distorted.
"I do not know what you are referring to but if you had questioned the teachers it would br quite immaterial to me."
"You ask your teachers what I say to them."
"I have never at any time asked my teachers what you or any other manager has said to them."
"You did question them."
"I beg your pardon; I have never done such a thing."
"You have – you said so in your Log Book. You said I questioned your teachers at the sale of work."
"I do not remember what entry I made in the Log but as it is a practise I need not indulge in I could not have made a statement, but I will get the book to prove my assertion."
As the Rector & Mr Boosey were standing by they were asked to remain as witnesses. Page 234 was read by Miss B and her accusation was found to be false.
"I apologise", added Miss Banning, "but it was unkind of you to make any entry in the Log Book."
I replied that it was necessary to make verbatim reports for future reference.
Miss B. said she was compelled to introduce herself as a Manager to the staff because I had never introduced her to them – we have only two strangers on the staff and when the classroom is crowded with parents & the Mistress is busy it is scarcely the time to introduce oneself.
The person responsible for the school or for the subject is the one capable of speaking of the quality of the materials used.

July 1st   "At Home" to Parents

Children gave a display from 2.15 to 3.30. in playground. Collection was taken on behalf of Childrens Welfare Funds. Messrs Bacon, Boosey and the Rector were present and spoke to the parents.

Oct 17th   Closed school room this morning owing to influenza. M.O.H. & Messrs Bacon, Whent & Boosey.

Nov 11th   The signing of the Armistice by Germany caused much excitement soon after 11o'clock this morning. There was considerable noise with the whistles from engines in both the railways and from sirens and the children were far too excited to work. They were sent home at 11.15. I wired to Mr Bell for a holiday and Mr Boosey and Mr Bacon – both managers thought the children unfit to return. In the afternoon I therefore put up a notice outside the school to that effect.

Peace Parade, Shoeburyness.

79

1919

Feb 10th   Wrote to Mr Bell re visit London specialist & that visit might be repeated twice at fortnightly period.

Staff :

Miss E. Brooks	C.T.
Miss E. May	C.T.
Miss C. Villa	C.T.
Miss E. Cox	U
Miss L. Cox	U
Pupil Teacher Albert Horner	

April 1st   Scholars sent home. Temp inside rooms 40° – no fuel.

Jun 11th   No. of children admitted from Hinguar St. Infant Dept Stand 11 – 45.
Average age of children – 9 years and 3 months
No. of children admitted from Richmond Avenue School Standard 1V – 46
Average age of children – 11 years 3 months.

July 19th   Saturday Peace Celebrations.
Children met at school – marched to field.
Sports from 1 o'clock to 7.30.
Tea 4.30 each child given a mug or a beaker.

National Peace Day 1919

July 21st   Left this A.M for Saffron Walden Geography Course. Miss Brooks left in charge.

Sept 8th   The following children have left to take up Scholarships in the High School. Jolly – Free School. Rowlands & Gooch – part School. Elsie Alexander – Art School.

Sept 10th   Went to London this P.M. to visit son in Hospital.

Oct 27th   Report to Managers – asked for another cupboard.

Oct 24th   School closed this afternoon for one week – to celebrate Peace.

Nov.3rd   School Sports
           It has been decided to introduce School Sports again among the scholars but to run them on slightly different lines. Each class will form a unit and will be represented on a General Committee, elected wholly by the scholar members and workers, without the help of the Staff. I wrote to Mr Bell informing him of our intention and suggesting Tuesday afternoons 2-30 to 3-45.

Hinguar Football team 1920-21 season. My Dad Ralph Harknett
front row holding football. Mr Hillyer left.

Nov 7th   Miss Viller absent today – illness.

Nov 12th   Owing to an attack of Influenza I have been attending late & leaving early for the last 3 days.

Nov 20th   The Visiting Committee has visited the school this morning – I had gone to an incident when they arrived. Mr Mitchell – the Chairman said it was intended to send down to me 40 children from Richmond Avenue School who were too old for the classes.

Dec 1st	25 boys & 18 girls have been promoted From Richmond Av. S.

Dec 1st   25 boys & 18 girls have been promoted From Richmond Av. S.

They consist of Standard 111 - 7, Standard 1V boys – 11, Standard 1V girls – 22.

Average age of Std. 111 – 11 years 5 months.

Average age of Std. 1V – 11 years 9 months.

Of the latter 2 are turned 13 years & 10 are over 12 years of age.

Standard 1V are poor readers & unintelligent; their work is untidy & English very weak. They have no knowledge of fractions or decimals, method of unit, Proportion, Areas, symbols & are very inaccurate.

1920

High Street, Shoeburyness Hotel, Garrison Gate and Jenkins Garage. C. 1920

Jan 9th   Children promoted are too old for Scholarships or else the standard of work & attainment is so much below necessary requirements of that Exam that it is quite impossible without undue pressure in making up arrears in the short time allowed.

My rule has been to promote scholars every half-year but for several years the amount of arrears has caused intensive teaching in this Dept. which has produced so great a strain upon the scholars and the staff that it is now decided to extend the period to 12 months.

Repeated application for reconsideration of the promotion age has produced no result. I have therefore altered my reorganisation and the syllabus to meet the attainment of the promoted scholars.

Jan 15th to 22nd   Miss Parris absent – father states through overstrain.

Mar 1st   Miss Parris absent – visiting doctor.

Mar 22nd   Pupil Teacher Horner absent this week for Certificate Exam.

On three occasions recently the children of Class 2 (Std. 1V) have been sent to play in the playground owing to there being no teacher for them & I have been engaged on other work.

The work of the school continues to deteriorate. With some of the staff continuous supervision is a necessity but I am confined to one room & am neither able to supervise nor to help.

Mar 19th R.A.N. Hillyer, appointed to temp. Asst. till July. London Matric 1914. Birth

Dec 19th   1899. Taking Class V1.

Mar 31st   School closed for Easter.

Apr 12th   Student Teacher Laura heading commenced work as from 1st. Born Feb 23rd 1903. Passed Camb. Cert.

Am now able to give Miss Parris a lower class and 2 classes (3& 4) have been split to make 3.

Oct 1st   Mr R. Hillyer left today.

Oct 8th   Miss E. Cox terminated her services this morning.

Oct 8th   Managers Meeting 3.30. Extract from Report.

This shortness (of staff) necessitates re-organising to enable remaining teachers to take other classes whilst their own are at recreation.

Extract from Report to Managers Nov 7th 1920

I enclose Med. Cert. From Miss Howard who has been absent since Nov 1st. This additional shortage gives me now 4 classes or about 200 children to take care of. Teaching or even adequate supervision is entirely out of the question. The children are not only not making progress but are going back and seeds of trouble in the matter of discipline are being sown that will take years to eradicate. It must be understood that I can be in one form only at a time & whilst I am in one, I cannot be seen by the children in the other three, & sometimes the children get into such an excited condition that I am compelled to send some of them into the playground or, if the Time Table permits, to send them home earlier.

Nov 2nd   Miss Howard absent – illness.

Nov 10th   Am compelled to get away this afternoon to keep appointment with a Physician in London. It was originally fixed for 11.30 but that at present is impossible. The continuous overstrain is compelling me to seek other medical attention.

Nov 16th   Mr Cunningham a County supply teacher commenced duty on Nov 8th at 3 P.M.

Nov 19th   Miss Cox was too ill to remain at school this morning. She returned in the afternoon.

Nov 23rd   Miss Villa absent through illness today.

Nov 24th   Miss Villa returned to duty.

Nov 25th   Miss Villa absent today.

Nov 26th   Miss Villa returned.

Dec 6th   Mr Cunningham absent today. Mr R.A.N. Hillyer commenced supply duty.

Dec 7th   Mr Cunningham recommenced.

Dec 10th   Mr Cunningham recalled to Tilbury.

Dec 13th   Mr Rex Hillyer absent – illness.

1921

Mr Hillyer and class, 1921.

June 21st   School Sports today Saturday.
Class A. Invitation & Relay Hinguar St Juns V Richmond Av Juns.
10 events open to both Infant and Junior Depts.
Class B. Open to Hinguar Street Senior School.

22 Events comprising Flat, Hurdle & Skipping races, Hop, Step & Jump, Long & High Jump.

nter-class competitions & Relay races.

Class C open to Old Scholars.

Class D. Invitation Relay races – Gt. Wakering, Eastwood & Benfleet.

July 4th   School Report for June submitted to the Managers this evening
Average Attendance for month 464.

The school is staffed for 285 children and Miss Heading, the Ex-Student Teacher is not able to be left for more than a minute at a time.

In Nov. 1915 two men teachers left for the Army and one Mistress was appointed to the vacancies, since that date the school has never been fully staffed. It is questionable whether the parents of scholars of any school in any part of the of the County would have quietly submitted to such neglect of their children. Five cert. teachers are required and so far only one is promised and he has scarcely any experience. Miss Howard leaves us in August.

I feel the added strain is severely injuring my health and that of the competent staff for this latter share the xtra work. Today I had no teachers for 3 classes and a fourth I had to maintain contact with – making 221 in all.

Everything has been done to maintain the tone of the school by means of Sports etc but there is a limit to human endeavour. The teachers sent by the County are practically worthless and I trust some effort may be made to give the Shoeburyness children an equal chance with those in other parts of the country. In eagerness and ability they are unmatched but they demand one who can control them.

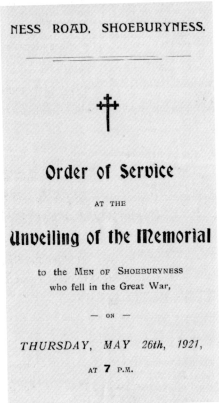

NESS ROAD. SHOEBURYNESS.

✝

Order of Service

AT THE

Unveiling of the Memorial

to the MEN OF SHOEBURYNESS
who fell in the Great War,

— ON —

THURSDAY, MAY 26th, 1921,

AT 7 P.M.

In Memoriam.

C. BIRD	W. JOHNSON	W. SMART
A. S. BOSWELL	A. C. JOLLY	W. SMART
H. J. BRAZIER	E. A. KEYES	H. SOUTH
H. G. BROWN	S. C. KINGSLEY	W. SOUTH
W. J. BRYANT	S. KNIGHT	F. SPREADBOROUGH
D. BUXTON	G. H. LIVERMORE	J. M. STEVENS
A. E. CASTLE	S. MARSH	J. SWANCOTT
F. CAUSE	V. MAY	E. J. TAYLOR
J. CORK	T. E. MACNALLY	E. W. THOMAS
C. W. DEADMAN	H. G. MACNALLY	G. TRIGG
H. DEAN	A. J. MOTT	W. TURNER
A. F. ENDERSBY	J. H. MOTT	E. TURNER
W. EVES	F. K. MOTT	G. TYLER
J. E. FISHER	E. N. NICHOLLS	F. TYRRELL
H. W. FOSTER	F. NOON	F. G. TYRRELL
E. A. FRENCH	H. NORDEN	W. D. VILLA
O. L. FUGGLE	J. NOTLEY	A. WATTS
S. GAGE	P. ODELL	F. S. WEST
W. H. GOODCHILD	J. PEACOCK	J. T. WHALE
C. W. GREINER	W. PELLETT	C. T. WHITEHOUSE
E. C. HALL	J. O. POTTER	E. C. WIGG
J. J. HARDEN	S. J. POTTER	C. B. WILDISH
H. S. W. HERBERT	J. PORTER	H. R. WILSON
A. E. W. HUNT	S. A. PRIOR	J. J. WINTER
A. V. HUMPHRIES	G. ROBERTS	L. WOOD
J. HUMPHRIES	A. ROBERTS	F. WOOD
J. B. HOWDLE	G. H. SCARROLD	C. WOODS
C. J. R. HURRELL	H. A. SELF	
W. J. JEFFS	W. G. SIMONS	

Smalls, Printer, Southend

Unveiling the War Memorial at Ness Road, Shoeburyness 1921.
The old Palace Cinema can be seen.

C	Miss E.Brooks	V1 &V11	76 on Register
C	Mr A.E. Allaway	V1	67
T.C.	Miss Villa	V Upper	63
Supply	Miss Cerson	V Lower	43
T.C.	Mr Hansen	V R.A.	62
T.C.	Miss Knott	1V	63
T.C	Miss Cox	111	71
Total no. on Registers 445			

1922

School Report for Meeting of Managers October

Mr Hansen is making satisfactory progress. Having had only a few weeks of Practical Teaching before coming here some allowance must be made.

Miss Cerson, the Supply Teacher from Wakering is making great headway and I am quite pleased with the progress she is making.

Mr Allaway is not great as a Disciplinarian or as a Teacher but his genial manner helps him considerably. Being the Proprietor of two businesses he finds the work too exacting.

Miss Knott is almost hopeless.

May 5th The attention of Mr Hamm, (C) & of Miss Trevett (N) was drawn this morning to the fact that they were teaching examples of Arithmetic (exactly similar except as to number) like those selected for the Term Exam which will be commenced on Monday.

The custom here is for the Class Teacher to draw up the questions & submit them to me for suggestions & alterations. This was done yesterday and Monday's Exam work would have been the farce of reproducing, except for numbers, an example taught today.

Miss Trevett appears to be the injured party & was very rude in her manner.

May 24th Celebration of Empire Day 9.30 – 10.15. Infants joined us round the flag staff. Mr Bacon, Mr Boosey, Miss Banning asked the 'King' sung as flag unfurled, addressed by myself. Mr Pollard spoke on symbols of colours of flag. Hymns, National Anthem, returned school, dismissed 11.40. Sports at Southend.

May 31st School Year altered to September & combined registers are to be used from the last week in June to tide over the interval.

Sept 4th   Advanced class for children up to 16 commenced. Desks requisitioned in July not to hand though wire was sent to Mr Bell on Thursday last.

40 children consequently sitting on the floor, and another complete class of 56 sitting 3 to a desk.

Goody's Dairy,
Richmond Avenue,
opposite
St. Andrew's
Church.

Sept 4th   Mr Eley called this morning to make enquiries concerning requisition for desks sent to the office in mid July notwithstanding that the fullest information concerning past, present & future numbers was sent to Mr bell with the requisition in order to expedite the order.

Sept 29th   Desks delivered yesterday afternoon. Much of stock not yet in. Further letter to Chelmsford.

Sept 29th   Mr Green has very little knowledge of class control and I have spent considerable time hovering about the class.

Nov. 20th   The work of Standard V1 is very poor in quality and neatness. Mr Green a student from training and without much experience does his best and is most anxious but he knows neither what to teach or how to teach, and the children are the sufferers from employing inexperienced and unqualified teachers. The deterioration is very evident.

Shoeburyness Council School Report by H.M.I. Mr. J.E.Hales.
Inspected on 16th Nov. and 22 Nov 1922

1. An interesting experiment is being made in the upper part of the school. A special class of about 40 children has been formed with the object of taking them through a two year course of study on the Dalton plan. The Head Master and two assistant teachers are sharing the work, each being responsible for two or three subjects. Energy and enthusiasm are being shown by all concerned and in due course good results may be looked for. At present however, the actual attainments and capabilities of the pupils need more consideration. The text books chosen are difficult, and the language is beyond the comprehension of many scholars.

   For this reason and also because the work had been done almost entirely by private study and too much had been attempted, it was found that the children had not really assimilated what they had studied. Further, their power of expressing themselves at any length either orally or in writing, is as yet rather undeveloped. It may also be pointed out that both teachers and children should be conscious of a definite purpose with regard to the study of each subject and the means should be found to encourage initiative and resourcefulness. Further, it might prove possible to differentiate between the courses of work for the boys and for the girls, and due regard should be had in the case of the boys to the practical side of the work.

2. There are seven other large classes in the school. Two of these (one of 93 and one of 56 pupils) consist of children who attended Richmond Avenue School up to Standard 1V. On account of the difficulty of fitting these children into the system of organisation at Hinguar Street it seems essential that some method of collaboration between the two departments should be instituted. Another large class of girls, it is understood, is composed of three heterogeneous groups.

Gothic Row.

3. All the classes were seen and tested in the course of the two visits. The work, regarded as a whole, is of moderate quality and there was much unevenness. The staff carry out their duties carefully and industriously. It was felt however, that there was a lack of unity of purpose and aim. In a large school like this there is every need for complete co-ordination of effort. Some of the schemes need revision and it would be well to take the opportunity of recasting the plans as a whole.

Jackson's Shop, Rampart Street.

1923

Jan 8th   As Mr Green has proved himself incompetent to maintain the class of ordinary size, the whole of the upper school has been re-organised to give him a class of 34.

Feb 12th   Mr Green absent owing to death of his mother.

Feb 19th   Mr Green returned.

Copy of Reply to Rochford Hundred D.S.C.
H.M.I.s Report may be divided into two parts
Section 1 Special Class
Section 2 General School Report.
Section 2   After years of insufficient and inefficient staff, during which time the standard of the work of former years had to be abandoned and the whole system of organisation changed to meet the deteriorating conditions, H.M.I.s report on the work of the school 3 months after stable conditions of the staff had been assured.

Previous reports of mine verify the accuracy of H.M.I.s statements, but I hope that two or three years will see us re-established. I note even in this one term's work a move in the right direction.

Unfortunately such a report does not give sufficient credit to the few teachers who have borne the burden and heat of the day.

With reference to Section1 on the Experimental Class, one or two points require explanation. The class is on the individual system, and not on the Dalton Plan, the latter being impossible under the present staffing accommodation and apparatus available. The children were chosen from all classes, grades and conditions of mentality in order to afford us information as to the effect of this system.

Here again the inspection was made 6 weeks after commencing the experiment, and the report is premature to say the least. I have received unsolicited testimony from several parents, that the distinct advantages of the system are apparent in their children even at this early date, and they speak well of the change in their children's' outlook, deportment, language and of their conversational powers, and of their anxiety to do and stand well in the eyes of their teachers.

Our plans and methods are not perfect and some of the results have been disappointing but the lessons learned are of great permanent value and we are convinced that we are on the right lines and that from the normal and sub-normal child, the individual work is superior to that gained by mass teaching, and in time, with an assured staff, it will be possible to introduce it, in a modified form, throughout the school.

Hinguar Street Council School, Shoeburyness Mixed Department.
Inspected on 1st. March 1923
Report on Needlework.

1. The Needlework scheme here is arranged on sound practical lines, and many of the girls were making garments for their own use. In all classes but one, the numbers are large, and individual attention is therefore difficult; it is all the more creditable to the teachers that in spite of this, the principle of letting each girl cut out her own garments has been adhered to.

2. In those sections of Standards V, V1, and V11 which are taught by the Certificated Assistant who is in charge of the Needlework, the work was very satisfactory. The sewing was in the main neat and clean, and the girls were

bright and interested in what they were doing. The planning of the work in these classes is evidently carefully thought out, and the teaching effective.

3. The work of Standards 111 and 1V, and the other sections of Standards V and V1 was not so satisfactory. Many of the garments seen in these classes were not being kept clean, and it looked as though interest had flagged, and the work had been on hand too long. Care had not always been taken to ensure that the most reliable methods of construction for the different materials were either definitely taught, or applied in their proper places.

4. The "Special Class" girls showed much interest in their needlework and many of them had constructed their own patterns and schemes of decoration. The standard of neatness and finish however in this class might well be higher, and the methods of decoration more interesting and varied. This class is exceptionally small in numbers, and some really good individual work should be possible.

Whent Stores, on the corner of West Road and Seaview Road c.1920

May 4th   **Copy of Report sent to Managers**

Mr Green has now been with us 8 months, but although he has had continuous help and advice he is still not yet capable of managing a class of even small size. In order to give him a fresh chance he was given at Easter a completely new set of children who had not previously been in contact with him in anyway – a class about half the size other teachers are taking -, but these children like his former class are already beyond his control when he is left alone with them.

When a class has a weak teacher it suffers not only during that period, but the ill-effects are shown throughout the rest of its school career and succeeding teachers are handicapped in their efforts.

July 9th **Copy of School Report for June.**

An endeavour is being made to raise the standard of attainments and in most cases with some success but the results of Mr Green's work will remain as long as the children, at present in his class, are attending school. Other teachers will be expected to reap where he has sown and for 3 years at least an adverse report can only be given on a school which contains a class such as this and the one I was compelled to take from him at Easter. It is somewhat unfair to the other members of the staff that one member should be paid – for less qualifications and less work – at the same rate of pay as themselves and as teachers depend for their advancement upon the school report, it is certainly not fair that their future should be sacrificed to another teacher's incompetency. The parents too, have grave cause for complaint.

Oct 6th **Needlework Report from County Needlework Instructress.**

In the Upper school the work is good. Suitable garments are made, the sewing as a whole is neat & clean and simple decorative stitches are taught.

In Stand.s 111 & 1V the work is decidedly poor, the stitches are most irregular and seams and openings badly made. Apparently careless work is overlooked & insufficient supervision is given.

Extract from accompanying letter:- It is suggested by the Director that Needlework of Stand.s 111, 1V, might with advantage be taught by some other member..

Reply to above; I have now been able to transfer Miss Cox & give N. To Miss Brooks. It means of course, that the former is taken from a subject in which the results obtained are palpable to an ordinary individual & given another in which the results are not so evident to even a keen observer. She is a teacher of limited ability & is not really qualified for a higher standard school.

9th Oct The Managers have given consideration to the question of the transfer of children from Richmond Avenue to Hinguar Street School, and have adopted proposals as follows:-

(i)   That the normal age for the main promotion in September of the scholars from Std. 1V at Richmond Avenue to Std. V at Hinguar Street be 10 years 6 months.

(ii)   That at the end of June a list of all scholars in the Richmond Avenue School who will reach the age of ten and a half years on September 1st shall be prepared by the Head Teacher for consideration of the Managers at their next meeting and that in the few cases where it may be desirable to retain pupils in the Junior School a further six months the special reasons for doing so shall be fully stated.

(iii) That, on March 1st following, a further promotion be made of the scholars who have during the previous six months reached the age of 10 years 6 months

1924

Extract from Report of Horticultural Instructor For the month of July 1924

SHOEBURYNESS HINGUAR STREET COUNCIL SCHOOL

This garden has again proved difficult to keep in order, owing to its size. Part of it now to be laid down to grass which will admit of more effective work being done on the remainder.

Nov. 10th Monthly Report to Managers

The two new Mistresses have now been at work rather more than two months – sufficient time for them to show their ability – if they possess it. Miss Grimes, although of an extremely nervous temperament, will with time and patience make good, but Miss Duke is hopeless in a Senior School where the classes are large. I gave her a class of the youngest children in the school and have spent considerable time with her, knowing she had no previous experience, but, despite all encouragement, she seems to have made up her mind that she is incapable of managing, and the work of the children as well as their behaviour is deteriorating. Miss Duke is a refined girl, but is only 20 years of age, and until she came here had never been responsible for a class. She is therefore overwhelmed. I am sure the Managers will appreciate the fact that in a Senior School, it is particularly necessary to have strong and experienced Teachers if we to do the work which is possible with such children as ours. In addition to these two beginners I would like to remind the Managers there are two Uncertificated Teachers who are really insufficient for older scholars.

Shoeburyness Hinguar Street Council School. Inspected on 14th October 1924
Report by H.M.I. Mr. J.E. Hales.
Mixed Department

As the last report made various suggestions about the methods adopted in training the children at the top of the school it should be placed on record that much success is now being achieved in this part of the school work.

The two top classes, one for boys and the other for girls, are known as "Student" classes and are limited to scholars who have made sufficient progress with their studies and who intend to remain sufficiently long at school to put in at least two years of comparatively advanced work. In these classes the scholars are required to study for themselves and to exercise their own judgment in various ways; e.g. as regards the books they consult and the amount of time they devote to each subject. They produce some very good and interesting written work and are able to discuss what they have been doing quite intelligently. They apply themselves industriously to their studies and evidently appreciate the methods by which they are being trained. The two teachers in charge of these classes are much to be congratulated on the results achieved.

The numbers in the two 'the student' classes have wisely been limited to 40 but in the rest of the school the work is at present much hampered by over-crowding and large classes. There are 9 classes and 7 rooms so that two classes have to be taught in the Hall. Two classes have 60 on the books, two have 58, one has 55, one 54 and the last 27 only.

The total number on the books is 456 while the accommodation is only 340. Additional school accommodation will, it is understood, be provided at Shoeburyness

Shoeburyness Hinguar Street Mixed School 20.11.24

In the May report of the Horticultural Instructor on the garden at this school, it is stated that "difficulties are experienced in securing the time to do full justice to this subject and to some extent we see this reflected in the condition of the plots."

Hinguar pupils, 1924.

Gardening is placed as a subject on the school time-table for Tuesdays and Thursdays; weather permitting and the Head Master reports that an average of about 2 hours per week is devoted to the teaching. He teaches this subject himself, but for the last two or three years he has felt that as his staff included a proportion either of weak or inexperienced teachers or both who could not well be left, it was his duty to help them in their work and consequently he has allowed the garden somewhat to get behind. There are of course occasions when the gardening will be taken on two or three days in succession if operations have been delayed by weather and his presence with the gardening boys meant leaving these teachers too long without guidance or help. The garden is however, separated from the school by the playground and it is therefore within easy distance. And the Head Teacher has agreed that now he should be able to find opportunity at least to superintend the work of the boys on the garden. He has now three male Teachers on the Staff one of whom has been selected this year for a course of instruction in Gardening at Chelmsford.

A great deal of work in the garden is now due to be done. The tools are stored in a long wooden shed on the site and, as a door has now been fixed, they are reasonably safe and there is no reason why a tool-shed be supplied.

1925

May 11th   Mr Hillyer absent. Post pneumonia convalescence.

Extract from the Report of the Horticultural Instructor for the month of July 1925.
Changes wrought recently in the lay-out of this garden have already produced satisfactory results and from the practical standpoint the work is of high grade quality. Little correlation is attempted except in regard to nature study. The subject, however, is receiving sympathetic handling and indications are not lacking that it will become increasingly useful.

Shoebury Fire Brigade 1925

1926

June 18th   This morning Cicely Pipe, aged 14, entering the classroom about 8.59 from behind children assembled in the Hall and endeavouring to do so quickly and quietly as possible to avoid being late for prayers, put her head through the glass panel of the door. In addition to superficial abrasions she received a deep cut of semicircular shape on her forehead which bled profusely. I phoned to the doctor, hired a cab to take her to the surgery after having rendered first aid. She was then conveyed home.

Nov 5th   The House System has been instituted and the House Captains were invested this afternoon

Nov 16th   First Social – Eton – this evening 5/30 – 7/30.

Nov 17th   Old Scholars Social.

Dec 14th The last House Social – Winchester.

1927

Apr 12th   At the Managers Meeting Last Evening Miss Banning gave the names of three children whom she implied had been put in the Special Class when the parents wished them to be presented for the Scholarship Exam. The following is an extract from a letter sent to the Chairman after investigating the facts this morning.

The three names given are 1) Ella Smith 2) Doris Foster 3) Ronald Cook.No.s 1 7 2 were from April 1915 so it is evident that all opportunities of sitting for the School Exam were over before they entered our school eligible scholars being retained at Richmond Av. S.

In the case of Ronald Cook the mother decided against the Exam preferring our Special Class. She promptly communicated the fact to Miss Whitehead who having then no object in detaining him sent him up to us. As the mother's decision was made whilst the boy was attending the R.A. School I may be able to escape suspicion in the matter.

June 3rd   Gardening Instruction Shoeburyness Council School

This garden was found to be in capital order. Cropping had been carried out well and some attention has been given to fruit and flower culture.

Sept 25th   A boy named Maurice Phillips this afternoon whilst under Gardening Instruction injured his foot with a garden fork. The wound was carefully washed, the foot bound up and the boy was then taken home in Mr Horner's side car.

Copy of H.M.I Report

Shoeburyness Hinguar St. Senior School

Inspected on 10th March and 25th May 1927. Report by H.M.I. Mr J.W. Veysey.

There is a noticeably good tone in this well – conducted school, and, on the whole, some highly successful work is being done. The organisation is in some respects unusual. The senior classes contain a comparatively large proportion of scholars, many of whom have received accelerated promotion on account of their greater capacity or higher attainments. After passing through Std. 1V and at about the age of 11+, the scholars are drafted either into the "Standards" (V, V1 & V11) or into one of the two "Special Classes" – one for boys and one for girls. It is understood that scholars are selected for this class only if their parents give a written promise to keep their children at the school for a further three years. For these children a special curriculum, with more extensive scope than that used in the standards has been prepared, and the scholars are taught very largely by the method of independent study supplemented by oral teaching. In English, History and Geography monthly assignments are arranged by the teachers and the scholars are allowed considerable freedom in the choice of a Timetable. The tone, the industry and the attainments of the scholars in the special classes are noticeably superior to those of the scholars in Stds. V, V1 & V11. This is probably due to a number of reasons. The special class teachers are perhaps among the ablest on the staff, and give considerable thought to the preparation of lessons; the method of conducting the class helps to develop self-reliance in the scholars; while the practical nature of some of the subjects tends to arouse greater interest, and the scholars work with more purpose and energy.

Most of the subjects – Mathematics, including Practical Geometry and Algebra, English, Geography and History were tested in both classes, and generally speaking the results were highly creditable. Some excellent Geography and English books were seen in both classes.

Although the work of Stds. V, V1 & V11 may be regarded, on the whole, as satisfactory, it compares unfavourably with that of the special classes. It is understood that the Head Master has for some time been considering the advisability of extending the special class curriculum and methods to all classes above Std. 1V. As there is no examination qualification for entrance to the special classes there appears no good reason why all the children above Std 1V should not get the best the school can offer.

Some of the boys in Std.s V & V1 show very fair skills in Pencil Drawing, but Brush Drawing is not taken by many, and with a number of boys in the Special Class, Drawing is regarded as an optional subject.

Std. V11 girls are very proficient in Sight Reading from the Staff Notation, and they sang some well chosen songs in a creditable manner.

The Needlework is now arranged so that each of the three larger groups is taken by the chief woman assistant for two one - hour lessons per week. This teacher is experienced and keen on the subject, and the work is in the main progressing satisfactorily. Minor points of criticism were discussed with the teacher, including the advisability of keeping systematic records of each girl's work.

The work of the special class which is taken by the class teacher, shows distinct improvement on that seen at the time of the last report. Some of the garments showed good and careful work, and definite tests had been set with a view to raising the standard of work. Quality and finish still need emphasis.

The school serves the needs of the scholars in other directions. All scholars are expected to take part in Netball or Football in the Winter and Tennis. Swimming or other games in the Summer. A Sports Day is held annually and the Junior School and the local schools are invited to take part in certain events. Parents' Days are also held annually. In connection with the school there is an 'Old Scholars Club' which holds monthly meetings from September to April.

Essex Education Committee
County Offices Chelmsford   **31st October 1927**

Dear Sir,
Shoeburyness Hinguar Street Council School
The recent report upon your school made by H.M. Inspector after visits on March 10th and May 25th was before the Committee at their last Meeting, when I was instructed to convey to you their congratulations upon the receipt of so satisfactory an appreciation of the work being done by yourself and your staff and in this expression of the Committee's pleasure, I should like to be allowed to share.
W.O. Lester Smith M.A. Director of Education.

1928

Feb 27th – 29th (inclus) Miss Cox absent
    The parents of a lad named M. Enticknap reported that on the 17th Miss Cox punished their son in such a way as to cause a wound. A crude letter of apology was received by them from Miss Cox which they brought to me. As so many complaints of this Mistress are received all future cases will be entered. I knew nothing of the case until the parents came to me.

Mar 22nd H.M.I. Mr Vassey called this afternoon and made enquiries respecting the method adopted for the teaching of adolescents.

May 24th Empire Day Holiday in afternoon.

May 30th   <u>Typewriter</u>

The Managers at their May Meeting agreed to the purchase of a Typewriter. In answer to an enquiry made to Mr Bell he states the Committee " cannot see their way to sanction the same." Such a machine is a necessity under the present adopted system which is reorganised by the County Council. The original expense was borne by me, if afterwards passed onto the teachers but the C.E.C. would and does not expect teachers doing original and first class work to pay for apparatus by which County benefits.

Jun 1st   Thundersley – whole day holiday for Rochford Hundred Sports.

SHORE HOUSE, SHOEBURYNESS.   1564.

Dec 4th   Two boys – forcibly entered the Junior Dept. last evening and gained admittance to this school by way of windows in the cloakroom. All the desks were ransacked and 6/2d from Miss Brooks room and 2d from Miss Ruegg's taken. The Police were called and the matter reported. A third boy shared the money.

During the investigation it was proved that the same boy carried out the robbery last February and gave some of the money to two younger boys.

Just after this one of the boys was found hiding upon the school premises when the Caretaker was locking up to go home. A special appeal was made to the Committee to have the boy sent to a reformatory school but met with no response.

1929

Jan18th   An explosion which blew out the front of the stove in No 2 room occurred this morning. Mr Morris had his hair and eyebrows burnt.

Mar 27th   Closed today for Easter. My duties cease on March 31st . *Nicholas Hillyer*

ENJOYING A DIP, SHOEBURYNESS.   1585.

Mr S. Tilson

April 8th 1929 to August 31st 1931

1929

Apr 8th   1929 1 was appointed Head Master of this school as from April 1st.

Owing to reduction in staff numbers the school was re-organised today as follows.

Class 1	Miss Wintle
Class 2	Mr Morris
Class 3	Mr Palmer
Class 4	Miss Cox
Class 5	Miss Grimes
Class 6	Mr Ruegg

May 2nd   A dental clinic was held at the school today.

May 8th   George Head was accidentally kicked on the toe by John Bennett while playing football in the playground. Apparently the kick opened a wound, which had no protection owing to the very poor boots which the boy was wearing. First aid was rendered by Mrs Grimes but the boy was not sent to the doctor as medical treatment did not appear necessary.

Statement by John Bennett

"When I was playing with George Head I accidentally kicked him in the toe & soon afterwards I noticed that it was bleeding".

May 10th   The school was closed for the afternoon session the school having made 92.6% for the past month.

May 22nd   An Empire Pageant was held in the playground this morning.
The Chairman was N. Hillyer Esq. (late head) & the speaker was Archdeacon Phillips.

May 30th   The School was closed today for the General Election.

June 4th   A Cinema Lecture on Tuberculosis and its Prevention was given by Dr. Webb the Pres. of the Tub. Soc. was attended by the older children at the Garrison Theatre.

19th June E.D. Edwards Esq. H.M.I. visited the school to discuss schemes of work and courses for the proposed senior school. He suggested that the age of transfer should be 10 yrs.8 months in order that the children should have an opportunity of completing a 3 yrs. Course.

June 21st School closed today to enable staff to attend Dunmow Summer School during next week.

July 1st The school was closed today for the pm. Session on the occasion of the opening of the Sunshine Home by Prince George.

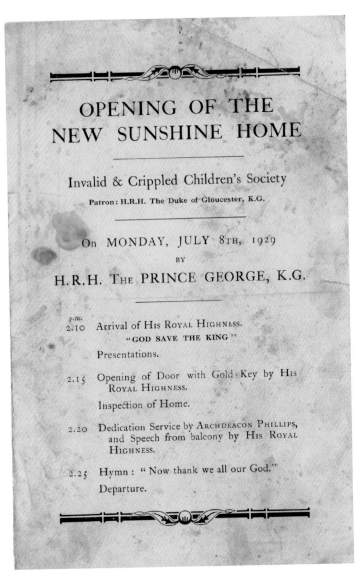

OPENING OF THE
NEW SUNSHINE HOME

Invalid & Crippled Children's Society

Patron: H.R.H. The Duke of Gloucester, K.G.

On MONDAY, JULY 8TH, 1929

BY

H.R.H. THE PRINCE GEORGE, K.G.

p.m.
2.10 Arrival of His ROYAL HIGHNESS.
      "GOD SAVE THE KING"
      Presentations.

2.15 Opening of Door with Gold Key by His ROYAL HIGHNESS.
      Inspection of Home.

2.20 Dedication Service by ARCHDEACON PHILLIPS, and Speech from balcony by His ROYAL HIGHNESS.

2.25 Hymn : " Now thank we all our God."
      Departure.

July 17th   The   school was closed today for the afternoon session to hold the Children's Sports in the Brigade Football Ground.

Sept 2nd   Re-organisation came into effect in regard to the schools in Shoeburyness, in consequence of which 104 children of 11+ were transferred to this school from Richmond Avenue.

Richmond Avenue and Richmond Avenue School.

Sept 17th   Mr MacDonald (asst. Architect) visited the school today with reference to the proposed Manual & Science Rooms. The suggested site for the Manual Room being on the site of the old shed, & the present brick building reconstructed to form a temporary Science Room.

105

Nov 7th   The girls of Year 1 visited the Infant Welfare Centre under the supervision of Miss Grimes.

Nov 11th   Armistice Day was celebrated by a short service in the playground.

1930

Feb 6th   The top 4 classes visited the Health Exhibition, organised by Dr. Bellough at the Council Chambers, this afternoon.

Feb 26th   Piano tuned by J.G. Harding.

Mar 15th   The Staff & 80 children visited the Science Museum & Imperial Institution.

Mar 19th   This afternoon was treated to an open day when about 100 visitors looked round the classes & witnessed the Gym display.

May 23rd   Empire Day was celebrated today. School closed for the afternoon session.

Aug 31st   Miss Grimes appt. ceased owing to marriage.

Sept 1st   Miss Maloney commenced duty today as Senior Mistress. Miss Banning presented 10 medals to be used at the discretion of the H.T.

Sept 8th   Mr Lewis absent owing to death of his brother in Wales.

Sept 10th Mr Lewis returned to duty.

Sept 16th The school was re-organised today with definite year groups with sections as follows:-

Organisation

Year 4	32	Miss Maloney	C.	Needlework - Lit
3x	34	Mr Morris	C.	Science - Lit
3a	37	Mr Palmer	C.	Geog
2x	36	Mr Cousins	C.	Arts - Maths
2a	36	Miss Wintle	C.	History - Hygiene
1x	37	Mr Lewis	C.	Handicraft
1x	40	Miss Ruegg	U.	
Prep	25	Miss Cox	U.	

The scheme was placed before the Managers at their last meeting (Sept. 9th) and they recommended that an additional certificated teacher should be appointed to take charge Mr MacDonald (and assistant) visited this school with reference to the proposed Manual & Science Rooms. The suggested site for the Manual Room being in the site of the old shed, and the present brick building reconstructed to form a temporary Science Room.

Sept 19th   I attended the National Savings Conference at Cambridge. Oct 27th   Under the supervision of Miss Maloney 20 Senior Girls visited the Rochford Hospital for a demonstration in 'baby care'.

Nov 3rd   Senior Boys today visited the Garrison Power Station in connection with their electrical course.   Mr Morris in charge.

Nov 31st   Mr Crombie – caretaker retired after 32 years service.

Dec 1st   Mr Cooper appointed temporarily.

Dec 3/4th   Concert by the school given in Garrison Theatre at 7.30.

Dec 10th   Miss Maloney and the H.T. visited the Exhibition of work by the Shoreditch Trade School.

1931

Shoeburyness

Jan 8th	30 boys of Year 3 visited the Schoolboys' Exhibition under the supervision of Mr Morris and Mr Lewis.
Jan 28th	16 Year 3 girls visited the St. Lawrence Nursing Home, Crowstone Rd., Westcliff, under the supervision of Miss Maloney, for a demonstration in bathing and dressing a baby of 3 weeks.
Feb 20th	Acting on the instruction of the Managers Mr Cooper commenced duty as temporary assistant caretaker.
Fe. 28th	On the advice of Mr Bell I informed Mrs Cooper that her engagement has only been sanctioned by the Committee for week-end cleaning at 7/6, and advised her to discontinue until she received further instructions from Mr Bell.

Postman G.Crump
outside Shoebury Post
Office Dane Street

Mar 2nd	Mr Cooper has apparently returned to duty in the Junior Dept: on further instructions from the Managers.
Mar 4th	Miss Banning sent 25/- to be paid to Mr Cooper for last week's salary
Apr 21st	30 Year 3 children visited the Exhibition of the Southend Arts and Crafts School this afternoon.
May 22nd	The Empire Pageant was held today at 10.45 am. The Speaker – Rev. Phillips. Chair – R.I Cook Esq. (Chairman of Managers). School closed at the end of morning session for Whitsun.
Oct 6th	Under the supervision of Miss Wintle and Miss Lewis a party of 47 children from Yrs. 2, 3 & 4 visited the Historical Pageant at Barking during the afternoon session.

June 11th	With the sanction of the Chairman of the Managers the afternoon session commenced at 1.0pm (registers closed at 1.10pm) and finished at 3.10 pm so that the staff could visit the Educational Exhibition at Ingatestone.
May 28th	Medical Inspection continued today at 2.pm.
June 22nd	Messrs Lewis, Morris and Deal visited the Electric Lighting Service Bureau, London.
June 26th	I attended the Dunmow Fellowship this afternoon, & for the remainder of the week.
July 10th	46 (boys & girls) under the supervision of 3 staff visited places of historical interest in Colchester.
July 15th	36 (boys & girls) visited the P.L.A docks with Mr Palmer & Miss Maloney.
Aug 31st	My duties as Head Teacher terminated today.
Oct 6th	Under the supervision of Miss Wintle and Miss Lewis a party of 47 children from Yrs. 2, 3 & 4 visited the Historical Pageant at Barking during the afternoon session.
Oct 9th	Thomas Tracey accidentally struck William Stevens in the eye with a stone shot from a small catapult. No complaint was made to the teacher Mr Palmer who was in charge of the playground or to the Class Teacher Miss Wintle. Hence it was not known until Monday Oct. 12th. In the meantime the mother of the injured boy visited Dr. Ryan who sent a Medical Certificate to the school 1 on Monday Oct.12th . A witness statement has been made upon Accident Form 4000/23/690 and forwarded to Mr H. Bell.

Mr Frank Cyril Dale

Nov 2nd 1931 to August 30th 1943

1931

Nov 2nd   Commenced duty as Head Master of this school today.
I, Frank Cyril Dale. Reg. No. 16/478.

West Road.

Nov. 4th   Test papers in Arithmetic and English set throughout the school this morning with a view to assisting the Head Master in finding out the level of attainment.

Nov.6th   Two staff meetings have been held this week with a view to giving the staff some idea as to my wishes in general school management.

Nov 9th   Mrs Alice A. Cooper of Wallace St, commenced duties as assistant to the Caretaker.

Nov 26th   The Head Master discussed with the Staff Arrangements for a new Time Table on Specialization basis.

Dec 1st	No Requisition Book was found on the premises for general stock when the Head Master took up duty on Nov.2nd 1931. A new one has been sent from Chelmsford. The Stock Book has no dates from 1928. A Stock List of Manual Tools has been compiled.

Dec 1st — No Requisition Book was found on the premises for general stock when the Head Master took up duty on Nov.2nd 1931. A new one has been sent from Chelmsford. The Stock Book has no dates from 1928. A Stock List of Manual Tools has been compiled.

No record of work or notes of lessons have been kept by the staff previously. Books for this purpose have been ordered on the requisition and will be put into use on arrival.

Dec. 8th — Tool List examined and items checked as per list retained in Stock Book. All old slates on the premises are not of use and condemned.

Dec 9th — The Head Master has instructed the Caretaker;
- that he must remain on duty in a morning till the session begins:
- that he must be on duty by 12. Noon and remain till the afternoon session begins:
- those urinals must be flushed at least thrice daily.

Dec. 15th — Mr Palmer was given leave of absence by the Head Master to attend an interview at Saffron Walden.

Dec 16th — One of the boys was sent home on 23-11-31 with scabs on chin & face. He returned to school this morning, but as his face was not yet well the Head Master sent him home & advised the mother by note to take him to the Welfare Centre.

Dec 22nd — The Head Master has explained to each member of the Staff that a weekly Forecast of Work is to be kept from 11.1.32 onwards. Brief notes of lessons – or digests of lessons – in Geography, History, Science, and Hygiene are to be kept.

1932

12th Jan — The school leaves room for improvement in cleanliness especially with regard to floors and walls, dusting never seem to be done.

14th Jan — Nurse Smith examined the heads of all the children present: 3 with nits. The Head Master sent two girls to the School Clinic this afternoon as they were suffering from impetigo. Both children brought a message back that they were to be excluded till better. (Verbal message.)

Jan 20th — There are 59 children less in the total present than there were this morning. A local Club is giving a "treat" to the boys and girls.

Feb 12th — Attendance very low – Snowfall 83.7% for the week.

Feb 17th   The Attendance Officer Mr. W. Cooper called. The Head Master pointed out to him that about a dozen boys were absent on a Tuesday morning 15th inst. because the paper train was late, yet the boys have no employment certificate, nor are they old enough.

29th Feb   The Head Master gave Mr. P. Palmer leave of absence to attend an interview at Ford End.
Mr. H. Robinson terminated duty as Caretaker.

March 1st   Mr Frank Anderson began duty as Caretaker.

March 4th   Seven boys examined by M.O.H. for certificate to enable them to deliver papers during permitted hours.

April 5th   School re-opened this morning. The school is decidedly cleaner. Mrs Cooper helped the Caretaker to 31st March, when holiday cleaning was done.

April 12th   Mrs C.A. Cooper recommenced as Assistant Cleaner.

May 24th   Empire Day. School assembled in the Hall. Hymns and songs rendered. Address given by Capt. Ashweek.

May 25th   On Thursday 19th and Wednesday 24th parties of 12 boys in the charge of the Head Master visited the Government Water Works and Electricity Station, through the introduction of Mr Cook.

May 25th   37 boys and girls entered in events at the Southend and District Sports went there in charge.

May 26th   School closed for the day for Rochford Hundred School Sports.

May 27th	The Girls Senior Championship Shield was won by girls from this department
June 15th	There is a Sunday School outing today 30 children less in attendance today than yesterday, both morning and afternoon, total absent 57.
June 29th	Owing to an outing arranged for children, there are 76 children less in attendance today than yesterday. 99 absent in total.
June 28th	The Head Master gave Mr Cousins leave to attend an interview this afternoon .
June 29th	The Head Master gave Mr Palmer leave to attend an interview for a post this afternoon.
July 7th	The Head Master gave Mr Cousins leave of absence to attend an interview at Canvey.
July 21st	The Head Master spent the afternoon at Richmond Avenue Junior School, seeing the work the pupils due to transfer in Sept. to the Senior School.
July 27th	86 pupils absent today. There is a Primitive Methodist Sunday School outing to Canvey.
July 29th	The following terminated duty in this school as they have resigned their positions as certified assistants, Mr. P.S. Palmer. Mr. G. Lewis. Mr. R. Cousins.
Sept. 5th	School re-opened this morning. The following began duty as certificated assistants Mr. J. Absalom Mr. A.C. Horlick Mr. H.Q. Harris.
Sept 5th	Children admitted:-

	From		
		Hinguar St. Junior	51
		Richmond Ave. Junior	53
		New Arrivals	7

Sept 16th	No. on roll 361
Sept. 19th	The Attendance Officer called. The Head Master drew his attention to several cases where children stay away on Friday afternoons.
Sept 30th	Attendance for September 91.8%.
Sept 14th	The Contractor commenced the electrical installation.
Sept. 19th	Nurse Smith examined the heads of all children present and reported 6 cases where girls had nits.

High Street, Shoeburyness

Sept. 20th — The Head Master spoke to the above mentioned girls privately and suggested means for cleansing their heads.

Sept 22nd — Nurse Smith called to see if there was any improvement in the heads of the 6 girls noted on 19th inst.

Oct. 10th — Nurse Smith called to see the 6 girls reported with nits on 19.9.32.
1 clean: 2 nearly clean; 2 improved but still many nits; 1 at cookery class.

Oct 19th — Several boys are absent at a football match in the garrison. Special note to be made when the attendance officer calls.

Oct 27th — Nurse Smith examined the 6 girls who had nits on 19.9.32.
1 clean: 3 nearly clean; 1 many nits; 1 at cookery class

Oct 27th — The Head Master gave Miss Maloney leave of absence to go to arrange for lodgings where she is going to live.

Oct. 28th — Miss Maloney terminated duty having resigned her position as a Certificated Assistant Mistress.

Oct 28th — The Head Master checked the Needlework Stock – material and garments, Mr. Cook called while this was being done.

Oct 31s t — Mrs. N. King commenced supply duty.

Nov 3rd — Nurse Smith called. She saw girls with nits on 19.9.32.

Nov. 3rd	During the night the school was entered. A drawer lock was broken open, and a cupboard lock spoiled – both in the Head Master's desk, No. 7 room was entered – the sewing machine tampered with, cupboard opened.
Nov.9th	The Caretaker attended the local police court in connection with the case against those who had entered the school 2nd to 3rd in.
Dec. 15th	Nurse Smith examined the heads of all children in 3B and girls through the remainder of the Forms. The girls previously noted as unclean are now satisfactory. Two girls recently admitted in Form 1B, were taken home by Nurse to parents

1933

Jan 25th — Owing to Influenza and severe colds, attendance is very low. A large number present are going to the "Eagle Club" Treat this afternoon, therefore the school is closed as per instructions from the Managers. Roll 343.

Jan 30th	Roll	Attendance	%
344	280	280	81.3 A.M
345	276	276	80.0 P.M.

Attendance January 1933:- 75.5%

Feb. 10th — Attendance this week 88.6%

Feb 17th — Attendance this week 90.0%
Attendance for February 87.8%

Attendance for month of March 93.2%. thereby an Attendance half holiday has been earned. This is the first since I took charge of the school.

March 7th   At the morning break in Number 1 Room Alfred Reeves (13.3.20) lifted the lid of a desk to shield himself from a knife thrown by Lewis Foster (31.12.19) : the lid slipped from his hands the lock catches pierced his lower lip.
The Head Master took him to Dr. Ealand's but she was out. Dr. Ryan was phoned but he was about to go out to administer gas, so I took the boy home.
Reports to District Office and witness statements attached.
Inspector Clare, N.S.P.C.C. called about a girl who was excluded for Impetigo on 10.5.33: the child had nits in her head in last Autumn.

March 13th   Alfred Reeves; accident noted on 7th returned to school today.

April 12th   School closes this afternoon for the attendance holiday earned in March.

April 28th   Nancy Challis made perfect attendance for April 92.1%
Attendance May 91.6%

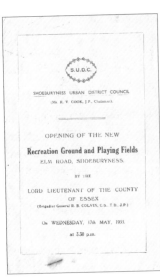

Shoebury Silver Band

May 17th   School closed this afternoon on the occasion of the opening of the Shoeburyness Urban Recreation Ground.

May 27th   Fredk. Evans has reached the standard qualifying for admission to the Junior Technical School.

June 24th   On Monday and Tuesday, Afternoons, 3rd period, a party of boys in charge of Mr. Eaton visited the local Gas Works.

July 4th   A third party of boys is to visit the local M.D.C. Gas Works this afternoon.
Each afternoon this week during the last period, a party of children will be taken to the Exhibition of Art in Southend.

July 17th	Mr Holbrook, Superintendent of School attendance Officers called this morning. To enable him to compile a list of residents in the area. The Head Master took him to various points on the proposed new Borough Boundary.

July 17th — Mr Holbrook, Superintendent of School attendance Officers called this morning. To enable him to compile a list of residents in the area. The Head Master took him to various points on the proposed new Borough Boundary.

Sept 29th — School closed all day on Oct. 1st to commemorate the extension of the boundaries of the Borough of Southend.
On and from Monday next, this School passes under the control of Southend. The Head Master and Staff have been offered appointments similar to those held at present.

Oct 3rd — Mr Barnard from the Education Office checked stock.

Oct 6th — Notification from the Office; that School number in future is Southend-on-Sea, Shoeburyness Council.22.

Oct 9th — Mr. J.W. Chambers H.M.I. visited the school for a short time this afternoon.

Mr.J.W. Chambers H.M.I.and Mr. Witts H.M.I. spent the morning here. Log and punishment book sent to the Education Office.

Oct 25th — The Head Master discussed with Staff points on methods to be adopted in Mathematics for the sake of continuity.

Nov 3rd — Sgt. H. Cheatle called to see me; a coat belonging to Donald Yarrow was missing from boy's cloak room on 2nd. Inst: the mother complained to the police on 2nd in the evening.
It appears that the coat was taken by mistake and returned to school this morning.

Nov 10th	Armistice Day falling on a Saturday this year, a short service and address was given in the Hall at 11 A.M. this morning (Friday.) by the Head Master.
Dec 14th	Children due to leave at Christmas interviewed by Mrs Evans, Messers W.G.Rainer, W.J. Clack, Mr. Kelly, (Borough Ed. Office) Mr. J. Knight, Sec. to Juvenile Advisory Committee; with the Head Master.
Dec 15th	Winchester House Party this evening 5.30 – 8 P.M.
Dec 18th	Eton House Party this evening 5.30 – 8.P.M.
Dec 20th	Rugby House party tonight
Dec 21st	Harrow House Party tonight.
Dec 22nd	P.C. Bates interrogated a pupil concerning some pigeons in his possession.

1934

Jan 30th	In charge of Mr Eaton 13 Year 4 & 3a boys visited the garage of Messers Wakefield and Sage this afternoon – subject – the internal combustion engine model in section.
Feb 8th	The glasses of Percy Cox, 1B, were broken by an unknown boy who shot something hard with a catapult. The Head Master sent Percy Cox to the clinic where the M.O. gave him instructions to see the eye specialist tomorrow. The Head Master assembled the whole school and gave instructions that catapults were forbidden.
April 10th	During the holiday the school football team won the Southend Cup Match by defeating Hamlet Court Rd, 3 – 0.
April 17th	As five of our boys were selected for the Southend Team V West Ham the Head Master gave Mr Lewis permission to attend the match.
May 3rd	Subject to the financial position of the parents the following will be offered admission to the schools as stated • Junior Technical:- Douglas Paton • Junior Commercial Leon O' Bee
May 11th	Last lesson this morning used for Empire Day practice in the playground.
May 15th	Senior and Junior departments combined for a practise for Empire Day celebration last lesson this afternoon.
May 16th	Southend Schools Football Cup was won by this school for the season 1933 – 1934 and was formally presented by the Head Mastr at the presentation of trophies last night by the Worship the Mayor of Southend –on – Sea. Each boy of the school team received a medal. Alec Mansfield has been awarded county colours.

| May 24th | **Empire Day.** Celebrations in the playground. Chairman F.W.Squier, a member of the Education Committee. |

The Prince of Wales, later Edward VIII.

Many parents and friends were present. A very pleasing function was the unanimous opinion expressed afterwards.

His Worship The Mayor (Mr Councillor H.E. Frith J.P.) provided portraits of H.R.H.The Prince of Wales. The top boy and girl of 3a, Reginald Parkins and Gladys Fean received these, they were presented by Mr. Squier. Country dances were performed by the two Junior School Classes, and in the Senior Department by 1A, 2B, 2A, 3C, 3A.

| May 31st | The girls of this school won the Senior Girls Championship yesterday with 16 points.
The boys were runners up to Leigh North St, 13 points to17. |

| 13th June | Open Day for parents.
An exhibition of country dancing was given; songs were rendered; work was shown in the various subjects; many parents praised the school and expressed pleasure with what they saw. |

18th June	County Sports at East Ham on Saturday. Ronald Parkins from this school won the 75 yds Hurdle race: he beat the record for the county and equalled the time for the National sports: he was awarded a cup, and obtained four points out of 7 towards the challenge cup obtained by Southend.
19th Sept	On Monday and Tuesday evenings, enrolments took place for the Junior Evening Institute.
24th Sept	Junior Evening Institute session began. 45 students present.
25th Sept	As the school is so cold the Head Master obtained permission from the Office for fires to be started,
15th Oct	The Head Master reported to the Office that fumes creep into Rooms 3 &6 from the stove joints; 3 children sick in Room 6 on Thursday.
Oct 19th	Arthur Grover was playing leap frog when he fell over Douglas Reeves' back. His left arm appeared to be broken. He was taken to Southend Hospital, by ambulance. (age 12).
Nov 20th	The boiler in No. 6 Room burst while Assembly was taking place in the Hall. The Head Master reported this to the Office by telephone.
Dec 12th	Dr'.s Certificate from Miss Newman that she is suffering from psycho-neurosis and will be unable to follow her employment for at least 6 weeks.
Dec 21st	School closes today Christmas Holiday.

1935

Jan 11th	Miss N. 18 + 8 = 26 absences.
Jan 18t h	Miss N. 26 + 10 = 36 absences.
Jan 25th	Miss N. 36 = 10 = 46 absences.
Feb 1st	Miss N. 46 + 10 = 56 absences.
Feb 8th	Miss N. 56 + 10 = 66 absences.
Feb 8th	Dr. Logan examined all present in 3a & 2b. From these two classes Diphtheria contacts are excluded.
Feb 11th	Nurse R.R.Ody examined the throats of all present in 3a & 2b.
Feb 20th	Nurse R.M.Ody examined the heads of all children in the 4 lowest classes.
Feb 22nd	Nurse R. Ody examined the heads of children in the 4 upper classes.
Feb 28th	Nurse R. Ody examined the throats of all present in 1B – Diphtheria contacts excluded in this class .

March 6th	Medical examination began for 1 entrant, 19 leavers, 39 re-examinations, 11 milk cases.
March 7th	The Head Master stopped the examination of children's eyesight by Nurse R. Ody during the time set apart for religious instruction.
March 18th	Miss Newman absent – Laryngitis.
March 19th	Dr's Certificate received from Miss N.
March 19th	Nurse Newman examined the throats of 22 present in 3C. (William Attewell is away in that class with Diphtheria). At the suggestion of the Head Master , names and addresses of absentees, since the above named boy was absent were also supplied.
April 4th	Miss N. was unwell towards the close of the morning session, and returned home at midday.
May 6th	School closed for Celebration of the Silver Jubilee of His Majesty King George V.

| May 7th | Alderman Cook J.P. presented a book, The Silver Jubilee, to a boy and a girl from each class as a representative. All received their books in their form rooms afterwards, also chocolate. Mr Cook addressed the children and on the proposal of a senior boy, received a hearty vote of thanks. The Proceedings terminated with the singing of "God Save the King". |

May 9th	Staff and pupils went by bus to see the film "Royal Cavalcade" at Ritz Cinema as part of the Jubilee celebrations.
May 19th	The Head Master spoke to the Members of the Staff with reference to empire Day Celebrations.
May 20th	School closed all day – extra day granted in connection with His Majesty's Silver jubilee.
May 24th	Empire Day Celebration at 11A.M. Mr. J.G. Drysdale M.A. took the chair. He addressed the children briefly and expressed his appreciation of the dances and songs. Mrs Campbell was also present on the platform.
June 4th	Miss N. has leave of absence from the Committee as from today to go to Canada.
June 17th	On Saturday last, 15th inst., the Headmaster, accompanied by three members of the Staff took 40 3rd year boys and girls to London. Tower, White Tower, Chapel, and Crown Jewels. Houses of Parliament. Whitehall, Trafalgar Square, Strand, St. Paul's – Whispering Gallery and Crypt. Finance was aided by the grant from R.A. Jones "In Memoriam " Fund.
July 26th	As the junior school will be closed on Friday afternoon for an attendance holiday, the Managers agree to the closing of the senior department for the same period.
Nov. 24th	The Head Master pointed out to the Staff the necessity for accuracy in the Absence Slips and duplicate Registers.
Dec. 1st	The Head Master told the Staff that they must not send children off the school premises without his permission during lessons.

1936

Jan. 17th	Children attending Labour Party Treat allowed to go at 4 P.M., similar to those attending Garrison Treat last Friday.
Jan 28th	A Service of Remembrance was taken in the Hall this morning:- His Majesty King George V. who passed peacefully 20th January 1936 – followed by –Accession of King Edward V111. After the service school was dismissed for the day.
Feb. 26th	The Head Master left school at 10.A.M. to take his daughter to a Nursing Home for an operation: Office notified previously.
Feb. 24th	Nurse Crump examined Ringworm contacts, 3 pupils.

May 25th	Empire Day Celebration as the 24th was a Sunday. Chair was taken by Mr J.H. Burrows.
May 27th	The Head Master visited the Littorien Shirt Works this morning from 11.15am as several leavers may consider places that are known personally.
May 29th	Notification received: Special Place Examination Results: Admission to Junior Technical School. Ronald Curtis, 3a & Colin Bishop 3a.
Sept 9th	Jean Hollands. 3c. Died from Dropsy.
Sep t 10th	A collection for a wreath was very well supported.
Sept 11th	A member of the staff:- Miss N. & 2 children from her class will attend the funeral tomorrow Saturday.
Sept 29th	Pupil from George Street excluded by Head Master for what appears to be ringworm. Education Office notified accordingly.

Copy of H.M.I.Report

Southend – on – Sea, Shoeburyness. C. School. No. 22.
Inspected on various dates in June 1936.
Report by H.M.I. Mr F.C. Bishop.
Senior Mixed

Organisation: The children in this school are promoted from the contributory Junior Schools in the calendar year in which they reach eleven. Classification is by attainment, & at the visit there were 276 on the roll distributed among three third, three second, & two first year classes. The annual entry is somewhat in excess of 100 & the plan at present adopted of dividing it into two classes results in a unit too large for the type of work which is being developed in Senior Schools. It is suggested that a more suitable organisation would be to divide the first two years into forms 2A. 2B. 1A. 1B. & a small class of backward children drawn from these years.

Premises: The premises which were designed for a different purpose contains seven rooms grouped around a hall. A new classroom is being erected in the playground. There are no large rooms for practical work, & there is a general shortage of storage accommodation & especially for Needlework & Craft. There is only one playground for both boys and girls. This is too small to be used by two groups doing Physical Training simultaneously a necessary arrangement in a Mixed School. An adjoining piece of land, originally a school garden, might well be paved or turfed & added to the playground. The only available playing field is some twenty minutes away. The Practical Subjects, though taught in rooms at some distance from the school, come under the jurisdiction of the Head Master, & the teachers are members of his staff. Domestic Science is taught in a room in the Richmond Avenue School playground, of which room this school has exclusive use. The Woodwork room is in High Street.

Staff: The Head Master in spite of the difficulties is attempting to re-organise his school on modern Senior School lines. There is specialist teaching in all subjects except Arithmetic & English, & praiseworthy attempts are made to the ordinary classrooms into subject rooms.

Nov 13th — Inspector Pim of the Borough Constabulary gave a talk to all the school on "Safety First" & "The Dangers of the Road".

Dec 11th — Abdication of Edward V111

Dec 17th — Nurse Crump examined the heads of all children in the school.

1937

Feb 11th — In boy in Form 8:- Had what appeared to be a fit. The child was put at ease and at 4.15 sent home in charge of his sister, 13 years.

Feb 15th	Two pupils were given meals owing to low state, confirmed by S.M.O. and also milk.
Feb 23rd	An Attendance Order has not been complied with and as a result the Mother has been warned to attend Court today. She accosted the Head Master in the street at midday, and stated that she would come to the school in the afternoon to see where her boy John was.
Ma y 4th	The boys and girls taking part in the Coronation display of Physical Training and Country Dancing attended the stadium for rehearsals during the afternoon in charge of 2 members of Staff.
May 10th	Boys and girls in Physical Training and Country Dancing went to the Stadium for another rehearsal this afternoon in charge of two members of the Staff in preparation for Coronation Day.
May 11th	All the school is going to the Southend Stadium tomorrow morning. In the afternoon the school will assemble for an entertainment, tea and presentation of books by Alderman S. Johnson J.P. Each child has received a medal from Messes Hinds, of Southend.
May 26th	8 children have reached the standard qualifying for admission to the Junior Technical and Commercial School.
June 4th	Mr Dean N.S.P.C.C. called with reference to Margaret W.
Aug 31st	Fire destroyed a portion of the hall roof during the Summer vacation. Repairs are in hand. Use of hall out of question except for Assembly & morning services.
Oct 4th	3rd Year Boys & Girls went to the Electrical Exhibition at the Kursaal this morning in charge of 3 members of staff.

1938

Feb 7th	Attendance for January 93.73% Top of the Borough. Shield for Attendance on show in the Hall.
Feb 21st	Tree Planting Ceremony School assembled in the Hall. Hymn sung. Prayer for H.M. King George V1 and Queen Elizabeth. National Anthem . All then assembled in the playground and saw the tree planted by the Head Girl Joyce Offord and Head Boy Edward Crisp. Alderman and Mrs R.V. Cook present.

April 7th   The Head Master attended a demonstration of Radio sets in Southchurch Hall
             School.

May 14th   Empire Day Service at 11 A.M. After Dances Mr. Alderman R.V. Cook
             addressed the children and a vote of thanks proposed and seconded by R.
             Tuckerand J. Offord was carried with acclamation and 3 hearty cheers. Cheers
             were also given for H.M. the King and the British Empire.

May 26th   Open Session and Exhibition of Work for Parents.
             About 200 parents visited the school, and at certain times were able to see a
             physical training lesson by boys, some dancing by the various classes and
             music from all three year groups.
             Specimens of work were displayed in the subject rooms, and articles made in
             Handicrafts and goods from Domestic Subjects in the Hall.

             Mr Collins, Deputy Chief Education Officer, Mrs Cook were present. All
             expressed pleasure at the end of their visit.

July 12th   Outing aided by R.A. Jones In Memoriam Fund. Miss L.Hood has taken a party
             of girls to Canterbury and H. Day has taken 20 boys to the London Docks, over
             a liner at Tilbury and Ford's Works Dagenham.

27th Sept   The Head Master left the school at 10.40 to attend a meeting at the Education
             Office.

28th Sept   School closed for assembly of gas masks. Staff and many parents helping.

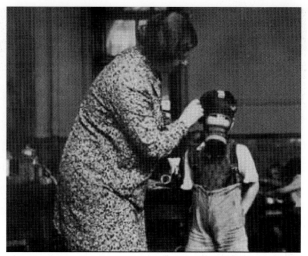

Oct 3rd   School re-opened this morning after use as a centre for the assembly and distribution of gas masks. 460 Assembled.

Oct 14th   A party of 6 girls in charge of Miss Hood took the collection of goods for the General Hospital Pound Day to the hospital.

Oct 20th   The Head Master was present at a consultation with the Chief Education Officer at the Caulfield Road Senior School.

Nov 11th   **Armistice Day observed.**
The whole school was assembled in the hall. First the Head Master addressed the pupils on the reason for the observance of this day. Then a hymn was sung "Now thank we all" and a prayer for "peace and charity among all men" was read. The National Anthem was sung.
Then the school listened to the B.B.C. service after the music from the massed bands, from 11.00 to 11.10 A.M.

Dec 2nd   The school has obtained the attendance shield for the 4 weeks ended Nov. 25th 94.65 %.

Dec 23rd   Attendance this week 70.33% owing to snow.

Dec 14th   Form E12 sent to the Education Office re one of our boys age 11 left forearm – suspected ringworm.

Dec 15th   Nurse Crump saw the boy at school after calling at his home to notify the parents that the boy should attend the clinic this afternoon.
At the afternoon session the above boy stated that his mother would take him to the doctor tomorrow.

Dec 19th   Pupil with ringworm to be excluded. Dec 22nd
Pupil re-admitted with a Dr's Cert. (private).

Dec 23rd   Attendance this week 70.33% owing to snow.

1939

Jan 30th   The Head Master attended a meeting at the Education Office on Air Raid Precautions at 11.15 A.M.

April 21st   The school obtained the attendance shield with the highest % attendance in the Borough for March: - 93.48

May 1st   Miss H. Newman was given leave to attend a meeting at the Education Office in connection with A.R.P. *at 11.30 A.M. * Air Raid Precautions
The Head Master attended a meeting of Senior School Heads at Leigh N. St. on A.R.P.

May 19th   Rehearsal for Empire Day taken this morning at 11.15 am. Combined with the Junior Department.

May 19th   School cupboards removed to Caulfield Road today.

May 26th   Pupils and Staff walked to the new buildings in Caulfield Rd. during the latter portion of the afternoon.

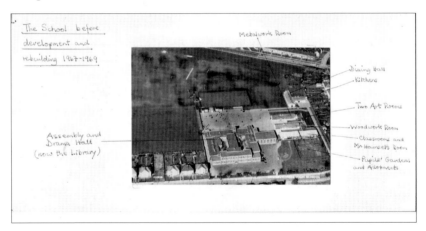

Original school buildings 1939

May 31st   School re-opened this morning after the Whitsuntide holiday, in the building in Caulfield Road. Miss M.E. Reay C.B.E. J.P. Chairman of the Education Committee, Alderman S.F. Johnson J.P. Chairman of the Elementary Committee. Mr H. Boyes Watson M.C. M.A. Chief Education Officer was present for the Assembly. After the usual morning service, the Head Master, Mr F.C. Dale, welcomed them and stated that the presence of Miss Reay was much appreciated in view of the many and varied calls on her time in the cause of Education.

The school had moved into a magnificent building equipped with the latest apparatus, that was no small achievement. But the committee under her lead and guidance had gone farther. It was situated so that it possessed what would be a wonderful playing field.

It would be a privilege to work in such a building which must have a marked effect on the outlook of those working in it. He then asked Miss Reay if she would speak to all assembled for the first time in that building.

She consented to do so and spoke of the facilities that would be at the disposal of this area, and stated that it was for the children to give the school a real spirit.

Alderman S.F. Johnson then spoke, and told the children that it was now for them to give life to every brick so to speak, and create the human factor.

The Chief Education Officer made the point that he had been associated with the school right from the closing of the site, the plans, the actual erection and furnishing and now here they were: and it was for them to cherish their possession. A tour of the building followed.

July 13th   Miss M.E. Reay C.B.E. visited the school and stayed for tea in the Flat at the invitation of the two girls using the Flat this week. She was accompanied by Mrs Oswald Reay.

June 16th   Betty Prior, Form 4 died and the girls have purchased flowers from the whole school and also from her own Form.

July 6th   Mr. H. Moorhouse H.M.I. called this morning re Handicraft. In the afternoon he expressed his views to the Handicraft Instructor – Mr E.V. Townsend and the Head Master, on the scope of the work as it should be taken in view of modern ideas of the subject as part of education in the fullest sense. July 7th Sgt F.L. Lawrence and Detective Hooper called to interview 4 boys found in Hinguar St. School on Sunday evening July 2nd

July 18th   The Head Master gave Miss Newman permission to leave school in time to attend an A.R.P. meeting at the Education Office at 11A.M.

This photograph was passed for publication on 15th October 1940. It was the height of the Blitz and shows an Air Raid Wardens post in London Road. Probably every town had its Spitfire Fund, as this was just a few months after the Battle of Britain. There were dozens of Air Raid Wardens posts in Southend and Shoebury. In the background posters proclaim "Careless Talk Costs Lives".

July 19th   A window reported broken in the pantry of the D.S. Room. A.R.P. used the school and playground last night.

July 19th   Open session. Parents assembled in the Hall & the Head Master explained the recommended Physical Training clothing and prices. Shower baths, lockers for clothes and changing rooms were discussed. The purpose of the Domestic Subjects Flat was explained.

Activities that it is proposed to commence in the Autumn such as Geography Survey Society, Cycling Clubs in connection with History and Geography, Hobbies Club, Sketch Club and Science Group were mentioned, and the Head Master expressed the hope that the parents would help and encourage their children in every possible way. Songs were rendered by Year 2, and the parents invited to go round the building and see the children at work.

Sept 3rd 1939 – Britain and France declare war on Germany.

Sept 5th   School occupied by A.R.P. casualty post. School work carried on in houses lent by parents.

Dec. 31st   R.E. Strong and R. Hogsflesh transferred to Hinguar St. as the Seniors living near Hinguar St. will be permitted to attend there.

1940

Jan 9th   As the shelters have not been completed the school cannot be opened. Work is being carried on in groups in houses.

Rescue teams posing for the camera, 1940. Two people were killed when a bomb fell near this Anderson shelter on Sunday August 18th , 1940. No entrance protection had been put in place at the time. Several bombs had been dropped in a line from Hobleythick Lane to Shoeburyness, the aircraft going on to bomb Shoebury Station. The air raid involved about 100 planes and 140 to 200 bombs were dropped.

Feb 12th   School re-opened this morning.

April 8th   Girls in Form 3 due for Domestic Subjects this afternoon retained in order to free the room for a demonstration in War-Time Cookery for parents. These will continue on Monday and Thursday afternoons for the next three weeks.
              The gymnasium has been released by the A.R.P. for school use as from today.

April 12th   Attendance this week is 90.52%. This is the first time it has been over 90% since school re-opened on Feb. 12th.

May 10th   Air Raid Precautions: - Practice held again 11.55 A.M. School cleared promptly, all children in shelters.

May 14th   Owing to the National state of preparedness, School hours changed from normal to 8.55 to 12.15 &1.55 to 4 P.M.

May 17th   Air Raid practise taken several times this week so that all the children will be familiar with the work and places to which they must go.

During the August 18th 1940 raid, bombs fell in Southend High School for Boys and Shoeburyness Station. The signalman, Mr Charles Speller, was killed on duty. Shoeburyness Railway Station was a particular target for the enemy as it was so close to the Garrison.

May 24th   Empire Day Service held this morning. The items on the programme supplied were taken with the addition of suitable hymns and the Head Master addressed the children stressing the

   • Origin of Empire Day

   • Loyalty to King Emperor

   • The present response of the Empire

   • Our Freedom of Religion

   • Our duties as members

   • Our Faith in Almighty God for a just cause.

May 28th   The Head Master attended a meeting at the Education Office yesterday at 4.30 P.M. in connection with evacuation preparations.

May 31st   Log Book, Admission Book and Summary Book taken to Southend Education Office. Registers of Classes to go with Party. (School to be evacuated).

May 28th   The Head Master attended a meeting at the Education Office yesterday at 4.30 P.M. in connection with evacuation preparations.

May 31st   Log Book, Admission Book and Summary Book taken to Southend Education Office. Registers of Classes to go with Party. (School to be evacuated).

1940. A German air crew prisoner of war, shot down during a raid on the estuary is being marched to a waiting train on Shoeburyness Station en route to a prisoner of war camp.

War damage in Shoeburyness 1940.

**One of the many bombs that fell on Shoebury in August 1940
fell on this house, believed to be in Ness Road.**

Soldiers guarding a crashed German Me 110 which crashed at North Shoebury in 1940.

An unexploded bomb which fell near Moat House in Shoebury Road
(Near Asda) during a raid in 1941 .

May 28th   The Head Master (Mr Dale) attended a meeting at the Education Office yesterday at 4.30 P.M. in connection with evacuation preparations.

May 31st   Log Book, Admission Book and Summary Book taken to Southend Education Office. Registers of Classes to go with Party.*

The school log book for this important event has been lost, but I have received accounts and spoken to a number of people who were evacuated from Hinguar Primary and Shoeburyness High School.

2nd June 1940 Evacuation Day by Maureen A. Andrews

Joyce, Maureen and Sheila Rawlings, twins and a sister two years older, were the youngest in a group of 18 Shoeburyness Hinguar Street School pupils to be evacuated from the Garrison Town on the 2nd June 1940

We left home, lunch bags, a small case and our gas masks in a box over our shoulder; we were kissed and cuddled, and told to enjoy our long holiday and not to look back to wave at mum.

We were lined up and put onto coaches outside the school and taken to Southend Central railway station. I remember there were lines and lines of us, too many for the station platform. Our school was lined up in Nelson Street beside the steps, three steps up to the forecourt of the Police Offices, and then marched up to the Station platform and onto the train. To us as children it was an adventure just beginning.

Evacuation Day June 1940. Children from all Southend schools queued outside Southend central station. Some 8,500 children were evacuated on a single day.

Our destination was Derbyshire, a lovely village called Castleton, located near Hope on the Yorkshire borders. The coach that had taken us from the train arrived at the village hall, there were lots of the villagers and their children there and we were sat on the pavement. Different people pointed out those certain children were to be taken in by them, we all had labels on our coats. When all but 18 had gone, the remainder were told that we were going to Holloway Hostel. When one set of parents said they could take another child in and pointed to my sister Sheila, she grabbed Joyce and myself and said very determinedly "My mother said we have to be kept together", and so we were.

Our new home was a Y.H.A hostel, to us at the time a huge place, one large oblong black wooden building, with a kitchen at one end, eating area in the middle and a lounge with a large piano at the other end. Behind this building was another long bungalow, this one painted green and had trellis and flowers around the doors. This was the private residence of a wonderful family named Rowlands, they were to be our family for the next four years. Mrs Rowlands, never to be called auntie or anything else, only Mrs Rowlands, her son Peter was about 19 years old and a brilliant pianist, her daughter Jean and someone known to us as 'Uncle Bill Twigg'. They took on 18 children from the ages 5 to 11. The children were: Maureen and Joyce Rawlings, Sheila Rawlings, Pamela and Derek Monk, Dorothy and Dennis Smith, Joyce and Christine Woods, Bernard Foster, Steve Sutton, Frankie Wakefield,

Isobell Whitton, Derek Crow, Roy Monk, Rodney Fry, Esme Smith, Barry Smith and Mrs Smith came as a helper.

As the village school was only a small one and it was summertime we were given our books and pencils etc., and we sat in a circle in the field to do our lessons. There were sheep, some of which were quite curious at first. There was a wide brook at the bottom of the field, the stones in the water were bright orange and the sides of the brook were rusty brown. The water running down from the mountains had lots of iron in it (mineral).

When the winter came we were able to use the bar and lounge of the Peverell Hotel, higher up the hillside but below Peverell Castle. Later the next year we all used the village hall as our school. We didn't integrate very much with the local children for quite a while until some of the children joined brownies and cubs etc.

Every six weeks my mother organised and brought up mums, brothers and sisters. A lot of older children, 13 and 14 years old etc., were evacuated to Ashbourne so my mum dropped off the coach some parents at Ashbourne and picked up my brother and sister, Pearl and Geoff, and came on to Castleton, so our little family were together every six weeks, except my dad, he worked for the Ministry of Supply on Foulness Island.

At the time of these visits we celebrated birthdays etc. All the children's mum's and visitors, as the Hostel was still open to visitors and walkers, came from Sheffield and Manchester. These regular visitors became our Aunts and Uncles and thoroughly spoilt the children.

Our Headmaster from Hinguar Street School, Mr. Bowyer, his wife and two daughters were settled in at Hope, he was our Headmaster whilst we were in Castleton. Also a teacher, Miss Standon had come with us all. Mr. Bowyer was like a dad to lots of the children.

I've mentioned that the first building was the reception, kitchen, lounge etc., the brick second building private to Mrs Rowlings and the family, the third was another long brick building and had our bedrooms or dormitories, a long building with one long central corridor and doors either side, small rooms each having two bunk beds, cupboard and a locker for our personal things. Every third or fourth set of bedrooms was a large bathroom and toilets down the corridor here and there.

There was a large wash house on one side of the building where we took turns to help mangle and fold sheets and all the wash, a young lady called Mrs Payne came in from the village to help with these chores bringing her young daughter Cynthia to play with us while she worked.

The hostel was set at the foot of the figure eight forest in a huge field. We had greenhouses, a large kitchen garden and we had to help Uncle Bill with watering and weeding. We had ducks and geese and chickens in pens dotted about the place. The Shetland ponies came down off the hills, they wouldn't let you get on them, they were quite wild. Half a dozen of us went down the lane about half a mile every morning for our milk from Eyres Farm, this was collected in open buckets and no playing about was allowed carrying it back to the hostel, two carrying a large bucket, one each side.

We were taken out on walks to the most beautiful countryside in England, and we explored down mine shafts into the 'Blue John' mines Peak Cavern. All these beauty spots were on our doorstep and then they were unprotected, now they are part of the National Trust and you have to pay to enter these areas. I have a large piece of 'Blue John I brought back from evacuation with me.

Mrs Rowlands who had always had very short straight hair and was a small cuddly lady was very strict with us, but if we were unwell or a bit homesick she was very kind and loving and had time for us all. After we had been there a couple of years there was a very bad Air Raid on Sheffield and aircraft were escaping the British fighters and gunfire and off loaded bombs just short of the village. The authorities were so worried it was decided that we should have an Air Raid Shelter, this was built. We did not take too much notice of this going up. It had been finished a few days and Uncle Bill had been busy going about some jobs inside finishing it off when we were told we had to go to the Air Raid Shelter as a practice in case we should ever need to use it. We queued up along the back of the shelter when we turned the corner and were taken inside the door. Our dear Uncle Bill, who hadn't wanted the children to be frightened at going into the dark shelter, had put fairy lights up and made a lollypop tree which was a large branch from a tree with the round chalky lollypops tied to the branches. This had been put into a large barrel and we had to take lollypop before going into the dimly lit shelter. We never actually had to use this shelter.

We were, it seemed, a million miles from the War, but not many miles away Sheffield, formerly the home of the steel industry making knives and forks, was now turned into making munitions and was a prime target for the German bombers and had been bombed flat. During one of these very bad air raids my mother had come to Hollowford to collect us as my father was very ill and had to have an operation. We sat on the train that had been run into sidings absolutely terrified, bombs exploding nearby, sirens, fire engines – the noise was deafening. The train continued and we arrived in London, after another air raid, crossed London and continued down to Shoebury. We were used to seeing soldiers as Shoeburyness was a Garrison Town but now all the houses that had been left empty by the people who had been evacuated had been requisitioned by the army and lived in by soldiers.

Our little school was used as a Civic Restaurant by soldiers and the local community. My dad recovered and we were taken back on one of the long coach trips with the visiting parents.

Gradually some of the older children went home but we also had children joining us. There was Rodney Fry's sister Jean, also Pat, Richard and Peter Done from Manchester, a girl called Deena. We were all brought up as brothers and sisters in one large family. We were accepted by the village families, went to church, brownies, cubs, Saturday morning pictures at the village hall and we always had the most wonderful day in May dressing up. There was a village band, all the girls in white with flowers decorating their hair and necklines, a huge May pole on the village green, dancing all the patterns around then a large party for all the village. Very, very, happy days.

We had lots of laughs remembering the goats eating our washing, one or two of us would have to play in the drying area near the washing lines to shoo the goats off as they would eat anything, sheets, jumpers, they were not fussy. We would go inside the pens of baby chicks and ducklings and play with the fluffy chicks. One memory that scares me still is the thought of the dozen or so geese that would nip the tops of our legs if we didn't run past quickly enough, they made excellent guards. We had a lovely sheep dog, brown and white, her name was Keeper, who we all loved very much. In the very hot weather and when the hostel was very busy we would move out of the brick dormitories to the wooden summer houses. We would lay terrified at night as the horses from the fields nearby would break into our fields and gallop round and round the buildings, it sounded so noisy in the dark.

We stayed at Hollowford for four years, very happy years and we had been looked after by folk who had loved us very much. All the other children had returned home and now it was our turn. It was a very sad day but we promised to stay in touch and visit again. This was awkward as travel and transport was not that easy then. No one I knew had a car until my friend's dad bought a Ford and we were then fifteen years old. We wrote letters to lots of the visitors that had taken us out and about for a few years after the war but then gradually lost touch. Mrs Rowlands and Uncle Bill with Jean, moved down to Wellington in Somerset. They had missed all of the children and couldn't stay at Hollowford any longer. I used to write at first and then I got married and decided to visit them. We chatted and laughed over lots of the past events with this now little old lady, Mrs Rowlands and Uncle Bill who had a great influence in my life. They had accepted all of us, bad tempers, feeling unhappy sometimes, sickness and given us the most wonderful four years any child could wish for when others were having very hard times.

We settled into school back at Hinguar Street easily as Mr. Bowyer was back as Headmaster there, Miss Standon was back teaching and slowly life returned to normal at home with Mum, Dad, sisters and my brother. M.A.Andrews

Evacuation June 2nd 1940 by Marian Jean Whiting (nee Osborne) and her brother Edward William Osborne (Ted). Pupils at Hinguar Street School Shoeburyness.

In June 1940 nearly the whole school assembled at school and were taken by bus to Southend Central Station, while trains awaited to take us from Southend to Chapel – En – Le – Frith in Derbyshire.

We then were taken by bus to the villages of Castleton, Bamford and finally Hope where we assembled in the village school.

We had not been allocated to any particular billet and therefore the eldest and the strongest were selected by our future guardians on the basis of who could work the hardest. Being only 7 years old and in tears I was left to last. The arrangement was that any family with a room had to take a child.

My first home was with Mr and Mrs Waterhouse who were newlyweds and were keen on walking in the Dales. I used to be left on my own with a paste sandwich for the day. I was lonely and subsequently was found wandering in the street, and then moved and lived with Mr and Mrs Chapman. My brother had been billeted with Mr and Mrs A.Noon. Mrs Noon was related to Mr Watson who was the local butcher and farmer. Ted was very happy in this position as he loved farming and working in the shop. He also accompanied Mr Watson on his rounds delivering meat, and to this day is referred to by the Noon family as 'Our Ted'. He sees them annually, but sadly Mr and Mrs Noon have passed away, but he still sees the children of the Noons. But I was still young and unhappy and my mother realised the situation. My cousin, Dorothy (Hedley) was also unhappy and her mother came to Derbyshire and brought us both home to Shoeburyness. My brother remained for a further period and was reluctant to come home.

We went to school in the Methodist Chapel which was a corrugated iron building and leaked, and Ted recalls that the evacuees were blamed for the Halls condition. Other Shoebury children that we recall are: Pat O'Dell, Dorothy Hedley, Jim and John Askew, Laurence Lee, Jean and Ron Comry

And the teachers were: Mr Bowyer (Headmaster), Mr Edwards, Miss Hogsflesh and Miss Thomas.

Notes taken from a discussion with Alf Hallums (aged 12 at evacuation and Don Pacey aged 9 at evacuation).

Alf and George Hallums right side of photograph. Don Pacey middle row 7th place.

Two busloads of children were taken by bus to Southend. Then they were taken by train to Chapel – Le – Frith and bussed to Bamford and Hope in Derbyshire. Although he wanted to go, when they got there they thought "What have we done"! There was only one road and when it rained it all went down the road.

We were taken to the Church Hall and separated. Don was the last one to be chosen. It was like a cattle market.

It was 'the worst time of their lives'. Alf was billeted with Mrs Thompson who received 5 evacuees and Don with Mrs Lister who also took 5 children.

Alf recalls that the postal orders his mother sent him were taken by Mrs Thompson " She used to take it all." The evacuated children used to eat after their own children and only had to eat what the family left.

"We slept in the attic 4 kids - 2 of them wet the bed and I used to be wet through. The two daughters never went to work and tipped the jerry out of the window – the toilet was down the bottom of the garden. The washing was on a rack on the ceiling.

They were 25 years behind the times – went to work along alleys in clogs."

The school was held in a working men's club, all ages were put together from little ones upwards. Everyone went to school in hob-nail boots. The area was surrounded by 3 farms and I once saw little pigs running down the road.

They were evacuated from September 1940 to August 1941. When he broke his arm he went to Sheffield Infirmary. His brother George had boils all round his neck due to the conditions.

Don's mum visited him and brought him back after a few months. Alf came home with his sister.

Alf went to Caulfield when it first opened and walked to school 4 times a day. Because of the war he lost much of his schooling, when he returned to Shoebury they went to school in other people's houses.. An aircraft landed along Herbert road and at North Shoebury Church there were old caravans for Jewish people from London.

His dad went to sea at 12 on a sailing barge the Harriet. His family were Salvation Army people and had barges. They were run by husband and wife. When loaded the barges could float in 6 feet of water or 3 feet if empty. Each barge held 40,000 bricks plus the skipper and boy. On East Beach there were 2 jetties, the bricks were loaded from barrows with 4 inch iron wheels. They took bricks one way and brought back coal – office and blacksmith – and chalk and breeze (rough stuff).

Before the war he knew everyone in every house. From 1936 onwards there was high unemployment and the Brickfield work was only seasonal. There was no dole for a lot of men and there was a soup kitchen set up on the corner of Southchurch Avenue and Shoebury High Street. You could get a house in Wakering Avenue for £25 down and 18/- a week. Alf's family lived in Shoebury Avenue 3,5, and 8, his parents, aunts and uncles.

June and Pamela Edmunds from Richmond Avenue.
Evacuated June 1940 aged 9 and 7.

There were lots of rehearsals before we were evacuated. On the day, only one boy had a car, all the rest of us were taken in double decker buses to Southend. All the shops gave us sweets and toffees – whatever was left. The journey to Derbyshire seemed to take forever, people were crying or going to sleep. Mrs Lipscombe, our teacher, who lived in Shoebury High Street was on the train and another teacher, Mr Brown. Daphne Fitt went and the Crouchers. – about 14 children.

We were sent to Ashbourne in Derbyshire and lived with Mrs Skellan who was about 30 and had one little girl called Brenda. I had a double bed.

We went to school in the Congregational Church Hall, sometimes I ate a penneth of broken biscuits on the way to school. I couldn't hear the teacher, Mr Brown and so he made me sit with all the baby's. Pat Croucher stayed at the Garage and we used to play with all the bells.

I came home at Christmas 1940 because my mum couldn't stand it. She wrote me letters but it made her cry every night.

My brother was in the Army and he used to write to me and send me the illustrated John Bull.

He died in 1942.

I'm going back in April to Ashbourne as a Christmas present.

Ruth Dawson (Wise)

We were all evacuated by coach on the 2nd June. All the children wore labels and carried cases. We were wearing everything as we couldn't carry much and it was boiling hot. There were four of us, Margaret Adams and her sister and 2 friends. We were sent to the Church Hall at Bamford, before we were billeted. It was like a cattle market there, because we were 4 friends they wouldn't pick us. I had a sheltered life at home and had no idea what to expect.

I had 3 billets. In one they starved us, we were so hungry we were digging up radishes and I had to look after a child. Once a man was jealous of his wife so he threw all our rations on the fire and we tried desperately to get it out.

I didn't stay at Bamford all that long as I gained a Commercial College Scholarship my parents stayed and bought me a bike for passing it. I had to transfer to Mansfield in

September. It was terrifying travelling there, I got lost in Chesterfield and had to get off a bus and get on a train. I loved it in Mansfield, which was a mining area and I went to the Technical College and learnt French, German, Typing and Book Keeping. I was away 2 years, but I would have learnt Spanish in the third year.

I lived in Forest Town, back to back houses and 9 avenues and I lived in First Avenue, which was near the bus for school. The man I stayed with was a surface miner with one little girl – who was quite good to me. He worked in Castleford and mined blue john. One family we knew had supper – high tea – and the father took his teeth out and put them in a mug. They used to laugh at the way we spoke – said bath etc.

When we returned to Shoebury in September 1942 I had to sleep under the grand piano as there was no room in the Anderson shelter. I went to work in the New Ranges.

1941 Winston Churchill boarding a train on Shoeburyness Station after a visit to the Garrison.

Aug 25th	This Log Book was returned from the Reception area in July 1942. Meanwhile, since the opening of certain schools as Group Centres in December 1940, a record has been kept in a temporary Log Book.
Aug 25th	School re-opened this morning. Domestic Subjects on Tuesdays – at Southchurch Hall, and Wednesdays at Municipal College.
Sept 1st	Nurse V. Crump examined the heads of all children present.

Winston Churchill inspecting the Shoebury Guard.

Sept 9th The two top classes have a lantern lecture with slides provided by the Imperial Institute and lecturer – on Canada 11 – 12 A.M.

Sept. 15th Dental Clinic held in the Medical Room.

Sept 16th Second lantern lecture held on the Empire

No1. Sept 9th Canada by Mr. N. MacIntosh.

No2. Sept. 16th South Africa by J.H. Koens.

Second World War shelters, now demolished.

Sept 23rd	14 Roman Catholic children withdrawn for Religious Instruction. This is to take place each Wednesday and Thursday.
Sept. 23rd	No. 3 Lecture New Guinea lecturer Miss D. Hosegood .

1st In accordance with Circular 1.40/42 par. 3 the Head Master instructed the Staff that on the sounding of an alert, children are to be taken to the shelters, provided that no air activity at the time would make this dangerous.

Use of the Hall was discussed now that permission has been granted from 9A.M.- 4 P.M.

Oct 12th	Lecture on China, No. 6 in series was much appreciated – Commander Partington.
Oct 16th	Dental Treatment finished yesterday.
Oct 20th	Lecture No. 7 – Japan – by Commander Partington.
Nov 4th	Lecture No. 8. Empire Sea Routes by The Rev. Jandin Cruce.
Nov 11th	Lecture No. (Lt. Col. Thwaites. The Bahamas and West Indies.
Nov 18th	Lecture No. 10 – India by Mr. G.P. Dessai.
Nov 25th	Lecture No. 11 S. Rhodesia by Mr. F. Davies.
Nov 27th	Record of temperatures taken this week forwarded to the Education Office.

Room 10	M	T	W	T	F
9.30 A.M.	51	48	50	50	52
1.30 P.M.	47	49	51	52	50

Dec. 2nd	Lecture No. 12. Nepal by Mr. M. Milward.
Dec. 4th	Record of temperatures this week

Room 10	M	T	W	T	F
9.30 A.M.	50	51	49	52	54
1.30 A.M.	50	50	50	52	53

Figures forwarded to Education Office, and a note from a parent E.G.Weston., 7 Vincent Crescent re. cold classroom.

Dec 7th	Nurse Crump examined all children present in J3 and S3, owing to a case of Scabies in a family where all are suffering.
Dec. 9th	Lecture No. 13 The Mediterranean Mr. J. Wolusemore.

Dec 11th	Room 10	M	T	W	T	F
	9.30 A.M.	56	58	57	58	60
	1.30 P.M.	54	56	60	58	58

Dec 16th   Lecture No.14 Miss W.B.Yeatman – Nigeria.

Miss R.Dobie represented this school at a service at Prittlewell for Women's Voluntary Services.

This week on Tuesday 3.15 P.M. Junior Lantern entertainment.

Dec. 17th   Thursday   11 A.M. All Entertainment

                         3.15 P.M. Senior Lantern Entertainment

Dec 18th   School closed for Christmas Holiday after the afternoon session.

1943

Jan 5th   School re-opened this morning.

Jan 11th   Siren 9.45 A.M. all children taken to shelters Surface drain in playground North – near cycle shed reported to Caretaker's Supervisor.

Jan 18th   Siren 1.50 – 2.20. Children taken to shelters.

Jan 29th   Many children absent suffering from colds, chicken pox and measles.

Feb 2nd   No Domestic Subjects for S1, S.B owing to illness of teacher.

Feb 3rd   Nurse Crump saw those children noted on 26.1.43 as suffering from nits. All children in S1C examined as contacts with Scabies.

Feb 4th   A.R.P. Wardens examined gas masks.

Feb 9th   Miss R. Dobie absent – heavy cold.

Feb 10th   Mrs A. Fortescue absent. She has gone to Derbyshire to nurse her son who is ill with bronchitis. (Many children evacuated to Derbyshire).

Feb 10th   Lecture by Commander Elwell Sutton – S. Africa – all Seniors.

Feb 15th   Routine Medical Inspection of all senior boys by Dr Spencer.

Feb 16th   Ditto girls Medical Inspection.

Feb 23rd   Mr J. Johnson absent chill, and his son has some form of Scarlet Fever.

Feb 24th   Canadian Industries – Mr N. Mackintosh.

March 8th	Mr Strong absent with influenza cold.
March 12th	Attendance still only 85.1% - many children with colds.
March 15th	The Head Master absent during the afternoon - unwell.
March 19th	Attendance for week :- 86.9%.
March 19th	Lecture on New Zealand by Rev. P. Steed in connection with Imperial Institute.
March 30th	Mr J.C. Scott gave a lecture on objects dropped from the air by enemy planes : 2.30 – 3.P.M March 31st Alert 11.0 – 11.15.
April 7th	Mr A.J. Findlay : Lecture – E.Africa to S3, S2, girls & S1C – chiefly Uganda and Kenya. Lists prepared of children needing Psychological Record Cards.
May 4th	Miss R. Dobie addressed all the girls, as usual at the beginning of a new term, on behaviour in Cloak Room and W.Cs.
May 12th	The Head Master addressed the boys on behaviour in W.Cs and Urinals, of writing on walls and similar actions. Lecture British Guiana – Mr E. Eytle 2.0 – 3.0 P.M.
May 24th	**Empire Day.** The usual programme was observed, and songs appropriate to the occasion were rendered by Years 1a and 1b and Years 2 and 3. The Head Master gave short address introducing the following points :- • Origin of Empire Day. • Unity of language over great tracts of the Empire. • Ties of relationship. • Membership imposes an obligation :- • The duty of members to the whole. • Freedom of decisions made. • Freedom of Worship within the Empire. • Empire spread over the globe – the phrase – "The sun never sets on the British Empire." • The present war – a righteous cause. • We pray for victory so that Peace may help us to return to a constructive policy, so that God's Kingdom on earth may flourish.
May 25th	Inspector Edwards called and asked about 5 boys re. use of catapults and damage to Shore House.
May 26th	P.M. Lecture J.H. Koens. W. African Colonies.

June 4th	Distribution of chocolate sent by the Optimists International Club, Ontario.
June 9th	Commander Parkington – Lecture on Borneo.
June 11th	Sgt Livermore, of Southend Constabulary called re. a complaint about a boy in 1c. The Head Master stated that nothing had nothing had been reported to the school. A reminder was also given of the request that members of the Police should visit school in civilian clothes.
July 2nd	School total effort in Wings for Victory £154 – 0 – 6. Half day holiday to celebrate total effort of all schools in the Borough.
July 7th	Low attendance due to Salvation Army Treat.
July 7th	Lecture – Australia : Mr J. W. Luxmoore.
July 9th	Mr Kelly called and saw Mr Cardwell – First Asst. re. plots behind shelters recently handed back to the Ed. Com.
July 12th	Mr Nock called with Mr Harvey and Mr Lister to judge the garden plots
.July 15th	Lecture on India by Mr Dessai. Inspector Cheatle gave 2 talks on "Dangerous Objects", 1.to the juniors and 2. to the seniors from 3 – 4 P.M.
July 22nd	Dig for Victory Competition – Allotments. This school was placed 1st and awarded the Silver Cup and 20 books on Gardening for the Senior boys.
July 23rd	The pupils made a presentation of a barometer to the Head Master in the Hall this afternoon and 2 pipes and a lighter. After the pupils had been dismissed the Staff presented the Head Master with a wristwatch, and expressed their appreciation of his kindness and thought for their welfare during the time they had worked together. The Head Mistress of Sea View Homes Miss E. Main and Staff joined in the latter function. School closes this afternoon till Tuesday August 31st 1943. My service in this school terminates on August 30th 1943, on being transferred to another department in the Borough of Southend-on-Sea. F.Cyril Dale.

Mr R. F. Poutney

August 31st 1943 to July 26th 1946

1943

Aug 31st   I began my duties as headmaster of this Junior and Senior Mixed School. R.F. Poutney.

Five new teachers joined the staff and these and these and the four remaining members of the staff were allocated to classes as shown below:-

3rd Yr Senior	*Mr H.E.Cardwell*
2nd Yr Senior	*Miss A.E.Coney*
1st Yr Senior A	*Mr. R.L. Strong*
1st Yr Senior B	*Mrs V. Mumford*
Remove	*Miss W.M. Barren (Special Class)*
4th Yr Junior	*Miss J.A.Danks*
3rd Yr Junior	*Mrs E.M. Segust*
2nd Yr Junior B	*Miss E.H. Brooks (Special Class)*
2nd Yr Junior	*Miss C.A. Picken.*

Mr Lewis reported that the garden shed had been entered during the holiday and certain tools stolen. This was reported to the Education Office and to the Police.

Sept 1s t   A police officer came to take statements from gardening monitors concerning the missing tools.

Sept 3rd   Mr Collins placed 3 bulbs in 3 of the surface shelters and 4 in the fourth shelter and these were locked in the lamp holders.

Oct 15th   Gas masks examined – whole school.

Oct 18th	Shelter drill.
Nov 11th	Shelter drill – time taken 3 mins.
Dec 14th	Concerts were given to the whole school. Each class contributed a play or some other item and two very enjoyable hours of entertainment resulted. On Wed 15th Mr Strong gave a short conjuring show for the entertainment of the children.
Dec 17th	School closed for the Christmas Holiday at the end of the afternoon session. The sum of £8.16.2 was sent to the Merchant Navy Comfort Fund.

1944

Jan 6th	Air Raid practise. Children rehearsed going to shelters as if an alert had sounded during playtime.
Jan 11th	Shelter drill.
Jan 21st	Air Raid Shelter drill this morning and children proceeding to the shelters from a full assembly in the hall. At 11.25 a short alert children went to shelters in about 3 and a half mins.
Feb 2nd	It was discovered this afternoon that the garden shed was broken open. On checking the tools it was found that one fork and one small hand cultivator were missing. This was reported to the Education Office and to the Police.
Feb 4th	Air Raid Shelter Drill this morning. Children went to shelters from the playground as if an alert had been sounded during playtime.
Feb 16th	Alert at 1.37pm children went to shelters all clear at 1.50.
March 24th	School closed for Easter Holiday – An extended holiday being given because of the fuel shortage.
April 18th	School re-opened after the Easter Holiday. All staff present. Twenty-eight children admitted from the Sea View Homes School.
April 28th	An alert at 9.20 approx all children proceeded to shelter according to plan. All clear 9.35.
May 19th	Sergt Bates visited the school in connection with some ammunition that had been stolen. A number of boys were questioned and it was found that these lads had been given empty cartridge cases by soldiers.

May 24th	Empire day. The usual Empire Day Service was held – concluding with the singing of Jerusalem by the Upper Juniors and all Seniors.

May 24th · Empire day. The usual Empire Day Service was held – concluding with the singing of Jerusalem by the Upper Juniors and all Seniors.

The Headmaster gave a short address - the main theme of which was the debt we owe to the hardy pioneers of old – that same courage is alive today – troops from all parts of the Empire came freely to help in the war. That spirit combined with a true Christian spirit will ensure the development of the Empire in future years.

June 1st · First inter school netball match since the outbreak of war played today against the girls of Hamstel Sch (score Shoebury 16 – Hamstel 4)

June 8th · Return match with Hamstel Sch which was won by Hamstel (12 – 7)

June 7th · **In aid of Salute the Soldier Week** a display was given from 3.40 – 4.40 to which parents were invited. Those children not taking part were sent home before the programme began. The programme consisted of

Songs by Seniors & Juniors   *(Miss A.J. Coney)*
P.T. Display by Senior Girls   *(Miss W.M. Barren)*
P.T. Display by Senior Boys   *(Mr. R.L. Strong)*

Dancing by children from J3, J4, S1B, S1A under the direction of their teachers – Miss J.A. Danks or Mrs V. Mumford being in charge.

Salute the Soldier Parades Carnarvon Herald 1944

The Display was well attended by an appreciative audience of parents. Miss R. Hart (P.J. Organiser) was among those present and she took the opportunity of saying a few words to the audience.

June 9th   The Salute the Soldier Week closed with the excellent total of £409 -12-6 – over four times the target figure of £100.

June 16th   The alert which sounded at 11.31 the previous night was still in operation when the time to open morning school came. At 9. a.m. 224 children were present. As all was quiet they came to classes, registers were marked and they then proceeded to the shelters. The Raiders Passed Signal was given at 9.25.

June 19th   During the dinner hour today a number of children were playing around the planks left by the builders constructing the shelters. Jean Key (who had come back from home early) was unfortunately near the end of a plank when E. Holland jumped on the other end; the plank sprang up and hit Jean just above the eye. The bruise was attended to by Miss Cobey and Jean continued at school. The bruise although nasty, did not appear to cause Jean any pain.

June 21st   An alert at 11.50 approx – children to shelters. Raiders passed at 12.5.

June 23rd   School closed at noon today - a half day's holiday being given in recognition of the effort of the elementary schools - the Salute the Soldier Savings Week.

June 30th   A sudden alert at 10.46 (playtime) followed at once by gunfire and the noise of enemy planes. The children behaved very well. Those in the classroom took shelter beneath the desks. Those on the way to the playground sheltered in suitable places in the passages, while children who had reached the playground went at once to the shelters.

July 3rd	An alert at 9A.M. the Raiders Passed Signal was followed by another alert – children did not leave shelters or begin work until 9.50.
July 7th	The alert at 12.10 approx – dinner children and others still at school went to shelters – the alert lasted about 10 mins.
July 10th	An alert at 2.45 approx.
July 14th	Dig for Victory Week Essay Competition – 1st Prize Kathleen Wall, 3rd Prize P.S. Cook Poster Slogan Competition – 3rd Prize Cyril Ayles

Great Wakering pea pickers.

July 26th	An alert 2.14 to 2.30
July 27th	An alert 2.17 to 2.40
July 28th	An alert 9.43 to 9.53.
Sept 8th	Norman Diack received a bump under his left eye (for which Colin Banks appears to be responsible). For a time I thought the bump was more serious than it was and so took Norman Diack to Dr Ryan the boy was then sent home in the care of another boy who returned to report that he had seen him home safely indoors.
Oct 16th	Message received that Mrs Mumford will be absent for the next two weeks owing to her husband being on embarkation leave. Mrs Patten to come as a supply teacher for half of each day.

Oct 24th   Wardens visited to inspect gas masks. New gas cooker installed in kitchen.

Nov 14th   Detective Constable Hooper asked for permission to question four boys in connection with some lamps missing from the Railway. The boys were questioned in my presence and all admitted having some connection with the incident.

German prisoners of war removing barbed wire defences which ran along the beach in front of Shoebury Common. The threat of invasion had gone by 1944. Bottom picture top right - higher defences visible. This together with mined beaches had provided land defences after 1939.

Dec 22nd   School closed for the Christmas Holiday. Over £25 was collected by the children for various charities. British Red Cross £11.5.0, Merchant Navy Comfort Fund £10.15 and Aid to Russia Fund £3.12.6.

The Festivities during the last week included :-

Weds Dec 20th Punch & Judy & Conjuring at 11. o'clock.

Play by J4 and Carols at 3.15.

Thurs Dec 21st Tea Parties in each class at 2.30.

1945

Feb 6th   Imp. Inst Lecture on Ceylon by Mr Luxmore.

Feb 14th   Parents meeting at 3 o'clock re how the New Education Act will affect Secondary Education. About 100 parents attended.

Feb 23rd   A representative from the Ministry of Supply gave a talk to encourage the Book Drive.

March 5th   An alert shortly after play – all children to the shelters.

March 9th   Book Drive ended today over 7,500 books were brought in.

March 28th School closed for the Easter Holiday 13 children came off the sch. Roll; 3 go to the Municipal College, 9 age leavers and one removal.

May 4th   The Primary section of the school transferred to Richmond Avenue School. This section consists of 4 classes totalling 148 children of the four teachers Miss Mullen has already been transferred.

May 8-10th **Three days holiday to celebrate Victory in Europe.**

V.E. Day St. Peter's Hall Shoebury 1945.

V.E. Day Caulfield Road, Shoeburyness May 1945, showing Sally,
Rose and Grace. This is the end table – the others stretching up
from the end of this one up the road – with a large gramophone in
the road itself – all the local children, people and dogs were
thoroughly enjoying themselves. Sally complete with party frock and
red white and blue ribbon.

VE Day, Richmond Avenue, Shoeburyness.

May 11th   School reassembled and a service was held giving thanks to God for Victory and Peace in Europe with prayers for our men in the Far East.

May 24th   Empire Day celebration held at 11o'clock. His Worship the Mayor – Alderman Miles O.B.E. J.P. presided & Miss M.E.Reay C.B.E. J.P. Chairman of the Education Committee and the Chief Education Officer were also present. The Rector, Mrs Sweeney and Father Toft completed the platform party.
The programme consisted of songs (England & Jerusalem) taken by Mrs Coney & Dancing by girls under Mrs Barren & P.T. by boys directed by Mr Strong. His worship the Mayor addressed the school on the subject of Our Empire. Later the Mayor was pleased to recommend that the school had a half days' holiday and Miss Reay agreed that the occasion should be marked in this way.

May 28th   Imp. Inst. Lecture by Commander Partington – Hong Kong.

June 1st   Mrs V. Mumford away as her husband is home on leave.
School closed at 2.50 to enable teachers to attend a special service of Thanksgiving at St. Mary's Church Prittlewell.

June 11th   Betty Chilton crossed the road (from the school) during the dinner hour and was knocked over by a cycle. Appeared to be suffering from shock. Phoned doctor – out. Sent for mother & ambulance – mother accompanied child to hospital. Betty retained at the hospital 3 days & then sent home. It appears that her injuries were not serious.

June 15th	All this week men have been removing blast walls, filling shelter trench and removing black paint from some windows.
June 18th	Mrs Mumford absent owing to her husband's leave all this week.
June 21st	Cook reported that during the evening a window in the pantry had been broken and a tin of spam stolen.
July 2nd	Detective Hooper called in connection with the incident on June 21st and questioned a boy in my presence.
July 18th	Dig for Victory Essay Competition. I was informed this afternoon that the following children had won prizes.

Class A (under 13)   1st Margaret Bates 2nd Betty Oatley 3rd Ellen Holden.
Class B (over 13)   2nd Maureen Lewis 3rd Kathleen Wall.
Art Competition Class A P.Taylor 2nd Prize Class B Dennis Smith 3rd

July 24th	The whole school (with the exception of 18 children) went to see King Henry V at the Odeon Cinema. Miss Bailey and Miss Coomber remained at school to look after the boys & girls who did not go.
July 27th	School closed for the Summer Holiday. 43 children are leaving the school.

16 age leavers
10 boys and girls going to the Municipal College
16 boys and girls going to Southend and Westcliff High Schools.
1 boy returning to Kent.

Sept 18th	School re-opened after the Summer Holidays. Caretaker reported that the children have been on the roof during the holiday & thrown small pieces of pitch into the Domestic Science Room. Children playing in the field had scattered the bricks left from the dismantled blast walls and heavy concrete slabs from the shelter trench were knocked over and broken. This matter was reported to Mr Dawson and the Education Office and the following recommendations were made by me.

• Padlocks fitted to school gates.
• A notice Trespassers will be prosecuted put up.
• Wire netting along west fence where the school boundary fence is also the back fence for a number of gardens.
• The removal as soon as possible of the slabs and bricks.

Later it was found that the garden shed had been broken into and a considerable number of shallots taken. Reported to Police who were asked to watch building.

Sept 21st	4 children admitted 9 left Roll 213 Attendance 93.66%.
Oct 5th	Thanksgiving Week ends with a total of £173.6.0. As the target was £100 and the response rather poor in the beginning I think this can be regarded as a very fair result.
Oct 8th	It was discovered that during the weekend the padlock on the west gate of the school had been broken. It was ascertained who the boys concerned in this were and the incident reported to the Education Office and to the parents of the boys concerned. The parents were asked to pay 2/9 each to replace the padlock which (I am told) cost 5/6. Cash for padlock sent to Ed. Office.
Nov 19th	Nurse Crump came for a Routine Medical Inspection of heads and Reported an improved standard of cleanliness.
Dec 10th	Mrs Mumford absent – will be away for a week owing to her husband's leave from the forces.
24th Dec	Letter from Lt. R.H.Strickland, RTO Hagen, 48 Movement Control, BADR.

Dear children,

Today being Christmas Eve is the one day all our thoughts go to giving and receiving presents. I have had quite a number this week each marked with that usual phrase "Do not open until Dec. 25th," but an hour ago I had a parcel handed to me for all of my men here in Hagen. I was surprised when I opened it and found it a parcel of cigarettes and so I gathered my twenty nine men and we shared them out. In the parcel were six printed cards showing the name of the school which had subscribed to this fund. I saw the name of your town and I immediately took it for myself for I feel as if I belong to Shoeburyness, even if it's only slightly. Last Christmas I spent on Foulness Island with an anti-aircraft battery which was deployed against the attack of V1s (doodle-bugs). So I know quite a good bit about your homes and realise just how happy you must be this first Christmas since 1938 of peace. We are all looking forward to tomorrow also and we have made lots of preparations, some of the men have gathered evergreens and decorated the rooms, two others brought a Christmas tree from a neighbouring wood and they have decorated this, of course there are no silvery glass toys here so we made it shine with some cellophane and cotton wool. But we will have a happy time tomorrow and I know as we sit by the fire, after supper, talking we will remember you children of Shoeburyness School who sent to us all a very welcome Christmas present. Let me thank you very sincerely for the pennies and sixpences you all put together for this truly unselfish gift. One word about us before I close. You have all seen the letters R.T.O. on the station and as you know it means Railway Traffic Officer. Now here in Germany it's a similar job although we do not see so many passengers for our main job is to send coal to Austria from Hagen. Hagen is a marshalling yard for all coal going to the Ruhr to the south and south east. The countryside is very pleasant but unlike Essex, for here are lots of hills and woods. Still I would much rather be in Essex for Christmas than Germany.

With this I will say again thank you for your parcel, goodbye and God bless you all.

Wishing you a very happy New Year,

Yours Very sincerely,

R.H. Strickland.

1946

March 26th Initial Meeting held in the formation of Camping and Outdoor Clubs by Miss Danks and Miss Barren respectively. A large number of children are very keen but it was decided to have a small number in each club to begin with.

Football Match v Great Wakering Lost 4-2.

April 1st Mrs Mumford absent this week owing to her husband's leave from the forces.

Apr 4th/5th   Mr R.L. Strong away on a course concerned with the Prevention of Road Accidents.

May 24th   Empire Day – Miss Senier, Chairman of the Governors of the School took the chair and gave the Empire Day address.

June 6th   **VICTORY DAY**

A service of thanksgiving was held in the hall at 11. a.m. Appropriate hymns and prayers & an address by the headmaster were followed by the singing of Peaceful England and the National Anthem.

Winston Churchill paid tribute to the men and women who had laid down their lives for victory as well as to all those who had "fought valiantly" on land, sea and in the air.

In the afternoon registers were not marked we were blessed with a fine afternoon for the Victory Day Sports:- Events were keenly contested Blue House won with Green House a close second. Prizes were presented by Mrs Ginnis J. Ashbourne.

June 21st — Week-end camp held at Eastwood attended by 16 girls under the care of Miss W.M. Baren and Miss J.A. Danks. The week-end was fine & the camp proved an enjoyable & valuable experience for the girls concerned. Following week-end Boys Camp.

June 26th — Open Day. A good number of interested parents gathered in the hall at 2pm. for a demonstration of visual aids to education. The parents were then divided into three parties and taken on a 'tour' of the practical rooms, this was followed by a visit to the classrooms. Parents were very interested in the work done by the pupils and appreciated the effort made to give them an insight into the work done by the school & the facilities it offers.

July 3rd — School outing to Maldon, Langford Water Works & Beeleigh Abbey – 32 children from 2A went accompanied by H.T. and Mrs Wiseman. A fine day and an enjoyable and instructive outing.

July 9th — John Fisher while working in the garden stuck a garden fork through his foot…The boy did this himself & no blame can be attached to any other person. Mr Townsend in charge of class. Boy attended to by Mr Day & myself & sent home.

July 23rd — School outing to London, 3rd Form Mr Strong and Mrs Wiseman in charge. Informed this morning that I am to be transferred to Richmond Av. Sch. As from Sept. next. This alters, at very short notice, the arrangement by which I was to remain here until Christmas.

July 26th — The pupils and staff presented me with an electric clock & Mr Cardnell on behalf of all expressed his appreciation of the work I had done and the help I had given to all. My services terminate on being transferred to Richmond Av. School. R.L. Poutney.

July 26th — The pupils and staff presented me with an electric clock & Mr Cardnell on behalf of all expressed his appreciation of the work I had done and the help I had given to all. My services terminate on being transferred to Richmond Av. School. R.L. Poutney.

Mr Napier BA MRST

September 10th 1946 - May 31st 1954

1946

Sept 10th   1946 I took up my duties as headmaster of this High School.

All members of the staff were present and are taking forms as follows:-

3rd year boys	*Mr Cardnell*
3rd year girls	*Miss Wiseman, B.A.*
2A	*Miss Danks*
2B	*Mrs Mumford*
1A	*Mr Strong*
1B	*Miss Barren*
Remove	*Mr H. Smith*

The time-table involves a very high degree of specialisation, under which, subjects are dealt with as follows:

History	*Miss Wiseman B.A.*
Geography	*Mr R.L. Strong*
Science	*Mr H Day B.Sc.*
Music	*Mrs Mumford and Mrs Titford*
Art	*Miss Danks*
Physical Training	*Miss Barren & Mr H.Smith*
Gardening	*Mr Townsend and Mr. H. Smith*
Homecraft	*Miss Bailey*
Literature	*Mr Cardnell*

In taking up my duties I would like to thank my predecessor Mr Poutney and to Mr Strong for the help they have given me to "pick up the reins" during the summer vacation.

10th Sept   Mr Rye, a student joined for teaching practice Sept 11th Visit of Mr Dagley, P.T. organiser, bringing details of lay out of hockey and football pitches.

Sept 23rd   Visit to the Ford works. A party led by Mr Strong and Mr Cardwell consisting of 30 boys from the top boys' class left at noon by Westcliff Motor Services conveyance and arrived at the Ford Works at Dagenham. After an exhaustive & exhausting tour of the works the party were provided with light refreshments by the management. The party then left and were in their homes by six p.m. A report on the visit was sent to the Chief Education Officer and a copy retained in the "School Visits" file.

Sept 24th   In the afternoon the school was honoured by the visit of Miss Reay vice chairman of the Education Committee. Miss Reay visited the classes and welcomed back the masters who had recently returned from the forces.

Sept 25th   Miss Bailey took a party of sixteen girls from the top class of girls to visit the London Co-operative Bakery.

Sept 28th   This Saturday marked the opening of the schools' football season, and the return to almost pre-war conditions with the re-commencement of the Southend Schools' Football League. Shoebury fielded a strong first eleven which beat Westborough by five goals to four.

Sept 30th   Today marked the resignation of Mrs Mumford after four years war time service with the Education Committee, on the return of her husband from the forces.
The occasion was marked by the presentation of a fruit basket and a cake-stand subscribed for by the pupils and staff, by the head girl and the school captain.

Oct 3rd   Visit and lecture by the Rev. Stead, lecturing under the auspices of the Imperial Service League on "British Honduras". This lecture was listened to and much appreciated by the first year.

Oct 4th   Visit for one day: Gebescope sound projector.
Our percentage of attendance the highest so far 93.8%.

Oct 7th   Savings week has realised £46.7.6d.

Oct 17th   Visit of Imperial Services Lecturer: Mr Blackam to talk on Jamaica.

Oct 18th   Visit of Dr Earle, Master of Kirkaldy High School, Fife, and a lady teacher from Baltimore, U.S.A. and another from Colarado, accompanied by Mr Dawson. Coming as these teachers do from schools with two or three thousand children on roll the visitors were shown all that a comparatively small school of 250 children could do.
At 2pm. Miss Wiseman and I left school to attend a conference of Head teachers and assistants – the final item in the conference on Comprehensive schools.

Oct 21st   Miss Bailey took a party of 15 third year girls on a visit to Thorpe Bay Laundry; left school at 2.40 and returned at 4 pm.

Oct 22nd   Major Harwood R.E. and his technical officer at the Garrison, Major Merrit, R.E. came to discuss the question of trainees in the civilian services of the experimental station, and how the 4th year (14-15) could provide a better grounding for trainees than had hitherto been possible with the leaving age at 14. After an informative discussion on both sides Mr Strong and myself were invited to visit the training departments and workshops of the Garrison engineering depot.

Oct 30th   Mr Strong and myself left at 10am to visit the Garrison Engineers shops and establishments. After the visit, the technical officer agreed to take parties of sixteen boys at a time over the engines and sheds, subject to permission being granted by the O.C. Experimental Station and the Chief Education Officer.

Nov 13th   Visit of Imperial Service Lecturer, Miss Hewitt to talk on Nova Scotia.
Dr Preston arrived to discuss the allocation of a room on one day a week for use as a speech therapist's consulting and treatment room.
Arrival of P/Sgt Bryan and Detective of the Shoebury Police Station. This was a 'courtesy visit' and after discussion of how the local police could help the school, Sgt Bryan agreed to referee the school's match on Saturday.

Nov 18th   Visit of third year girls to Garon's Bakery. The party left at 2pm.

Nov 19th   Lecture on the Ballet by Gryfyn Williams to 2nd and 3rd years.

Nov 20th   "2nd year girls and boys left under Miss Danks to attend performance of the Ballet.

Nov 28th   Mr Day took party of 15 3rd year boys to visit Ekco Works to see lamp making & other departments

Dec 16th   Christmas film show 2pm.

Dec 17th   146 children and 7 staff led by Miss Wiseman and Mr Strong visited the Britain Can Make It Exhibition. (depart 9.35, returned 5.30).

1947

April 21st   During recess, the school, chosen to represent Southend in the Robert Cook Cup played a match against Halstead Secondary Modern School at the Garrison Ground. This was kindly loaned to us by the officer commanding the Experimental Station, Brigadier Licknan O.B.E. The Shoebury town Supporters Club provided officials and advertisement of the game. This was played before a crowd of 3 to 400 and was won by two goals to one. Tea was very kindly arranged by some of the parents of boys in the team and the co-operation of certain shops in Shoeburyness.

| April 27th | Robert Cook Cup: 2nd round: against West Ham lost by 3 goals to 1: this was played on the garrison ground and arrangements were similar to those of April 21st. |

| Sept 9th | The timetable has needed considerable thought in order that the following courses might be run for the pupils between the ages of 13 -15. |

Age 14 – 15:   *Final year Course*

Age 13 – 15:   *Housewifery*

                         Pre technical Engineering

                         Handicraft course

(This last course in being until the appointment of a teacher for commercial subjects). In addition to the above courses the syllabuses of the "a" classes in the second and first years are being modified to admit of selected children being prepared for the London General Schools Examination.

| Sept 12th | Roll number 287 |

| Sept 17th | Return of overhauled wireless set. |

| Sept 24th | Visit of Mr Dawson and party to arrange for final clearance of the site in preparation for the opening of the school. |

| Sept 30th | Shoeburyness High School was formally opened by his Worship the Mayor.. The door was unlocked with a golden key. This was followed by a ceremony of dedication conducted by Canon Gowing. |

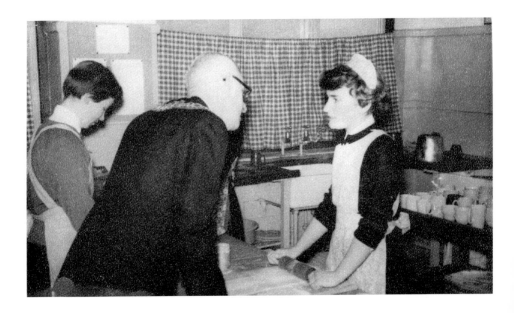

1948

Feb 6th   Visit of lecturer and film unit from the National Coal Board: talk given and film shown to first year at 11am.

Feb 10th   On Tuesday at 12.10 the following incident occurred. Miss W came to report that she had some difficulty with Miss B. I sent her to tell Miss B that I wished to see her. I heard her do so, Miss B's room being not far from mine. Miss W returned with Miss B's message to the effect that she was on her way to the cloakroom.

I proceeded to the dining hall. After lunch at 1.30 Miss B came to see me alone. I refused to do so without Miss W being present. Miss B offered the explanation that she was too upset to come when I had called for her and that she would have been rude. (In the dining room during the lunch hour she did not give any indication of a recent upset – rather the reverse in fact).

At 1.40 both were present and described the following incident. At 12.10 some boys from Miss B's class dashed from the classroom and knocked into Miss W who was walking along the passage. She remonstrated with them. While doing this Miss B recalled the class into the room and shouted at the children to whom Miss W was talking who were therefore left wondering to whom to obey.

After the class had been dismissed Miss W remonstrated with Miss B who in turn accused Miss W of being rude.

I listened to both sides and gained the impression that Miss B resented Miss W's actions in preserving discipline on this and other occasions.

I warned her that she must be prepared to back up Miss W in all efforts to improve the discipline of the school or that she must do the honest thing by sending in her resignation if she was not prepared to work with Miss W. Squadron Leader T.H.Sprowle addressed third and fourth year boys on the Royal Air Force, (3pm).

April 26th   **School to be closed for the afternoon in honour of the Silver Wedding Anniversary of Their Majesties, The King and Queen.**

May 21st   Mr Day and Mr Townsend took a party of 27 boys to the Model Engineering Exhibition at the Imperial Institute, South Kensington.

May 24th   Empire Day was celebrated during the afternoon when Councillor H.J. Bates was the Chairman. Councillor Bates expressed his appreciation of the way the ceremony was carried through – and was particularly pleased with the Sketch "Defence of the Commonwealth of Nations".

June 16th   A Lantern Lecture was given to the children of the second and third years on "Jerusalem and the Dead Sea", given by Mr St Clair of the School Lecturer's Association.

June 9th   Through the generosity of the late R.A. Jones whereby boys and girls leaving school could be taken on a School Journey, a party of 35 boys and girls went to London.

July 5th   On the arrival of the Caretaker it was discovered that the school had been broken into over the weekend and considerable damage done. The police were called and Mr Dawson informed at his private address. After the arrival of the C.I.D. personnel the school was opened. A report on the damages and losses sustained was forwarded to the Chief Education Officer.

July 17th	Miss Danks and Mr Holland took a party of 1st year children to the Tate Gallery. The party left at 9.5 and returned at about 6.30.
Sept 7th	Opening for the Autumn Term.
	In addition to the painting carried out during the Summer Term several repairs and additions had been carried out. The Assembly Hall has now been equipped with two hundred chairs. The former School Meals Kitchen has reverted to its former use, and is now occupied by the Senior Master and the Head of the Technical Department. The clock in the Tower now goes well. In addition two H.O.R.S.A. huts are nearing completion.
	During the course of the morning 145 children were admitted bringing the school roll up to 419.
Sept 30th	Mr Danks and Miss Strong took a party of 4th yr children to the "Meet South Africa Exhibition."
Oct 29th	Mr Ikoli, Member of the Legislature for Nigeria and Times correspondent in Lagos came to the school to lecture on Nigeria. He stayed to lunch and looked over the school.
Nov 30th	The school was dismissed at 3.35 in order to allow the children to get home quickly before darkness added to the difficulties of travel caused by the fog.

Mr Napier, Headmaster and Mr Aspinall, Football Season 1949-50.
Players include Henry Mercer, Johnny Hales,

1949

Jan 6th School re-opened on this date and all members of staff were present. The H.O.R.S.A. huts, completed last term, were being equipped during the holiday and several items still required attention. In addition sinks were being installed in the science laboratory so for the time being this could not be used. The engineering and metalwork equipment in use in the class room in the school building had been transported to the engineering hut and the classroom had reverted to its normal use.

Jan 13th Lecture to upper school by Mrs Hucks wife of a District Officer, on Tanganika. This was arranged by the Central Office of Information. (11am – 12 noon).

Feb 10th Headmaster and Chief Woman Assistant left school at 2.15 to see the Matron of the Sunshine Homes. Returned at 3.30 pm.

Feb 24th Visit of Mr Aspinall with four boys, William Nicholls, Andrew Patterson, Ford, and Derek Adkins to take part in the Essex Schools Amateur Boxing Association Championships held at Tilbury. They left at 2.30 pm. (William Nicholls won his bout and proceeds to the Semi Finals).

March 1st Headmaster and Mrs Lilley left the school at 10.50 am, taking a party of 40 children to see "Scott of the Antarctic." Returned at 12.45.
Mr Gregory Ward, lecturer from Empire Day Movement came to the school to talk on Canada at 11 am.
John Halsey of Form11 sent home by Mr Strong at 11.15 am who suspected he had chicken pox (spots extremely visible).

March 26th John Halsey returned with certificate from Schools Medical Officer saying he was suffering from "wucaria" (heat bumps!).

Nov 7th Gillian W (aged 13) was brought back to school having suffered with a tuberculosis condition of the knee. Her father who brought her to school was warned that although every care would be taken his daughter would enter the school at her own risk in view of the difficulty she might have in a crowd. The Headmaster informed the whole school at assembly of the need for care; a senior girl was deputed to accompany her when she moved about the school.

Nov 10th Miss Pollard and Mr Allen took a party of fourth year boys and girls to the House of Commons. The party was shown around by Captain Gunter, Member of Parliament for S.E. Essex (Shoeburyness being in this constituency).

| Nov 17th | Det. Const. Lavis attached to Shoeburyness Police Station asked permission to take a statement from John P in connection with thefts of cycle lamps. Since his statement was required as he was to be a witness, the Headmaster agreed to request. |

1950

| Feb 7th | Mr Thomas, (Eng. Hist and Fr), Miss Purseglove (Homecraft etc) Miss Beatley (School meals) Mr Sullivan (Commerce), Mr Pullen for Science and Maths, and Mr Truman music and general subjects, were present in the school during the course of the day. |

| Feb 8-10th | Inspection continued. As each specialist inspector completed his inspection he reported to the headmaster in the presence of Mr Thomas (leading the inspection panel), on the subjects he had examined. As the inspection proceeded Mr Thomas discussed the various aspects of the work of the staff, the equipment etc. and at the conclusion of his inspection said that he would report favourably on the school. The courses, run as an experiment would have the blessing of H.M.I. providing the implications as to additional and effective staffing, buildings and equipment were realised by the Governing Body. |

He commented in general on the welcoming manner in which the inspecting panel had been received and was very appreciative of all that had been done in that direction.

| Feb 23rd | Headmaster left school at 2.20 to attend Governors meeting at the Education Offices to receive the verbal report on the inspection of the school, given by Mt Thomas. (Col. Ames, H.M.I. also attended). |

| May 19th | During the morning Miss O. Pollard reported that during the course of the week her notecase containing six pound notes had been stolen from a cupboard in her room. The police were called and Mr During Lavis of the C.I.D. came in to investigate. During the morning he interviewed a number of girls. In the afternoon he interviewed two girls in the presence of their parents, because of the differing versions the girls gave of a visit by them to Miss Pollard's room. Mr Lavis left at 3.40 but without having discovered the culprit. |

May 24th   An Empire Day Service was held at 9.30am at which Councillor Brush took the chair.

The programme consisted of :

Hymn : Land of our birth (488)

Reading: Psalm

Singing : Psalm 23

Reading : from Burke's speech to the House of Commons.

Hymn : And did those feet in ancient times (446)

Prayers and address by the Headmaster.

Orchestra : Trumpet Voluntary

Choir :   Come let us all this day

School :   England by Parry

                School Song

                God Save the King.

At 2pm the Annual Sports took place amid the usual cold and windy weather characteristic of sports days at Shoeburyness.

Shoeburyness cross country.

June 12th	It was discovered at 8.30 am that thefts had taken place from Miss Pollard's room (37/-) from the refrigerator in the domestic science room, a quantity of eggs and that Mrs Lilley's room had been entered and the drawers of the table had been rifled without any money being found. The police were informed immediately and a uniformed man followed by a C.I.D constable (Glasscock) came to carry out investigations. These continued throughout the day but without result.
Oct 24th	Mr Townsend reported that he had discovered a boy in the act of stealing money (2/6d) from a tin in a cupboard in the wood store on the previous afternoon. The headmaster telephoned the probation officer since the boy was in his charge. He advised that the police should be informed.
This was done and in the afternoon Det. Sgt. Lavis took a statement from Mr Townsend. The headmaster informed the boy that the matter would be put in the hands of the police. After taking a statement from Mr Townsend Det. Sgt. Lavis interviewed the boy in the presence of the headmaster.
He first warned the boy that he was a police officer and that he need make no statement to him. He asked him why he had done it. The boy replied that he was tempted, and later added that he wanted it to spend on fireworks. He also said that he did not know what he was doing. Asked "Were you going to keep the money?" he agreed that he was. No notes were taken and Det. Sgt Lavis arranged to meet the boy at his parents' house to take a statement from him then!
Oct 25th	Governors decided to terminate the general certificate of education arrangements in the school although making provision for those in the 3rd & 4th years.

The Tideway Christmas 1950 to Easter 1953

The School Song

All men must be free,
March for Liberty with me,
Brutes and braggarts may have their little day
We shall never bow the knee.
God is drawing His sword,
We are marching with the Lord.
Sing then brother, sing, giving everything.
All you are and hope to be
To set the people free.

(Words by A.P. Herbert, Music by Edward Elgar, From Pomp and
Circumstance March No.4).

1951

May 24th   Empire Day Service held at 11am. G.E.Taylor, Esq., a Governor of the Municipal College was present as a representative of the Education Committee.

All sing:	Land of our Birth Hymn
Reading	
All sing	What Heroes Thou Hast Bred Hymn
Address	G.F. Taylor, Esq.,
Orchestra	March – by Eleanor Murray & Phyllis Tate.

Song for the Festival – sung by members of the Festival Choir.

Prayers :

Song of Liberty.   National Anthem.

Paris 1951 The Tideway

Final arrangements are now being made for our first school journey abroad. Very early on the morning of 2nd August a party of 31boys, girls and members of staff will be setting off via Southend on the first stage of the long journey via London, Newhaven and Dieppe to Paris. We shall be staying at a boarding school in this fine old city which this year is celebrating the 2,000th anniversary of its foundation. Names like the Eiffel Tower, Notre Dame and Versailles will become real to us as we are taken by English-speaking guides to see some of the most interesting buildings, museums and monuments which commemorate many exciting incidents in the history of Paris. Our great hope is the weather will be kind to us during our two cross-Channel trips.

Eastwood's Brickfields
Shoeburyness Elm Road.
Claudie Cole of West Road
and Bill Cox Friar Street.
Moulder and Runner Out.

A Trip to Star Lane Brickworks The Tideway

One week in September several classes visited Starlane Brickworks. We went on our bicycles with Mr Hedges. We went in twos, and when we got there we went to the pit where they were digging clay with a mechanical shovel, loading it onto a small train, then on to a conveyor, and so to the moulding shed.

The moulder shaped the clay into bricks and an "off-bearer" took the bricks to the "hacks" to dry the soft clay. A "crowder" took the bricks to the clamp where they were "fired" and later loaded on to lorries and taken away. The noise of the crush rollers and the heat of the drying shed also interested us.

Our thanks are due to the manager of the Star L ane Brickworks for an interesting trip.
T. SHEEHAN – Form 6. 4

The Festival of Britain

When I went to see the Festival of Britain it was nine o'clock in the evening and all the illuminations were on. The Skylon, Dome of Discovery and Festival Hall were conspicuous among other things. It was raining a little, which made the lights reflect on the roads and pavement as well as the River Thames. In my opinion, the South Bank was a very good place to have the Exhibition, because on one side of the river there were the Houses of Parliament and Big Ben, showing the stately side of London; and on the other side was the Festival, showing the colour and gaiety that London can also produce.

Everywhere I turned I saw people from other countries that had come hundreds of miles to see the Exhibition. Women from India wore their gaily coloured saris, and men from America had their thick crepe-soled shoes, their large hats and flashy ties. But however absurd to our English eyes these people looked, they made the festival a more exciting place.

I cannot wait till my next visit and I am sure the Festival of Britain will be a great success. *CAROLE DEACON – Form 5.*

1952

6th Feb   At 11am this morning the B.B.C. announced that His Majesty King George V1 has passed away peacefully during the night.

8th Feb   Children listened to the broadcast of the proclamation of Queen Elizabeth 11.

Feb 15th   In response to a complaint from the headmaster about the heating, Mr Smith (A.E.O. Sec. Ed.) and Mr Pickhaver, Superintendent of Caretakers visited the school at 8.20 am to inspect. The temperature in the hall was 48 degrees & that in the H.O.R.S.A. huts 48 degrees. The day was one of the brightest and sunny that we have experienced for some weeks.

At 1.45 pm a service in memory of His Late Majesty King George V1 was conducted in the hall by the Headmaster. At 2 pm. A silence for two minutes was observed

Order of the service :

Hymn :   *O God our help in Ages past.*

Two minute silence

Singing of Psalm 23

Reading from Revelations V11 v 9 to the end.

Hymn : Children of the Heavenly King

Address

Prayers

Hymn : Praise my soul.

Feb 21st   At 7.30 pm a school concert was held in aid of the grand piano fund and organised by Mrs Titford L.R.A.M. Owing to difficulties with the curtains the performance did not finish until 10.20 pm. The headmaster saw every child out and satisfied himself that they caught their respective buses.

March 6th   Douglas Tearrell (2B) had an accident on the way to school. While riding his bicycle he ran into a stationary van. He bruised his face and was badly shocked. Miss Barren took him to see Dr Dockery who gave him a sedative and a mouthwash and instructed that he should lie down. Since his mother was not at home he was put in bed in the medical room. He got up for lunch, attended afternoon school and returned to his home in the company of Derek Hunnibal (3A).

April 28th   The headmaster was not present since he was at Westcliff High School for Boys as a member of the interviewing panel for borderline cases

| April 28th | Headmaster continued on the interviewing panel in the morning and attended the official opening of Prince Avenue school in the afternoon. |

| May 12th | Headmaster left school at 2.15 to attend a conference of the local Head Teachers Association on the subject of "Backwardness in Reading". This meeting was held at the Education Offices. |

| 23rd May | Mrs Mussett member of the Governors of this school and wife of the vice chairman of the Education Committee attended and took the chair at the Empire Day Service held at 11 am. |

The service consisted as follows :

Hymn	*Land of our birth*
Reading	*by Mrs Henry*
Singing	*23rd Psalm*
Hymn	*Lord who hast made us for Thine Own*
Address	*by the Headmaster*
Prayers	*said by the Rev. Sweeney*

After the conclusion of the service, the choir and orchestra performed the following items :-

Non Nobis Domine

Land of Hope and Glory.

The proceedings were concluded by the singing of the National Anthem and the School Song.

| June 12th | **The General Certificate of Education examination, being held in this school for the first time, began today with the examination in English Language. Twelve pupils took the examination.** |

July 25th	In response to a request from Miss Pollard Inspector of the National Society of Prevention of Cruelty to Children was asked to come to the school. Investigation had revealed that two girls were involved in some unpleasant sexual incidents which were taking place in the railway sidings at Shoeburyness station.

July 25th In response to a request from Miss Pollard Inspector of the National Society of Prevention of Cruelty to Children was asked to come to the school. Investigation had revealed that two girls were involved in some unpleasant sexual incidents which were taking place in the railway sidings at Shoeburyness station.

The Inspector was accompanied by a police officer. After a discussion of the case, the inspector and police officer interviewed one girl in Miss Pollard's room. The inspector decided without reference to the headmaster to remove the girl to the Central Police Station in order that a statement could be taken by a police woman.

At 4.45 pm since the girl had not returned the headmaster telephoned the police station and was informed that application had been made to a magistrate for the girls' removal from her home and this application had been granted. The headmaster insisted that the parents should be informed. This was done by the police and the father eventually took the girl home again. As a result of the investigation proceedings would be taken against some boy and the girls were to be brought before the courts as in need of care and protection.

Sept 9th During the holiday notification of the school's success in the General Certificate of Education. .. Twelve candidates were entered of whom nine passed. Forty four subjects were entered and of these eighteen were successful.

Subjects entered
Successfully :

English Literature	6 candidates
Handicraft	6 candidates
Art	4 candidates
Maths	1 candidate
History	1 candidate

Sept 17th Det. Con. Hamblin visited the school to make enquiries into the firing of two hayricks at the end of Caulfield Road.

Oct 22nd Commencement of medical examination in the mornings by Dr Greenhalgh – 326 children to be examined.

Nov 28th Brian Dymock who had been taking part in boxing during a physical training lesson was distressed by a blow on the nose. Dr Kehoe was summoned and advised that he was probably suffering from concussion and that he should be taken home and if necessary seen by his own doctor.

Dec 1st Derek Hunnibal who had been boxing with Brian Dymock on Friday was discovered with a swollen hand..The headmaster advised the boy that he should attend his doctor's surgery for treatment.

| Dec 2nd | Derek Hunnibal reported that a small bone in the hand was broken.. He had it set in hospital, put in plaster and had been allowed to return to school. |

| Dec 9th | The nurse attended to read the results of the "patch test" for tuberculosis for 95 pupils in the fourth year. |

1953

| Jan 9th | It is worth recording that on this day the following work was being carried out in the school: replastering, window cleaning, repairs being carried out to blackboards and chairs by the carpenter and blackout fitted up by outside firm in Room 3. |

| Jan 21st | A boy from 3B was punched during a tussle at lunchtime. He felt very ill after this and Dr Dockery was summoned. He advised that he be taken home and if he had any more pain, the doctor should be summoned. |

| Jan 30th | Attendance during the week had reached the low of 87% owing to the onset of an influenza epidemic. In cases where children were not affected, often both parents were and the children were kept at home to attend to them. |

| Feb 2nd | **The attendance reached the low level of 400 owing not only to the severity of the weather and influenza epidemic but also to the floods which struck this part of the coast over the weekend. Foulness and Canvey Island were flooded. Canvey was evacuated but contact with Foulness was not made until this morning by the Southend lifeboat. Floods reached up to the Cambridge Hotel area and also to Greenways and in Lifstan Way – Southchurch Park being inundated last night. Boats were being used for deliveries along Shaftesbury Avenue.** |

Peter Pan's Playground during the Great Floods of January 31 and 1 February 1953.
The whole of Peter Pan's Playground was submerged.

Feb 4th   A collection was started today for the relief of victims of the flood disaster.

The Tideway July 1953

THE FLOODS

From the last week of January to the middle of February, 1953, were weeks of national disaster. All along the east coast people were flooded out of house and home. Thousands of people lost their homes and many hundreds lost their lives.

In Holland the floods were even worse than they were here in Britain. The disaster came in the night and nothing could be done to prevent it, as it was totally unexpected. The worst flooding anywhere near us was on Canvey Island. People woke up in the night to hear water washing around them and found themselves partly submerged in water. Many of them were forced on to the roofs of their houses, others into upstairs rooms. Newspaper reporters said that cars, buses and houses were swept 6away downstream like toys.

At one time Canvey was all under water. It was not, therefore, really surprising that the naturally high spring tide helped by an unusually fierce gale should have broken through the sea wall. Many of the houses on Canvey are bungalows and are made of wood, people in bungalows did not really stand a chance.

Many homes have been broken up as a result of the floods. It will be a very long time before Canvey Island is built up again, and it will probably never be the same.

Many people sent food, clothes and even furniture to relief centres. A good deal of money was sent from countries abroad, and many funds were started in aid of flood relief.

In short, everything possible has been done to help the unfortunate people whose homes were destroyed by the floods.

Julie Dartnall, 3A.

Feb 6th   The attendance this week reached the low level of 76.25%

Feb 20th   First performance of the school plays – excerpts from Hamlet and As You Like It and Shakespearean songs by the choir.

Feb 26th   The second performance of the school play. Miss E.O. Dowsett vice chairman of the governors was present as was Mr S.M. Smith (Asst. Ed.uc. Officer, secondary education). During the course of the evening a small fire was discovered in the boys' lavatories. On investigation it was found that a sheet left by the plasterers was smouldering probably from a cigarette end having been thrown into it. The police were notified together with the names of the suspected culprits.

28th Feb   The final performance of the school plays. This was the best performance. It is worthy of note that the boy who played Hamlet was from Seaview Homes.

March 6th   At 5.30 a patrolling policeman discovered the windows at the back of the school had been broken into. The classrooms as noted below had been entered and the drawers forced and removed from the teachers' tables. The drawers had been searched and put back on top of the tables.

Entry was also made to the H.O.R.S.A. hut and from Mr Henry's room were taken a hoe to open the drawers in that room and a pair of secateurs later found in Mr Strong's room.

The only articles missing were the keys from Mr Henry's drawer and about ten shillings from the art room. This is money that had been collected by sales of handwork materials by Miss Headle. This was the room into which entry seemed to have been made first since the window was broken here. The Chief Education Officer was informed and Det. Con. Hamblin came in to conduct inquiries. The rooms entered were : Room 1,2,3,4,5,6,8,10,15,16,18, (Horsa Hut) senior Master's Room.

March 12th   Det. Con. Hamblin came to school at 11am to interview a boy in connection with a waterproof canvas sheet that he bought into the school in order to cover his canoe. He admitted stealing this. The det. Constable went to the boy's home to take a statement after the close of morning school.

March 20th   A number of children had to be sent home from school owing to their having German Measles.

1953

THE TIDEWAY

As the magic day draws nigh

Flags and banners wave on high

Calling children everywhere

For this is Coronation Year.

Lesley Fox, 1D.

| June 1st | At 2.30 Councillor Townsend supported by Councillor Crush came to the school to present the souvenir books provision for which had been made by the Southend town council in honour of Her Majesty's Coronation. The proceedings, in the form of a service were as follows. |

Hymn :

Reading : Psalm 100 read by Miss Pollard

23 Psalm sung by the choir.

An address given by the Headmaster

Prayers were said by the Headmaster (these were taken from the order for the coronation service to take place in Westminster Abbey.

The books were then distributed to one boy and one girl in each class. After this Councillor Townsend gave a short speech.

The proceedings were closed with the singing of "Land of Hope and Glory", the School Song and the National Anthem.

THE QUEEN
THE TIDEWAY

"The Queen, God bless her," the people shout
Their loyalty you cannot doubt,
She passes by and waves her hand,
Our Queen, the ruler of the land,
Amid the tumult and the toil
Comes the monarch, shining, royal,
Here amid her pomp and state
The Queen is loved, there is no hate,
We all rejoiced when she was wed,
We rejoiced far more when on her head,
Was placed the crown that made her Queen,
The loveliest that has ever been. *Diane Fry, 3B.*

| June 2nd | Coronation Day and June 3rd were observed as holidays. |
| June 5th | At 2.45 pm. The school was assembled to watch the planting of two trees by Mr Waller chairman and Miss Dowsett, vice chairman of the Governors of the school in celebration of the coronation of Her Majesty Queen Elizabeth 11. |

The proceedings of Coronation Week were closed by a concert held in the school hall at 7.30 pm.

Elizabeth II

THE QUEEN'S CORONATION

THE TIDEWAY

On June 2nd, 1953, we celebrated one of the greatest events of our time. Although the Coronation is an ancient ceremony it was new to the children of our generation.

We in this school celebrated our gracious Queen's Coronation with a holiday. Each pupil received a Souvenir Book, so that in years to come we may look back and remember our schooldays, and look upon this year 1953 as one of the happiest we have had.

Let us hope that the courage of our Queen and her great calm in undertaking the numerous duties which she will be asked to perform for many years to come, will inspire us too, to serve her well throughout her reign.

May the Queen, Prince Philip, and their children have long, happy and peaceful lives together. Ruth Armstrong 1B.

EVEREST HOPES

Up from Nepal
Into the mountains tall,
They attempt to climb Mount Everest,
We only hope for the best,

Those brave men are equipped well,
You can never tell
If they will come down again.
In the biting wind,
And cold soft snow,
With a little tent
The brave men go,
We will still hope for the best, that they will climb Mount Everest
We have to give them time,
For it is very hard to climb.

Marion Pinkey, 1A.

22nd June   Whilst clearing the stage Robert Henn of 4A who was moving a ladder stepped back and down the trap door. He was able to get up and was taken to the medical room. He had a large graze on his shoulder and some bruising. He was taken by Miss Pollard to Dr. Dockery. Dr Dockery examined him and said he was all right. He was to go home and take things quietly. Miss Pollard took him home and handed him over to the care of his mother.

COBRAS VERSUS WASPS

When I went to summer camp in Buckinghamshire, we found on arrival, that in the middle of the camping ground was a wasps' nest.

Our tent (the Cobras) was very near to it. We tried to kill the wasps by pouring hot water down the hole, but that did not help. We next tried putting "bangers" in it, and then we lit fires on top of it. I got stung three times. One boy killed a hundred wasps.

One day we went up the river to Windsor. On a free day we had, I went to Marlow. It was a very eventful camp.

Robert Allsopp, Form 2C.

SECRETS

To learn the secret of the wood,
To know the wild wind's every mood,
To talk with birds, to understand
The magic of the meadow land
To watch the clouds, to realise
The silent story of the skies.
Brenda Sanderson.

1954

Jan 8th   The Inspector for the N.S.P.C.C. came to report that he had received anonymous letters regarding the ill treatment of two girls. Miss Pilcher and the headmaster saw one girl who reported that they were not well enough fed. After two slices of bread for breakfast they had to wait until after 4pm for their main meal, despite the fact that their brother who worked on the brickfields and the two young children belonging to their "mother" received something to eat at mid-day. This was reported to the Inspector who said he would visit the mother and the father.

Jan 11th	Dr Patterson and Nurse McGrath came to school to carry out the medical inspection of the girls.
Jan 29th	Headmaster absent all day to attend for an interview in connection with the leadership of the Silver Jubilee Secondary Modern School at Bury St. Edmunds. He was successful in obtaining this post and arrangements were made for him to take up that position on June 1st 1954.
Feb10th	During the lunch hour a boy twisted the arm of a girl behind her back. In view of the pain she felt from this action she was taken by Miss G. Pilcher by car to the Southend General Hospital and her mother was informed. After X-ray examination it was discovered that the arm was merely badly strained and she was allowed to return home.
	This incident occurred at about 1.30 pm when the boy was instructing the painting club and the girl was present with other girls who were either weaving or attending to the library. She taunted him and he retaliated although in no way intending to do the damage he did.
	Since both were prefects and this was a bad example to the others their badges were taken from them.
April 6th	Mr Francis Mills, BSc. Econ, A.K.S. who on April 5th was appointed head of Shoeburyness High School from September 1st 1954 came to visit the headmaster.
April 27th	School reopened for the Summer Term. During the holiday the corridors had been painted in bright fresh colours. Instead of the traditional two colours, a number of colours had been used to good effect. During the first part of the term the painters were engaged on painting the outside of the school.
	A boy in 3B while playing in the playground at lunch time received a cut in the leg from a scout sheath knife carried by another boy. After this had been dressed he was taken to his home by another pupil in 3A.
April 28th	A warning given to the school that no sheath or other knives were to be brought into school.
May 21st	Miss M.E Reay, C.B.E., J.P. Vice-Chairman of the Secondary Education Committee came to say "good bye" to the headmaster.

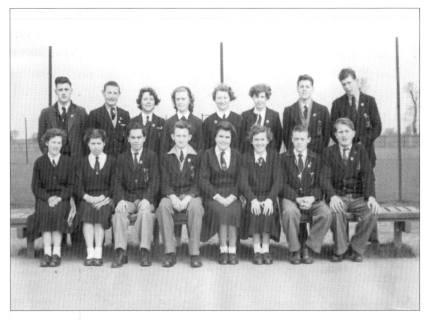

Prefects 1954 – 55.

May 24th   Empire Day A service was held at 11pm. The address was given by Mr E.W.Penn, a member of the No 1 Group of Governors and the prayers were said by the Rev E Jenkins M.A. rector of St Andrews. The order of service was as follows:

Hymn

Reading by Mr E.H. Hagger BSc.

Hymn : He who would Valiant be.

Address by Mr E.W. Penn

"Rule Britannia" sung by Gillian James of 2A, accompanied by the choir.

The prayers said by the Rector.

The singing of the 23rd Psalm & Brother James Air.

The service was concluded with the singing of the National Anthem.

May 28th   At the morning assembly, the headmaster R.W.J. Napier, B.A., who is leaving to take up leadership of the Silver Jubilee Boys School, Bury St. Edmunds Suffolk, was presented with a beautiful travelling alarm clock by the head girl, Gloria Everitt and Leonard Silby. Janet Ball presented on behalf of the choir two records of songs made by the choir prefaced with introductory remarks by the head girl.

During the day numerous visitors called to say "Goodbye". In the afternoon, a tea party was called at which were present Mr W.A. Waller, Chairman, Miss

E.O. Dowsett vice chairman of the governors of the school and many past members of the staff. A presentation was made of a dispatch case to the headmaster and of toilet requisites to Mrs Napier who was also present. The arrangements for both the morning and afternoon ceremonies were ably carried out by Miss G.R. Pilcher, deputy head of the school. They had been kept secret from the head who was not a little overcome at both these ceremonies.

May 31st   Today I hand over the keys and reins of office to Miss G.R. Pilcher who will deputise until the arrival of the new headmaster Mr Mills, BSc,. A.K.C., on July 5th.

My sad thoughts at leaving are vying with the memories of the achievements and difficulties of the eight years I have been head of this school. The fame of the school is widespread; its work has been done well. Several times the impossible has been tackled with success. This is the first secondary modern school to have prepared pupils for the University of London General Certificate Examination. Not only were nine children from the school successful but in almost every case they have added to the subjects they gained at school. One, Janet Rowley is this year to enter St. Osyth's training college. Another Paul Heywood is taking his Inter. B. SC. Examination this year and is intending to proceed to a degree. Not only these children others throughout the school have had success in other fields. Boys have obtained admission to the T.S. Worcester, one boy has obtained a cadetship with the Metropolitan Police Force and a large number of girls have entered hospitals as student – nurses.

All of these were reckoned to be jobs for grammar school children only. The dramatic performances, the concerts and the plays have all been "beyond our capabilities" but have been carried out in first class style. The standard of music, the work of the choir and orchestra have reached a very high level of performance, credit for which must go alone to Miss Titford. Great efforts have been put forth in the field of sport. The girls have been outwardly most successful in that last year they brought to the school the swimming championship shield.

The greatest difficulty has been that of obtaining women teachers. No one can be recommended for promotion without the feeling that it will be almost impossible to replace her. The older members of staff retired in due course, and of the other four, Miss Wiseman, Miss Barren, Mr Day and Mr Rice have obtained headships so that the staff has always been young and largely inexperienced.

The number of points of responsibility is now five and every teacher who was teaching before 1939 with one exception, has a post, three for men and two for women. The allowance for the chief assistant (a woman) has been raised from £40 in 1946 to £95 today largely through the efforts of this school.

I have been well supported by the staff and the parents and particularly loyal and enthusiastic service has been afforded me by those who have held posts of responsibility. Their loyal assistance in the early days helped me over many of the mistakes I made, and now they bear the brunt of a good deal of the task of training the newcomers to the staff.

I have too, had the assistance of good secretaries in Mrs Jackson, Mrs Dubour, and Mrs Otten, (who will be going into the Bishop Otten Training College in September). First Mr Dawson, then Mr Smith and Mr Perry of the Education Office have helped me a good deal in this task of attempting the impossible. The ancillary staff – Mr Anderson and his cleaners, Mr Brown the grounds man and Mrs Penneche and her school meals staff have all formed a happy band with whom it has been a pleasure to work.

The growth of the school in eight years from 200 on roll with 10 teachers to 600 on roll with 22 teachers has been rapid. The film strip of its opening, the film of its activities which Miss Danks took with her to California, the films made in school by the scholars, the records of the school journeys abroad, the description of the first school journey by air, together with these items noted from time to time in the log book are the archives which store some of the history of this period. The vast amount of work put in by staff together with their loyal support has enabled the school to gain the reputation as a good school. To them and especially to the hardworking chief assistants is due the praise for all the school is. I cannot thank them or the parents enough for their support.

R.W.J. Napier 31st May 1954

Mr Francis Mills

July 5th 1954 to July 1973

1954

July 5th   Mr Waller (Chairman of Governors) introduced the new Headmaster E.F. Mills at morning assembly.

July 21st   Mr Townsend, Mr Rush, Mrs Telford and Miss Danks and a party of approx. 45 to Switzerland 1pm.

The Tideway July 1955

Boxing Club

With the kind help of Mr Hickling a boxing club was formed at the beginning of the Winter Term. The club meets every Wednesday evening.

Steady progress is being made although the equipment is inadequate. Steps have been taken to meet this difficulty, however, and the members each subscribe threepence a week. With these subscriptions more and better equipment will be bought. *J. Hole, 3A.*

1955

April 29th   New Building: the actual building of the first of two new mahogany huts has been started. The footings for these were made last term.

May 24th   • Empire Day Service held at 9 am. The Rev. Jenkins Vicar of Shoebury addressed the children.
              • Parties visited the Municipal College and
              • The Army Engineering Workshops.

June 10th   Party from third year visited Royal Tournament as guests of Capt. Townsend of South Shoebury Farm.

June 16th   Fourth year (leavers) visit to Royal Tournament assisted by Jones Fund.

July 26th   Party left for Switzerland

<u>During the Summer Holidays</u>

- Gravel square at back was asphalted
- New road was constructed from E. Road to playground
- E. Road was re-surfaced, and the Dining Hall path was also re-surfaced. Both were curbed.
- The Switch room was damaged when a grab, working on asphalt square hit an electric cable unguarded at 10 -11 inches down. This cable was re-laid at correct depth & instruments in switch room replaced.
- New pair of classrooms (wood) were completed
- Girls lavatories were extended
- Cycle shed: 2 sections were moved shortly after beginning of new term.

Sept 28th   New Style Timetable was started this term.

- Each 'year' of children was re-graded according to arithmetical ability. Years 2, 3, 4 had arithmetic from 9.15 to 10.00 each morning. Year 1, during first period after break.
- Children were graded into English groups for English and other basic subjects taken in single periods (French, Music, R.I., P.E.) and these were taken during three periods each day forming a 2 hour session either from 10.15 – 12.15 or 1.45 – 3.45.
- Craft, games, art and a variety of courses were taken during the remaining 2 hour session. All children have a balanced programme e.g. all girls take some needlework and D/S even though they specialise in (say) maths and science.

Girls in the Rural Science class.

Oct 26th	Old Students Social and inauguration of Shoeburyness High School Old Students Association.
Nov 9th	Inaugural meeting of Christian Fellowship, over 100 children attending
Nov 23rd	Representative of Olympic Gymnastic Co. called to examine gym apparatus. Girls went to General Hospital for a visit and talk by the Matron. (Miss Pilcher & Miss Lark).

Nov 26th	First visit of school party to S.S. NOWSHERA (British India Line) the ship recently adopted by the school. 25 children with Mr Strong, headmaster and Mr Monk (school attendance officer) who is an ex-third mate of the earlier Nowshera sunk in Indian Ocean. We were shown over the ship and entertained to tea by Capt. & Mrs Smythe.
Dec 16th	Mrs Peters (Thorpe Bay Horticultural Society) gave a lecture demonstration to a group of girls on floral decoration.
19th Dec	In the morning the Mayor and Mayoress visited the school. She was shown models, the work of the printing club, and some of the 46 Christmas cakes made by the girls (and boys), and the school song sang to her. She addressed the children.

1956

Jan 24th   Staff versus school First X1 Football Match. Staff won 1: 0 Mr Pedrette twisted knee badly.

Jan 25th   Mr Pedrette absent with twisted tendons in knee.

Feb 1st   Mrs Doonan joined on supply to help out in view of Mr Pedrette's continued absence.

Feb 15th   Interviews all day with parents of children in 1A with Mr Popham. This is a new routine. Children meet their parents at certain times, entertain them in the flat (tea and biscuits provided); take them round the school and to two interviews – with form tutor and headmaster.

March 8th School photo taken by Pandora during the afternoon.

May 6th   Mrs Titford took three girls (Pauline Yorke, Gillian James and Joan Langston) to sing at the Royal Albert Hall in the 3rd of the National Festival of the School's Music Association of Great Britain.

May 9th   Mr Pedrette took 4 boys (Allen, Rowley, Lintott, Archer) to Southchurch Hall Sports to compete in Jones Memorial Cup. Won it: the first time this cup has been held by a (sec) modern school.

May 16th	Essex County Sports at Colchester. The Southend team included 3 boys and 3 girls from Shoebury of whom Archer got 1st place in 440 (under15) Lintott got 1st place in 880 (under 15) and three others got places.

May 18th	Interviews – Mr Merlin appointed for geography, visual aids and general subjects.

School Wear

TAYLOR'S

24-26 SOUTHCHURCH ROAD,   SOUTHEND-ON-SEA

NEAR GAUMONT CINEMA   TEL. MARINE 6655

May 24th	Mr S.C. Jones, M.B.E., M.C.J.P. addressed the school at the Empire Day Service. 49 children and three staff left after break to visit the Thames docks by launch.

May 31st	This is the school's 17th birthday in the sense that the first assembly ever held in this building was on 31/5/1939. The School's 1st & 2nd X1 Football Teams went for tea to Garon's Centre House where the Mayor presented three trophies to them: The Southend Cup, the Hunt Cup and the 2nd Division Shield.

June 6th	Two German women teachers visit the school (Frauline Baumgarten & Ningberg).

June 12th	Southend -on-Sea trial certificate examination in Arithmetic: all fourth year children sat. Mr O'Donnell visited the school and appointed to staff.

June 13th	30 boys and Mr Townsend on visit to Ekco works.
	Southend-on-Sea trial Certificate examination in English: all fourth years took it.
July 3rd	Mr Bott called to say goodbye: he is leaving the district as our HMI…He asked me to congratulate the school on the very sensible way boys and girls cycle to school – he has seen them most days for years and has never seen any example of silly or careless behaviour.
July 9th	I was informed the Police had knocked up the caretaker at 1.30 am this morning following the report of lights on and a motor cyclist leaving at 12.30. The school was searched but nothing out of place. The explanation is that Mr Popham was working in the school from 8.30 Sunday until 12.30 am Monday reading and correcting the proofs of this year's TIDEWAY.

Arrangements for the School Year 1956-7

Only four classes are expected in the incoming first year instead of the five anticipated. The second year will now be the only five stream year so far.
The main features of the timetable are:

• Maths is now spread throughout the morning.
• Special Sets as before for 3rd year on Monday am, 4th year Tuesday am.
• The sets are Woodwork, Metalwork, Rural Science, Radio work (new), Art & Craft, Domestic Science (two sets) Needlework.
• French is taken by A classes. Forms 4b&C and 3B&C will this year, as an experiment choose a cultural course to compensate for not taking French from Craft, Literature and Film Appreciation.
• The Fourth Year children will have an opportunity to proceed for G.C.E. engineering etc. Also the boys can choose between Experimental Science, Technology and Technical Drawing (mainly for those proceeding towards apprenticeships) or Science in the Modern World. Girls Science in the Fourth Year will be Mother craft (Nurse McGrath) and Science (Miss Lark) consisting of Nursing, Physiology, First Aid etc.

| Sept 11th | Mr D.M. Hounsell –(student) joined for three weeks of observation and teaching practice. |
| Nov 12th | Miss Curtis absent to perform for Southend on Television (Top Town Programme) also 13th. |

1957

Feb 27th   The School's First Eleven, which had already obtained the Southend 1st Division League (the first time for 50 years) played against St. John's School, Thundersley in the first round of the Cooke Cup to determine the best school football team in the county. It was held at home to a good gate and displayed some very fine football. Result Shoebury 7. St. John's 5. (Bright scored 5 goals).

28th Feb   This School's First X1 beat Southend High in the first round of the Southend Cup. They met the same team in the final last year and, unexpectedly, won.

March 18th   Attendance; Top of the Borough with 98.8% last week.

April 1st   Increase in school meals started today children 1/- Staff 1/10.

May 24th   Empire Day Service at 9am. Mr Celearer gave talk.

THE TIDEWAY 1956-57

Boys Sports Notes 1956-57

The sporting activities as a whole have been very successful this year.

The 1st X1 football team has been outstanding in Southend and has again won all the Borough's trophies. Rowley, the school sports captain, and Culham were the most improved players this year and played exceptionally well. Bright has always been the best forward, and as an outstanding footballer he gained a county trial. Keane, cousins, Matthews and Smith were always reliable and played consistently well. Other members of this team combined to make the team the most successful the school has ever had.

In the athletics sphere Archer has been the first outstanding member of the school. Gaining places in District, County and National events he has achieved all a schoolboy could wish for. Rowley and Bright have also achieved successes in sprinting and jumping. Paterson, Halsey, Cheek, O'Malley and many others have contributed their best and helped the school in athletics. *J. Pedrette*

1st X1 football team with golly the mascot (seated) third from left.

THREE VICTORIOUS YEARS IN THE 1ST X1

The present 1st X1 football team has always been a strong one, as this brief history shows.

3rd X1, 1954-55 – 3rd Division Shield

Although the team started off badly by losing to Eastwood away and drawing with Wentworth, it soon found its form. The best goal average in one match was against St. Helens, when Shoebury won 21 goals to nil. Unfortunately this team dropped out of the league and the points gained did not count.

At the end of the season Shoebury had the same number of points as Eastwood and the deciding match was played at Jones Memorial Ground where Shoebury won and so gained the shield.

2nd X1, 1956-57 – 2nd Division Shield

Despite two drawn and one lost match Shoebury finished top of the league and also won the Hunt Cup by beating Wentworth in the final. Five of the team played for Southend Junior Boys: A.Bright, K. Matthews, D.Keane, L.Archer and I. Rowley.After a few matches, the Hunt Cup finalists turned out to be Wentworth and Shoebury. In the early stages of the game it looked like a win for Wentworth, but after the interval Shoebury were put in the lead and then Matthews settled the issue, giving Shoebury the win by 2 goals to nil.

1st X1, 1956-67 – 1st Division Shield

The last season was the most successful of the three, as Shoebury not only won the League and Southend Cup but got into the last eight teams in the Cook Cup (all Essex). In the League Shoebury dropped only one point out of the possible twenty.

The team before Christmas was: R. Culham, P. Cousins, W. Rayner, R. Smith, A. Bell, L. Archer, A. Dods, K. Matthews, A. Bright, W. Frost and I. Rowley.

After Christmas the forward line was weakened by the loss of Matthews and Frost, but fortunately the place was admirably filled by B. Harkness who played extremely well in so short a time.

In the first round of the Southend Cup Shoebury knocked out Southend High by three goals to two after Shoebury had been 2-nil down. In the semi-final Shoebury beat Wentworth and so went on to play Southchurch in the final which was played at the Jones Memorial Ground.

Shoebury won the toss and decided to kick uphill. Archer was the first to score and then Shoebury were really on top. Bright got a hat-trick, Jupp scored two, Robinson and Archer got one each and the final score was Shoeburt seven, Southchurch one.

The Cook Cup is open for all Essex and in Southend one team represents the Borough. After defeating Eastwood by three goals to one, Shoebury played King John School (Thundersley_ at Shoebury and won by seven goals to five. In the second round the team had to travel to Ongar where they lost their only game. Shoebury played well and were leading by three goals to one, but Ongar fought back and won after extra time by four goals to three.

Out of the six trophies entered for, Shoebury won five. The total of games lost or drawn is: five games drawn and four games lost out of forty games exactly.

Boys Athletics

In the District Sports we had several successes, Archer easily winning the 44o yards in 56.4.secs., Rowley the 100 yards 11.2 secs., and Bright the high jump at 4ft. 9in. The relay team (Bright, Halsey, Paterson, Rowley) came second.

At the County Sports at Hornchurch, Southend School's Team included L.Archer, I. Rowley and A. Bright

E.D. Jones Cup (Inter Schools Relay):

I) T. Paterson (220) 2) A. Bright (110) 3) D. Halsey (110) 4) I. Rowley (220)

Under the eye of L.Archer as team manager, this team for the second successive year has defeated all Southend schools. We remain the only Secondary Modern School to win the E.D.Jones Cup.

School Sports 1957

Records.

Girls' Senior Javelin: Helen Brown, 79ft. 10in.

Boys' Senior Discus;: I. Rowley, 118ft. 2in.

Girls' Senior 100 yards, Pauline Yorke, 11.5secs. (which is 0.4 secs. Better than the National Standard for 19-year –old girls).

Girls Senior 150 yards: J. Loft, 18.5 secs. (National Standard for girls of 16). Her Long Jump record of 16 ft. 0 & a half in. is 3 & a half in. better than the National Standard for 19 year old girls.

Boys Senior 440 yards: L. Archer, 56.5.secs. (National Standard for boys of 17).

Mile: L.Archer, 4 min. 57 secs.

Jennifer Loft now holds 4 school records: Junior and Senior Long Jumps and 150 yards.

L. Archer also holds 4 records: Junior 220 yards, Junior and Senior 440 yards, and Mile.

I. Rowley holds 3 records: Senior Discus, Shot and 100 yds.

Pauline Yorke holds Junior and Senior 110 yards records.*

Helen Brown holds Senior Rounders Ball and Javelin records.

A. Bright holds records for Junior Cricket Ball and Senior High Jump – at 5ft. 1in. a National Standard for 16-year-old-boys.

* Pauline Yorke represented the school at the Empire Day Athletic Meeting at Southchurch Park. Having won the 100yds. Final 1n 11.9 secs is to represent Essex in the National Championships – a great achievement.

Sept 23rd   5 children were sent home unwell: signs of rapid drop in all attendance: fear of onset of anticipated epidemic of Asian Flu.

Oct 4th   One of our 4th year girls died this morning of Asian Flu and pneumonia. She had been sent home on Wednesday but did not appear to her parents to be seriously unwell until Thursday night. She died shortly after admission to hospital on Friday morning.

There is an increasing number of children absent mainly from senior School.

Oct 7th   BCG Tests due to start today have been postponed owing to the influenza epidemic.

Oct 9th   Memorial Service at School 9am. Funeral at Baptist Church at 11.15. Headmaster and Miss Pilcher attended.

Dec 20th   Concert and end of term assembly in afternoon. The concert was put on by children and organised by Simmons and Jones of 3rd year.

Carol Collection amounted to &12.19.6. £10 sent to Dr. Barnado's, &2.9.6. to Polio Research Fund.

1958

March 10th — An entry was made into the school during the week-end. A window in the D/S store cupboard (Room 12) was opened by tilting the fanlight window. Food was taken, cooked and eaten. 2 shirts were stolen from the men's' cloakroom. Police and CEO informed.

April 22nd — The new Art/Craft Building (Rooms 29-30) used for the first time as classrooms (Mr Jones & Miss Campling).
During the night time the window in the D/S store was broken. Also HM's and Secretary's Office were entered. 18/- and stop watch were stolen.

April 25th — Police woman called to interview a girl (with Mother's permission).

May 23rd — Empire Day Service. Rev. Blore, Vicar of Thorpe Bay spoke to the children.

July — During the holidays Mr. Strong conducted a visit to Golling in Austria. The party consisted of 25 pupils and three adults.

TELEVISION

The school has the use of a large classroom type television set during the past Summer Term. This was arranged by the L.E.A. It was installed in Room 14 and used frequently in connection especially with Science, English, Geography and History. It was found to be very stimulating and many programmes were very good. It was however difficult to fit them in with the right groups of children.

SCHOOL YEAR 1958-59

State of Staffing

Permanent Staff Joining in September

Mr. P. Quigley B.Sc as Head of Maths and Science Dept.

Miss C.J. Hartley to take charge of Girls P.E. (3 year trained first appointment)

Mrs M.E. Heap for English and Drama (from Thorpe School).

Mr D.B. Moore for Maths and Science (First appointment from Westminster College).

Mr A. Trovell for Art

Mr J. Duffy (unqualified) rejoined on supply half term to take Science and Games (He plays football for Southend United).

Mr J. Pedrette rejoined after completing his Loughborough Course.

Temporary Supply Staff Joining.

Mr D.M. Hounsell for full time Social Studies and backward classes.

Mr J.S. Guthrie B.A. joined 25th Sept full time for one term

Mr B.S. Taylor (Q) half term for D/S.

Mrs M.J. Pett B.A. increased her time from 2/10 to 5/10.

Mr M.J. Sheridan (Q) rejoined until 26th Sept when he left to take a special course for deaf children

Mrs F. Bailey LRAM and Mrs J.A. Hobbs GRSM worked half time each to do Music until new teacher joins in January.

Mr M. Allen (Unqualified) joins full time on October 6th when he became 18. He left this school in July 1956 and has gained 6 passes at age at the Municipal College and intends to go to College next year.

Mrs V. Keyte joined on 2nd Sept on same basis.

Staffing During the Autumn Term

Headmaster	E.F. Mills B.Sc
Deputy	Miss G.R. Pilcher
Senior Assistant Master	Mr Strong (Geography)
Head of Maths 7 Science	Mr D. Quigley B.Sc
Head of English Dept.	vacant
Graded Points	Mr Briggs B.A. (English)
	Mr Jones (Art)
	Mr Milverton (Metalwork)
	Mr Merlin (Science & Social Studies)
	Mr Martin L.I.O.B A.B. (Woodwork)
	Mr Pedrette
	Miss Lark SRN (Needlework)
	Mrs Wicks (French)

Permanent Qualified Assistants

Mr Melville (RI)

Mr Moore (Maths)

Mr O Donnell B.A. (History)

Mr Talbott B.Sc (Econ & Eng)

Mr Trovell (Art)

Mrs Bacon (D/S)

Mrs Cramp (Eng etc)

Mrs Heap (Eng)

Miss Hartley (P.E.)

Temporary Qualified Assistants

Mr Sheridan (Full Time until 26/9/58)

Mr Guthrie (Full Time until Christmas 58)

Half Time:

Mrs Coombes LRAM

Mrs Hobbs GRSM

Mrs Petty B.A.

Mrs Taylor

Temporary Unqualified Assistants

Mr Hounsell (Full Time)

Mr Allen (Full Time from 6/10/58)

Mr Duffy (Half Time)

Mrs Keyte (Full Time From 22/9/58

Nurse Mac Grath visited to teach Mother craft.

The Size of the School

The Autumn Term started with 711 children on roll an increase of 102 on the previous year. The first year intake was 225 (as compared with 146 the previous year). There were 30 on the staff. An average of about 360-379 stayed each day for school lunch.

There were twenty classes: 5 in the 4th Year, 4 in the 3rd Year, 5 in the 2nd Year and 6 in the 1st Year.

1959

Jan 13th   Mr Brown called to see about the heating of the school which is unsatisfactory. It appears that neither the main boiler nor the anthracite heaters in the new Art Block are being adequately stoked.

Jan 15th   The news came of the death of James Hartop in the Fourth year. This boy has had leukaemia for 3 and a half years but has spent most of the time at school. Last year he was made a Cornwall Scout for his courage and fortitude for his protracted and painful treatment. It was agreed between parents and school that he should not know of his fatal condition – it now appears that he has known for two years (he told his minister). But he has never shown to parents or anyone of his knowledge and has remained always courteous, cheerful and co-operative. This is a remarkable case of real courage.

Jan 19th   Headmaster and Mr Strong attended funeral of James Hartop.

April 20th   The school received an honourable mention on Sat 18th at the News Chronicle School Films Competition showing at the National Film Theatre. The school's first film 'Stamp Trouble' was in the final list for assessment.

June 15th   BBC Television Team were at work today and yesterday shorting pictures of our own Film Group making their own film on the end of the pier and recording and photographing interviews with Mr Merlin and the children.

June 17th   Mr Hounsell absent again today for degree examination (17th & 18th).

June 19th   Party of 3rd year children went by coach to the Royal Tournament as guests of Captain Townsend.

June 22nd   This afternoon Roger Harris scored what is believed to be the School's first cricket century (105 not out) in a match against Eton House.

June 26th   The school was featured today in a B.B.C. Television programme in 'Looking at Film' 2.05 – 2.25 pm., showing the School's film Group at work making a film and interviewing the actors and production team. The children of the school saw it on our own and a hired TV set and some went to small parties to the homes of parents.

Shoeburyness School archives.

July 1st   School Party (1Vth Year) off for the day to Boulogne.

July 2nd   The other section of the Year 1V children went to Canterbury today.

July 9th   Mr Godfrey Winn (BBC) called to talk to Head & Mr Merlin.

The Tideway July 1959

COURAGE

It must be an exceedingly rare honour for a school to have four pupils who, in the space of a year, have received national awards for acts of courage, but this has happened at Shoebury.

We are very proud of the girl and two boys who risked their lives to save three others from drowning at sea. We salute the memory of a fourth boy who faced personal crisis and suffering in a manner which puts him alongside that other boy, Jack Cornwall, V.C. after whom his particular award is named.

Pamela Offord of Form 3B was awarded the Girls' Life Brigade's Distinguished Service Medal, First Degree, "for saving life," at the Royal Albert Hall on May 10th 1958. A boy got into difficulties some 150 yards out in deep tidal swim way in August, 1957. Pamela, who was then only twelve, swam out to help and managed to bring the boy in, despite his struggles, and supported him until other help arrived.

David Williams of Form 3D was presented with the Royal Humane Society's Testimonial on Parchment in March, 1959. David and a friend noticed a boy getting into trouble in difficult currents off the Westcliff Baths in July 1958. The boy sank and did not re-appear and both boys dived repeatedly and ultimately located the unconscious boy on the bottom. David dived and brought the boy up and dragged him to the shore, where he recovered after artificial respiration and hospital treatment.

John Travers Cornwall VC (8 January 1900 2 June 1916) known as Jack Cornwall posthumously received the Victoria Cross at the Battle of Jutland for gallantry "in the face of the enemy". He was 16 when he died, but his bravery led to the Cornwall Award for Boy Scouts.

Terence Moffatt of Form 3C was presented with the Bronze Medal of the Humane Society in January 1959 in recognition of his gallantry in saving a heavy man from drowning, when their dinghy capsized in a squall one and a half miles off Southend in August 1958. The man was a poor swimmer and became unconscious, Terence, who was then only twelve years of age, supported him for some fifteen minutes in rough water until help arrived. This is the highest award given by the Royal Humane Society in the Southend area of which the police have any record. Terence was also given the Silver Cross of the Boy Scouts' Association.

James Hartop of Form 4X was presented in February, 1958 with the Cornwall Certificate the Boy Scouts' Association's highest award for courage 'in recognition of his high standard of character and devotion to duty'. The real nature of James' courage was only realised after his death in January, 1959 when it became known through the one person in whom he had confided that he had known of the fatal nature of his illness for two years. Nevertheless, he remained cheerful, courteous and active and gave no hint of his knowledge to parents or friends in the Scouts or School. He took a full part in all School work, including games, as far as he was able until a few weeks before his death. Only those who were privileged to know this boy during those last two years can realise that his conduct and bearing could not have been more magnificent.

It is right that the School should mark such an occasion so that those in the School may be reminded of what they themselves may be capable of doing should the need arise. It has been decided to mark such acts of courage by acquiring for each act a worthwhile picture to have in School. This will carry on its frame a brief description of the act it commemorates. We hope, therefore, to acquire soon four such pictures.

> *"It is not wealth or ancestry*
> *But honourable conduct and a noble disposition*
> *That maketh men great."*

Summer Term Records

Results of Southend School Leaving Certificate Exams

All children (in all streams) attending school in June took this examination.
44 gained the certificate out of a possible 102.
(30 out of 38 in 4A; 14 out of 29 in 4B)
17 failed because of Arithmetic, 0 because of English.
2 failed because of insufficient internal subjects.
Only 11 children got less than 40 in English.

Sept 4th — There was an illegal entry between 5.10 on the 2nd and 7.30 on Mon 3rd. There was no obvious break – although one window of Head's room and door to roof in Room 7 were open. The Head's Secretary's Rooms had obviously been entered drawers and cupboard's were opened. Nothing of value appears to have been taken except several bunches of keys. Police and Office were informed.

Sept 10th — Mr Southworth called to discuss the large numbers. The first year contains five classes. Children from the new housing estate continue to join and swell numbers in all years. There are six classes in the second year. Some re-arrangement is possible but there is not sufficient space to make an extra form.

Sept 11th	The three men responsible for the illegal entry of 2/3. September have been apprehended. They were P.T.I's staying at Shoebury who were running the tattoo at Southend Week. The keys have been thrown away in the grounds. (A search has led to the recovery of some). Other small items had been taken.
Sept 16th	Mr Hounsell who passed his degree (BA) examination last term was officially appointed to the permanent staff.
Oct 2nd	Called in Police because one boy has been discovered with a cut-throat razor on his person, and there were indications that a small 'gang 'was being built up involving other lads not in the school.
Dec 14th	Christmas Cake Competition held in the hall this morning. There were 110 cakes (fully iced) by 100 girls and 10 boys. All the school voted for the best.
Dec 18th	The School has collected over £50 to be sent to the Spittel Refugee Camp in Austria. Here the children are building their own workshops. They were sent via the Mayor's fund. During the term the school has purchased out of the School Fund a second-hand pottery kiln – gas fired, in good condition and of large size. We plan to build a brick and asbestos shelter for it adjoining the end of the Metalwork Shop. Parents of two children are helping with mixed cement (for the foundation) and bricks. The Governors have agreed that cost of removal (from Exeter) £10 and installation of gas fittings to main be met from official funds and we may use B.S.A. for miscellaneous building material.

1960

Jan 3rd	Mr Pountney the Head Of Richmond School died early today. He was head of this school for a short time after the War.
March 23rd	'Panora' visited the school to take photo of the whole school.

The Tideway July 1960

SCHOOL UNIFORM

It has been fine to see, during the past year, children so smartly turned out in full school uniform and we do most sincerely thank all parents who have provided their son or daughter with school clothing. It is most encouraging to all of us on the Teaching Staff, for though we do not make school uniform compulsory, it is clear that we have a wide measure of support

from parents and that children take a real pride in their school community as well as their own appearance. materials available at 2/11d., 3/11d., and 4/11d., a yard so that school wear can be very inexpensive if made up at home and a girl can easily change into another frock for the evenings.

HEADMASTER.

Sept 6th   Many children unexpectedly joined, many from the new housing estate north of the school. Total School Roll at the end of the day was 755 against July estimate of 733 and official number of 725.

Oct 24th   United Nations Day – Special Service arranged by Drama Group.

Jan 9th   7 new children joined today
              The painters were still in the school painting the corridors in the main building. The deep primary colours which have been here for 7 years disappeared under pinks and grey pastel shades with bright coloured doors and black against white skirtings and architraves.

Jan 19th   Parks Department at work on Part 11 of the Front Gardens Development: Trees planted, new paths, extended grass and pond to be dug.

March 23rd   Party of girls visited Ideal Home Exhibition

After school our First X1 won the Southend Cup at the Jones Ground against Eastwood.

May 24th   Commonwealth Assembly conducted by Seniors at 9am with Councillor Fortescue talking to the children.

June 9th   Billy Graham in hall at 6pm.

June 14th   Visit to Kew Gardens of most of the third year children in connection with science. 148 children led by Mr Eling and 7 staff.

This is the last entry made by Mr Mills. The Log Book for 1961 to 1973 is missing .Mr Mills retired in July 1973.

Mr Mills and prefects

The following extracts from the Tideway, however, show some of the key events during those years.

MILK TOPS

The milk tops you place in the metal receptacles in your classroom are collected, washed and, with foil from other schools and other sources, they are sent to a depot where they are melted down to obtain the aluminium they contain. The money received for them is put into a fund and this is used to help those in need.

You can play your part in the operation by taking care to remove the milk top without ripping it, which facilitates washing, and by placing it in the classroom container.

Thank you for your help and co-operation in the past.   *G.P.R.*

THE SCHOOL FILM

Last year, I took part in a film which was being made by the Photography Group. In the film, Nicholas Snelling and I were supposed to be fishing off the Pier. Other people caught fish, we caught a bottle. But in the bottle was a message in code and the rest of the film tells how the message was worked out. That's how the film got its title "Message Received".

The film was entered for the "News Chronicle" Film Award and was placed on the short list for the final awards.

During the making of the film, we were very excited to learn that the B.B.C. was to come and film us at work. They brought their cameras and microphones down to the end of the Pier as we were filming. It took them a day and a half to get all the shots they wanted. Graham Minshaw, who was our director, Margaret Carr, our continuity girl and I were interviewed by Mr. Stanley Reed of the British Film Institute. Mr Merlin, who was in charge of the Film Group, explained how it fitted in to the work of his group.

About a fortnight later the film was shown on television in the Schools' Service. It lasted about five minutes and although I was very excited at seeing myself and my friends on the screen, I couldn't help but think of the hours of work that the B.B.C. producer and his camera team had put in to make it possible.

Sydney Horrocks 2AF.

The Tideway July 1961

Lunch in the Flat

The girls in the Domestic Science classes repudiate the rumour circulated by the boys. Teachers invited to the flat for lunch prepared by the girls do not have to sign the Poison Book first.

A Domestic Science class with Mrs Beryl Taylor and Mrs Bacon.

The Tideway July 1962

Shoeburyness Youth Centre

Some years ago the Education Committee made a survey of all youth clubs to see how they were meeting the needs of boys and girls for evening recreation. It was decided to have six youth centres situated in all parts of the County Borough. Three of these Centres are already functioning, namely Eastwood, Southend and Wentworth. Two more will open in September 1962, one based at Shoeburyness High School and the other in a Youth Wing attached to Fairfax High School. The Sixth will be a completely new Centre at Leigh, the building of which has just been started.

In the first instance the Shoeburyness Youth Centre will open on Wednesday, Thursday and Friday of each week. Table tennis and other indoor games will be centred upon the dining room, where various refreshments will be available throughout each evening, such as tea, coffee, minerals, biscuits, confectionery, etc. A record player will be provided to give background music for those playing games, to give opportunities for playing the latest popular music for informal dancing. From time to time the centre may organise formal dance evenings with a suitable band to provide the music. These functions will be held in the main school hall.

Members who wish to take part in more formal recreation activities such as Judo, fencing physical education, football coaching and various organised games, will find such activities arranged for them in the gymnasium as soon as sufficient members are interested to form a group. Opportunities will also exist for those wishing to participate in cultural activities such as Art, Music or Drama. Boys and girls attending, or who have attended Shoeburyness High School have had training in dramatic work and quite a number have taken part in various types of dramatic productions. The Youth Centre will provide an excellent opportunity to continue this interest, thus providing entertainment for others, whilst having wonderful fun in doing so.

Mr Copping and six members of the 1962 Gymnastics team that won the Southend Schools Gymnastic Cup. Back Row: S.Corstophine, R.Dean, A.Ames. Front Row: B.Westaway, D.Johnson, S.Horrocks.

For the practical minded, the various craft rooms will be available – metal work, wood-work, boat-building, dressmaking and cookery – and remember, the various groups are open to all members of the Centre; thus boys will be welcomed in the cookery group just as girls will be welcomed in the wood-work shop.

The success of a Youth Centre depends very largely on the efforts of the members... Why not be a founder member and help to build up such a fine club spirit that in years to come you will be proud to say "I helped to lay the foundations of Shoeburyness Youth Centre". *M.A. Shepherd, A.C.P.., M.R.I.P.H.H. Officer for Youth and Community Service.*

Journey into Adolescence7

Last July instead of the usual Open Day we staged a School Festival consisting of exhibitions, demonstrations, displays, mannequin parades, concerts and a religious service. The central exhibition in the Hall was entitled "Journey into Adolescence" and was intended to show how the school was helping parents to steer their children through adolescence to become mature and well-balanced men and women.

Suspended from the ceiling, just inside the Hall, was a huge mobile in constant motion, each of whose suspended symbols represented one of those difficult tasks which a teenager must complete during the years of adolescence. These are listed here:-

1. Discovery of one's talents and weaknesses to make the best of oneself.
2. Intellectual skills for work and citizenship.
3. Choice of, and preparation for a career.
4. Effective use of one's growing body

School gym showing mannequin Parade.

5. Manual skills for work and hobbies.

6. Learning for leisure and the appreciation of the Arts.

7. Emotional independence from parents and adults.

8. Making close friends and how to be accepted in a group of one's age mates.

9. Learning how to behave as a young man (or young woman).

10. Understanding and getting along with the opposite sex.

11. Responsible behaviour and consideration for others.

12. Self-control and self-respect.

13. Building a moral code and a way of life.

Altogether a staggering programme. No wonder there are so often difficulties and problems! Some of these tasks are very much the school's business – for example, learning intellectual skills, some are more the business of the home and some have to be tackled partly at home, partly at school and partly in one's church, or club, or even in the playground and streets. The exhibition showed how the school was playing its part in this complicated and difficult process.   *E.F.M.*

Mr Mills and Connie Hardy, Deputy Head, right.

Where Do They Go?

Our readers – both pupils and parents are often puzzled about what further education or careers are open to them after they complete the basic four years course at the school. They may therefore be interested in the following analysis of what happened to the boys and girls in the last year's fourth year. Remember it was an especially large group (250) and that in the future the school itself will be taking over more and more of the further education.

We can first divide the children into three main groups:-

    1) 83 proceeded to further full time education.

    2) 104 went to jobs which involved some further education either as apprentices, traineeships or in clerical posts.

    3) 38 took employment of a more routine nature.

This makes only 225 – the 25 unaccounted for are those who left the district or went abroad during the year or about whom we have no clear record.

Further Full Time Education

Taking the first group of 83 who continued their full time education we find that 30 joined courses that would lead to G.C.E. Examinations in a wide variety of subjects. 27 stayed on at the school for the one year commercial course or to strengthen their general education. 5 proceeded to private comptometer or commercial school or grammar school and 51 went to the Municipal College to join the following courses:-

9	G.C.E. Professional Courses
7	G.C.E. Commercial Courses
8	G.C.E. Science Courses
10	Pre-Nursing Courses
10	Engineering
8	Building
3	Art School
1	Music and Drama
2	Catering

An analysis of the successes which our old students have had in G.C.E. examinations at the Municipal College shows that they have passed in some 20 different academic subjects at "O" and a few have continued on to take "A" level subjects, either to go into training college or even university. I have tried to make a comparison with national figures for secondary modern schools which attempt G.C.E. and find that this represents a slight improvement for those getting 1-3 passes at "O" level, but although only a few are sufficiently able and persistent to pass five or more subjects, nevertheless this represents five times as many in proportion as the national average (for secondary modern, not grammar schools, of course).

What sort of careers are aimed at by those students who continue their full time education? Here are the intentions of this group:-

34	Office work - including Civil Service, banking, accountancy, Shorthand/Typing, etc.
12	Teaching - 5boys and 6 girls, plus 1 girl who wishes to become a teacher of Speech and Drama.
9	Apprenticeships at Student Level.
6	Building Apprenticeships.
5	Commercial Art.
5	Nursing (excluding cadetships and child nursing).
2	Catering.
2	Merchant Navy.
1	Optician.
1	Photography.
1	Receptionist.

Jobs with Training

The second and largest group of 104 left for jobs which involve further part-time studies and many of which will lead to apprenticeships when they reach the appropriate age – generally 16
.

45	Trade apprenticeships (radio, electrician, carpentry, catering, printing, mechanical trades, horticulture, gas fitting and building) – 24 have reasonable hope of getting craft apprenticeships; 21 will probably get traineeships.
24	Clerical posts in banks, insurance brokers, accountants and other offices.
12	Hairdressing (most of these have hope to get an apprenticeship).
12	The Services (including Merchant Navy and Police).
5	Nursing Cadetships or Child Nursing.
1	Receptionist.

Routine Jobs

The third and remaining group of 38 left to take jobs with no systematic training.

18	Retail trades.
9	Machinists and Needlework trade.
7	Factory work.
2	Stable girls.

FORMER PLAYGROUNDS (1)

"CHICK'S DUMP"

The name "Chick's Dump" was well known a few years ago. It was the old waste piece of ground by the railway bridge in North Shoebury Road. It was always called "Chick's Dump" but I never knew why. There were two buildings there. One was an old brick house with no roof, but we had lots of fun playing around it. The other building was an old empty tin shed which was locked, so we crawled through a small hole in the side and covered it up when we went home. We always enjoyed ourselves looking for things amongst the rubbish and often found worthless treasures.

   As we grew older we stopped going to "Chick's Dump" but it is still remembered by many boys. Unfortunately they have now cleared all the land to make rooms for bungalows.

John Lynch The Tideway 1963

Photograph from school archive.

FORMER PLAYGROUNDS (2)

"FREEZERS"

In 1959 work was started on factories in Shoebury. The clearing of the site was to be a hard job for the workers, not only because of the bad ground but there were gangs of boys who did not want buildings in that area since they thought of it as their own personal playground. The site, formerly a sand-pit, was called "Freezers" by the boys and consisted of about six acres of hills, trees, streams, ditches, ponds and flat ground. The work began with bulldozers clearing the hills, filling in the ditches, and the first foundations were laid.

But it was then that the trouble started. These gangs of boys went to the site and broke up bricks and pipes, also put out of action any machinery they could find. This did not stop until the police were called in.

Now in 1963 there are about eight factories completed and several more under way and by 1965, it is hoped by the managers that everything will be completed. Although the action of the boys is not to be commended, frequently we wish that Shoebury was once more surrounded with fields as it was not so long ago, but we know when we leave school, many of us will be glad of the employment offered by these very same factories.

William Perks 3AE The Tideway 1963

GOLDEN AND SILVER JUBILEES

1964 is the Golden Jubilee year of Southend as a County Borough and at Whitsun it marked the quarter century of the opening of Shoeburyness High School. What a lot has happened during those years! My earliest recollection as a small boy was to travel by tram to Thorpe Bay Corner and then balance on the kerb as I made my way to Shoebury Cottage. One hesitated to walk on the "promenade" as that consisted of fine sand into which the walker would sink and shoes would soon be filled with the stuff. Where the yacht Club slipway now stands was Mason's boathouse and across the road in the car park was a red brick building which housed a lifeboat. Behind this on the cliff stood the Coast Guard Station which was demolished this year.

At this point the road narrowed to a mere cart track which led round what is now Ness Road as far as the Cambridge Hotel. On either side of the track were blackberry and gorse bushes. How easy it was in those days to gather a basket full of fine juicy berries for few people passed that way. My pal Cyril told me his mother, when a girl, used to walk along the sea wall from Shoebury to St. John's School, a little church school built on the sea front near Burdett Road, just by the Kursaal.

As the years passed and I had a bicycle I remember my father and I loading our machines with all the paraphernalia needed for a picnic which we enjoyed in the buttercup field to the east of Shoebury Cottage and it was on one of these occasions that I met my wife-to-be, a pretty young slim lass who came visiting for the day. We decided to settle and took one of the eight houses in St. Andrew's Road, which had been built in the lark field. So the tale went, larks were caught, dyed yellow and sold in Club Row as canaries. Behind our house were haystacks; in front, nothing interrupted our view of the sea and we used to watch fire-work displays on the end of the pier from our bedroom window. Each morning, that summer, we were awakened by the song of larks as they winged their way on high. As the Thorpedene Estate developed the roads were full of holes and ruts and in winter a veritable quagmire.

Nearly following the line of Ulster Avenue was the church path and just to the west of St. Andrew's Church was the huge tumbledown red brick Rectory, with its spacious grounds all overgrown with weeds. This path led to the old part of the Church Road and on the corner of the road and Ness Road were the piggeries, or so we were told, and how they smelt when the weather was hot!

The first school in Shoeburyness was built in the Garrison grounds and later added to from time to time as the population increased and even St Peter's Hall was used as a manual centre. Once Shoebury was absorbed into Southend the local education authority decided to erect a senior school in Caulfield Road and so designed that only a half was built with the intention of erecting a duplicate on the east side of the gymnasium. A second gym was to be built on top of the existing one. Moving-in day followed the Whitsun holidays of 1939. I was appointed to the school in the following September.

After the summer holidays, imagine our consternation when we found the A.R.P. had moved in. The lovely maple floor of the gymnasium had been pulled up and the room turned into a gas decontamination place. All the rooms along the back of the school had holes knocked into the dividing walls and the rooms were intended for First Aid. The Staff Room was the mortuary; un-happily it was used for this purpose. The rear playground was lined with ambulances and official cars. In the playing field were trench dug-outs more of them anon. There was no schooling for several weeks although the staff attended each day. Later plans were made to teach small groups of children in houses. At first only in the mornings but later afternoons were included. In January 1940 I was sent with a Miss Hogsflesh to look after some of our senior children in the village and we were housed temporarily in two rooms in Hinguar Street School. Evacuation came in June and it fell to me to officially close the school.

I did not return to Caulfield Road until after Easter 1942. What fun we had. Assemblies in the front corridor at first but later we acquired the Hall and during Morning Prayers the smell of frying bacon wafted over a screen across the front stage. Despite the fact that we had a large billiard table in the corner we were able to use the Hall for P.T. and Country Dancing. School meals? Brought in a container and partaken in the Science Laboratory (now Room15). Later Mrs Penneck used my office as a kitchen and the annexe as a server for meals in the Hall.

Did you wonder about the dug-outs? They were great fun at first bit gradually they filled with water, so four surface shelters were constructed, two of which still remain for the use of our grounds men. With the advent of "Doodle-bugs" the shelters were of little use as the V1's often came over before the siren went so the children sometimes had to duck under the desks. What other excitement? An unexploded cannon shell was picked up on the football pitch. A suspicious round hole was also seen and barricades were erected with large notices "Danger – Unexploded Bomb". A disposal squad spent hours digging for the missile without success and had to refill the hole. They were rewarded however for the remains of a barrage balloon, which had broken away and was shot up by a Spitfire was sent from Rochford, came to rest near the sweating soldiers.

Alas for the original ideas for extending the school. When numbers grew and more accommodation became necessary all we could have were two HORSA huts – really unused prefabricated hospitals. Later we had more elaborate Hallums huts. Of the future? Mr Mills has a wonderful scheme but it will be some time before the plans come to fruition.

R.L.STRONG

The Tideway July 1965

Death of a Warrior

On Sunday, January 24th, the world learned that the "greatest living Briton" was no more. Sir Winston Leonard Spencer Churchill had died. With him went part of the 20th century and the thanks of the whole free world. For he had done more than any other man in history to ensure the freedom of the individual. When Britain stood alone against Nazi tyranny it was he who rallied the nation, instilled dauntless courage into the people and symbolised their tenacity and ferocity.

Churchill was above all proud of being British. He would rather see the Empire crushed than bear the degradation of defeat. He told the world simply but eloquently, "We shall defend our island, whatever the cost may be, we shall fight on the beaches, we shall fight on the landing grounds, we shall fight in the fields and in the streets, we shall fight in the hills;

we shall never surrender!" Probably this mastery of the English language and his gift of inspiring oratory did more than anything else to make him a great leader who could command the nation's respect. He had "Nothing to offer but blood, toil, tears and sweat" and he gave of these generously and unstintingly.

The Tideway July 1966

Shoeburyness to go Comprehensive

Our junior schools in Southend are already fully comprehensive: children of whatever ability, colour, creed or sex attend a conveniently placed junior school which deals with all needs inside one school...

In Southend, as from 1968, there will be no 11+ selection and junior school children will proceed to one of ten new comprehensive schools to be formed by combining, altering or extending the existing fifteen secondary grammar and modern schools.

Shoeburyness High School is planned to become an eight-form entry co-educational school by extending the present premises, for we are fortunate in having a large site. Whether comprehensive or not, the school must expand anyhow whatever the system, because the building is becoming hopelessly overcrowded. New housing has already forced our western boundary to move from Southend Gas Works to Maplin Way and within the next few years pressure of numbers will increase still further.

There are plans for new and even larger housing estates and the minimum school leaving age is rising to 16 years for those children who enter school in a year's time. As far as Shoebury is concerned, if major rebuilding is necessary in any case, this is obviously the best time to carry out any fundamental reorganisation. The cost of expansion is estimated to be £435,000, building permission has already been asked for, and it is hoped that it will take place between 1968-1970.

Fully comprehension will not be suddenly realised in September 1968: there will be a long interim period of six or seven years, not only for rebuilding and re-equipping, but for a new generation of children to work its way through the newly developing courses and curricula. The final capacity is planned to be 1,200 in the first five compulsory years with a sixth form of about 200. *E.F. Mills*

The Tideway July 1967

The Ten Commandments

1. I am Mr Mills your headmaster, who brought you into this house of bondage.

2. You will not like any teacher better than you like me.

3. You shall not draw funny pictures of me.

4. You shall not laugh at me, for I am free with detentions.

5. You shall not disturb me when I am in my room, for I might be snoozing on the sofa.

6. For five days you will labour and do all your work under the gimlet eyes of my slave drivers.

7. On the Sixth day you will not make your parents do your homework.

8. Honour the teachers and prefects and do not question the punishments inflicted in abundance upon you.

9. You shall not flick ink pellets or rubbers at the teachers.

10. You shall not bellow at the top of your voices when you thunder along the corridors.

If you obey these laws you will end up a prefect, or what is considered perfect by teachers, but by pupils, an unimaginative, unquestioning, degraded little worm.

Stephanie Barrell, 3A1.

The Tideway 1965. "Oh! They're too beautiful to live, much too beautiful". Dickens.
Photo: School Photography Group. Staff include: Mr Mills, Miss Pilcher, Mr Milverton,
Mr Prior, Miss Lark, Mr Quick, Mrs Bacon, Mr Hounsell.

July 1967 Junior Photographer of the Year

Christopher Partridge 3A1 won this national award and received his trophy from the press and television companies (under 15 class). Guests of honour were Captain Ridgewayand Sergeant Blythe who rowed the Atlantic.

Oh To Be In England

One day it was raining. It was very wet, and it was very dull. The sky was black. It was pouring down with rain. Then suddenly I heard thunder and saw lightning. The wind was blowing. The grass was wet. There was rain running down the window.

There were lots of puddles. I felt very sad and dreary and I thought to myself "Summer's here again." *Shaun Rudd* 1A

The Tideway July 1968

Thought for Food

At about 12.25 every day one may see certain members of staff heading at a brisk gallop for the dining room, and by 12.30 a chattering, shoving mob of girls is waiting outside. At one o'clock the mob becomes a horde of boys, all demonstrating what a large part the stomach plays in the lives of one and all.

It is certain that we seldom give a thought to the way the food comes to us, nor to the organisation that provides it. An interview with Mrs Swan, Canteen Supervisor, revealed some facts that few of us are aware of.

Many schools are provided with Meals on Wheels: that is, dinner cooked at a central kitchen and delivered by vans. At Shoebury we have our own kitchens, thereby ensuring hotter and fresher dinners and a certain amount of choice. Mrs Swan plans her meals a month ahead, and tries to ensure a daily balanced diet of proteins, fats and carbo-hydrates. She is allowed a daily budget of 1s. 7d. Per child per dinner, and has to calculate carefully so that this is not exceeded.

School dining room.

She has seven ladies working for her, her and the Cook working from 7.45 a.m. until 3.30p.m. others are part –timers, working from 2 to 4 hours each. Cleanliness in the kitchen is highly important, everything is washed and scrubbed daily. They even wash their hands after sneezing into a handkerchief, and clean clothing and caps for the hair are compulsory.

With the enormous numbers of meals to provide the staff need mechanical help and the Hobart mixer peels, chips, slices, shreds and dices very quickly.

When asked what changes she would like to see, Mrs Swan said that a choice of dishes should be available, and she hopes that this will soon be arranged by the Area Supervisor. She thinks the school is generally well-behaved and helpful, and has settled an age-old argument – girls are definitely more careless with water-jugs than boys!

For those of you who like a few statistics to chew(!) here are some figures concerning our food. We consume:-

10 cwt.	*of potatoes*	*per month*
140 lbs.	*of flour*	*per month*
56. lbs	*of sugar*	*per month*
30 lbs.	*of jam*	*per month*
7 gals.	*of milk*	*per week*
84 lbs.	*of dried milk*	*per week*
1 gal.	*of vinegar*	*per week*
7 lbs.	*of Custard Powder*	*per week*

340 knives and spoons are washed up every day with 680 plates, dishes, forks and 200 glasses.

Next time you start wrapping yourselves around your school dinner, spare a little thought for Mrs. Swan and her hard working Staff!

Shakespeare – End of Afternoon School – Friday

Mr Merlin who led the photography group.

For this relief much thanks.
(Hamlet) The Tideway July 1962

Our pupils at Shoebury Park.

Mr Harold Shaw

September 1st 1973 - August 31 1983

1973

Sep 1st   Harold F. Shaw B.Sc took charge of this school on the retirement of E. Francis Mills B.Sc.

Sept 11th   School Opened 899 on roll.

Assistant Staff. Mrs E. Bacon, Mr J. Barton Hanson, Mr P. Binns, Mrs M. Bright, Mr H. Brownley, Me E. Cooke B.A., Mr B. Coppard, Mr R. Cornish, Miss B. Dalton, Mrs Duval, Miss I. Grover, Mr R. Hamper ACIB, Mrs C. Hardy, Mr D. Horne B.Sc, Mr D. Hounsell BA, Mrs Y. Jones, Mr J. Kempster (Instructor), Miss E. Lark SRN, Mr F. Merlin, Mrs H. Michael, Mrs D. Morrison, Mr W.O Donnell BA, Mr J. Plowman BSc, BA, Mr A. Prior, Mr J. Puddick, MusB, Mr D. Quick, Mr B. Roberts, Mr G. Rye, Mrs C. Sellicks (Instructor), Mr C. Sharpe, Mr P. Sonnen, Mr D.Staveley, Mrs J. Stone, Mr A. Talbott BSc, Econ, Miss J. Tempest, Mr R. Thomas, Mr R. Wakeman Reynolds BA, Mrs T. Walker (Instructor), Rev Mr J.C. Whitney MA, BD, Mrs M. Wright, Mrs B. Yates, Mr N. Zafar, Mr H.R. Jenkins, Mr J. Milverton cookery part time.

1974

Oct 3rd   Meeting of parents of second year pupils protesting about no German in year two. This meeting was at the request of parents.

Oct 31st   Col. Kelly Chairman of Governors visited the school to discuss with the Headmaster, problems arising from the ban on wearing finger rings.

Nov 22nd   Pupils lined the road as funeral of Timothy Campbell (4WR) passed. He was killed in road accident. Headmaster, Deputy Head and 12 boys attended funeral. The Headmaster read the lesson.

Dec 6th   Demonstration at break. Pupils protesting that there was no day's holiday for Christmas Shopping. All finally returned to lessons.

Dec 9th   The H.M. met deputation on Christmas Shopping Holiday.

Dec 10th   Twelve boys and one girl left at break as protest. All suspended until parents bring them back for punishment for truanting.

The Miners Strike began on the 10th February 1974 and they returned to work on the 11th March. The country had been on a 3 day working week since 13th December 1973 and the IRA terrorist campaign on the British mainland was in full sway.

1975

Jan 15th   A number of girls, having previously been warned, were sent home to fetch shoes with heels of 2 inches or less. The protesters reported to local press.

Jan 21st   Headmaster met Editor of Evening Echo concerning recent reports.

Feb 4th   Special Governors Meeting to discuss problem of high heels. Resolution supporting H.M. passed but advised to modify.2

On the 10th February 1975 Margaret Thatcher becomes leader of the Conservative Party.

March 2nd   Informed that NAS members would not teach 3 boys (suspended).

April 11th   Informed by Co. Ed. Office that home tuition would be arranged for two of the boys. Attempt would be made to transfer the other boy to Southchurch Hall High School.

April 23rd   Wednesday League Football Team beat SEEVIC in Div 3 Cup Final.

School librarians in the Mills Resource Centre.

Sept 2nd   School opened. Intruders had caused damage to HM Study, door to Rm 11, Sewing machines, door of projection room. Also losses by theft.
960 on Roll.

Nov 3rd   V1th Form Girls may wear trousers until Easter – 2 did.

Nov 19th   Public Meeting in Drama Hall 8pm on reorganisation of secondary education.

Mr Quick and Miss Lark – School Sports. Miss Lark clearly enjoying the event!

1978

Sept 5th   1094 on roll, including 98 in the Sixth Form.

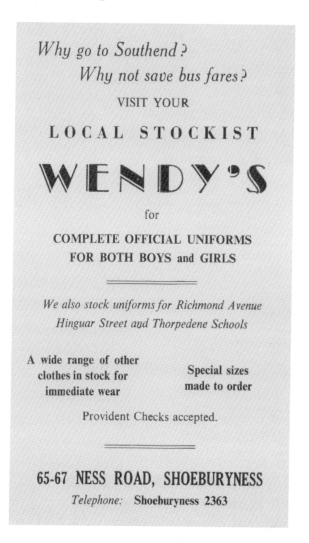

1979

April 27th   Notified by NUT representatives that members are being recommended to withdraw their goodwill and will undertake no voluntary duties or activities.

May 1st   Notified by NAS/UWT representative that members had been instructed to leave after five hours of attendance as from Tuesday 8 May. This means that they will be leaving at 3pm.

School bicycle shed.

**Britain's
Fighting
Lady**

Prime Minister
Margaret Thatcher

*3rd May 1979 General Election - Margaret Thatcher
becomes first female Prime Minister.*

1980

1119 pupils on roll. 7 form entry in all years except 4th.

July 21st   Marriage of Charles Prince of Wales to Lady Diana Spencer.

31st July   Took over all new extensions we are now a fully 7 form entry school.

1981

Sept 8th   School re-opened with 1155 on roll.

7FE up to and including year 4

Yr	1	2	3	4	5	6	7
	212	214	218	210	185	73	43

1982

April 2nd   Falkland War, start of hostilities.

The Royal Navy suffered its first casualties when 22 men were killed on HMS Sheffield when the destroyer was hit by an Exocet missile.

1983

July 22nd   I Harold F. Shaw ceased service on retirement as from 31st August 1983.

Sept 1st   Mr Quick acting deputy for term.

Mrs Bright acting senior teacher for term.

Mr Goodson is full time instructor.

Harold Shaw, Headteacher, Doug Hounsell, Jackie Pentlow Deputies and staff 1983.

Mr Arkell

January 1st 1984 to July 19th 1990

1984

Jan 1st   Kevin Arkell B.Sc. M.Ed. took charge of this school on the retirement of Harold Shaw BSc. Miss J. Pentlow assumed her post as Deputy Head having been Acting Head for the Autumn Term.

Jan 9th   School re-opened with 1159 pupils on roll.

The staffs were as follows:-

Miss B. Dalton, Mrs Y. Jones, Mrs S. Kirby. Miss I. Grover, Mr A. Prior, Mr. R. Thomas, Mr. M. Knight, Miss T. Chipp, Miss E. FitzGerald, Mrs S. Hammond, Miss C. Muir, Mr. J. Puddick, Mr E. Rye, Miss A. Wyllie, Mr R. Crane, Mrs B. Davison, Mrs D. Harley, Mrs I. Linssen. Mr. P. Mason, Miss B. Steward, Mrs J. English, Mr R. Campbell. Mr P. Denenberg, Mr A. Middleton, Mrs W. Owen, Miss M. Seal, Mrs J. Whitehead, Mr H. Williams, Mr J. Barton Hanson, Miss M. Copping, Miss A. Oakman,, Mr A. Patteison, Mr D. Piper, Mr C. Sharpe, Mr S. Smith, Mr T. Hammond, Miss J. Ward, Mrs C. Sellicks, Mrs E. Webster, Mr D. Horne, Mrs P. Stibbards, Miss G. Bainbridge, Mr A. Bareham, Mr P. Binns, Mrs M. Bright, Miss J. Foley, Miss S. Goodman, Mr S. Goodson, Mr D. Hounsell, Mrs J. Marshall, Mrs D. Morrison, Mr W.O'Donnell, Miss J. Pentlow, Mr A. Pomfrett, Mr D. Quick, Mr H. Singh, Mr P. Sonnen, Mr C. Thompson, Miss E. Towers, Mr J. Walker, Miss L. Walker, Miss M. Webber, Miss V. Frost.

Jan 12th   Coming from an area of very high youth unemployment I was agreeably surprised to find a much more hopeful situation existing in the Southend area.

Jan 19th   Mrs D. Morrison went into hospital and is not expected to return until half-term. Mrs M. Bright, the Senior Mistress assumed her responsibility for the First Year until Mrs Morrison returns.

Dilys Morrison.

Feb 3rd   The school is fortunate in having a potential Olympic swimmer, Sarah Hardcastle, as one of its pupils. Mr Hardcastle came to school to discuss the problems Sarah was facing attempting to combine her rigorous swimming schedule with her school work. I agreed to Sarah dropping 3 of her options so as to lessen her load,

April 30th   School re-opened with 1121 on roll.

May 9th   As a result of Industrial Action a number of pupils had to be sent home.

May 24th   As a result of Industrial Action a number of students were excluded for a brief time during the middle of the day.

June 4th   Owing to industrial action no formal meetings can be held during lunchtime or after school.

June 21st   An extremely busy day! Mr Barlow from the British Olympic Committee visited the school at 8.30 am. Mr Brevington and colleague (school architects) came from Chelmsford to look at our accommodation problems. Mr Barton, a photographer from the Daily Mirror visited to take a photograph of Sarah Hardcastle with a few of her fellow pupils – which eventually became the whole school! Fortunately we were able to combine the organisation of this photograph with a Fire Drill. Sports Day occupied in brilliant sunshine the remainder of the day.

Daily Mirror photo of Sarah Hardcastle and fellow pupils.

July 7th   Leon Garfield – author of children's tales visited the English and Drama Departments.

Sep13th   Sarah Hardcastle brought into the First Assembly of term the silver and Bronze medals she had won during the summer holidays at the Los Angeles Olympic Games. At that assembly she presented to the school her attendance medal and certificate. The presentation was covered by the Daily Express.

1984 Los Angeles Olympics Sarah achieved a silver medal in the 400 metres freestyle and a bronze medal in the 800 metres freestyle. The East European swimmer who won gold in the 400 metres was later disqualified for performance enhancing drugs.
Sarah won a World Championship gold medal and two gold medals at the Commonwealth Games along with many other medals.

Nov 11th   I attended the Remembrance Service together with the Head Boy and Girl. I was most impressed by the number of familiar Shoeburyness Comprehensive faces I recognise in the various units marching by, including Army & Air Cadets, Venture Scouts, Girls Brigade etc.

Michelle Stone England School Champion 1984 Intermediate Hurdles.

Nov 12th   The Governors expressed their support for the idea of a Community Sports Hall and asked that a more detailed document supporting it should be presented at the next meeting.

1985

Jan 25th   Interviews took place for the newly created Special Educational Needs post resulting in the appointment of Miss Hunt currently teaching at Laindon School.

March 19th Saturday Superstore – BBC Childrens TV. Programme spent day in school and at Warrior Square swimming pool filming Sarah Hardcastle led our girls swimming team to victory in the Southend Championships.

July 3rd	A very successful (socially & financially) Charity Walk took place from Chalkwell Station along sea front to school. Virtually whole school took part on a warm and sunny day. Raised £2,600 for an off-set litho machine.

Sept 3rd   School Re-opens with 1242 on Roll.

Year1	Year2	Year3	Year4	Year5	Year6
226	239	213	218	217	129

Sept 17th   The school is now becoming increasingly subject to industrial action. The Year Tutors Meeting will probably be the last 'formal' management meeting to take place outside normal school hours until the dispute is settled.

The first computers used in school.

Sept 19th   Owing to children being sent home as part of industrial action, the annual school photograph taking session has had to be postponed.

Oct 15th   The school is now subject to daily action by the NAS/UWT with individual staff taking action as part of an Essex Rota of action!

Oct 17th   Mr Passant – County Inspector for Drama visited the school and because of the excellent work undertaken by Miss Frost agreed to £4000 being spent on a new lighting system.

Touch typing lesson from school archive.

Nov 11th   Mr Christodides, Mathematics Advisory Teacher in school to discuss the school's difficulties in appointing two new Mathematics teachers. He stated that it was a problem throughout the county.

Nov 25th   The current teacher's industrial action is now having a serious effect on the day to day running of the school – teachers not attending courses, Parents Evenings etc.

1986

Feb 28th   Industrial action now means no meetings or out of school activities taking place. Only after delicate negotiations with respect to 'cover' was the annual Geography field trip able to take place.

May 9th   'Secondary Re-organisation of Southend 'letter' sent out to all parents.

June 16th	Public Meeting – Drama Hall over 300 parents attended with County Councillors and pressed for: 1) A fully comprehensive system 2) Retention of the Sixth Form. Considerable debate within Southend since two of the options would mean the closing of at least two of the existing Grammar Schools. All but six of my staff voted in favour of a fully comprehensive 11-18 school.
May 26th	After half term following agreement at National Level the various teachers unions and associations began to work on a 'normal' basis although a problem still exists with respect to no cover action. The school in some form or another has been subject to industrial action for nearly two years.
June 25th	Annual School Walk took place today along the seafront. Raised nearly £3000 towards textbooks, equipment etc.
Sept 2nd	The school re-opened with 1222 pupils on roll and the Headmaster and 68.8 staff.

1987

Jan 6th	Mr Hounsell takes over as First Deputy Head.
Jan 12th	The school unable to be opened because of heavy snowfall (2 foot) Both key holders failed to make their way to school. Public examinations unable to be held.

Jan 13th	The school remained closed except for Public examinations.
Jan 19th	Essex and Kent worst areas hit by snow. Local radio invaluable to keeping parents informed.

Jan 20th   School re-opened for all pupils. Snow still not thawing.

Jan 21st   Thaw now set in. Major leak directly over Boiler Control Panel/Pumping controls – complete breakdown of heating system at 9am! Repaired at 1.30 but school so cold that sent home pupils early at 2.35pm.

April 10th Difficulties in recruiting staff now affect almost all subjects on the curriculum not simply the traditional shortage subjects such as CDT and Mathematics.

June 15th   Site Meeting to discuss development of Library Resource Centre with special reference to Computing.

June 29th   School walk took place on a very sunny day raised nearly £4000 for the school.

Sept 9th   The continuing difficulty in recruiting staff shown by the fact that 10 new staff are in their probationary year. It is now becoming even more difficult to recruit experienced staff mainly due to the high cost of housing in S.E. Essex.

Nov 16th   Hurricane conditions occurred! School lost half the swimming pool roof. Much destruction caused by the 100.2 mph winds in local area although school (except swimming pool) only marginally affected. Only 100 pupils turned up. School closed at lunchtime.

Warrior Square swimming pool showing tree damage.

1988

Jan 15th   Agreed not to replace two staff at the end of current academic year. Falling Rolls only minimally affected School in number of pupils admitted. The main effect can be seen in the continued decline in the number of above average ability children admitted to the school.

This is unlikely to change since the County Council have decided in the light of the New Education Bill to postpone any changes to the 'Southend System' until the national perspective becomes clearer.

One of the proposed changes in the new Bill concerns the ability to 'Opt Out' of the existing system.

School disco!

Feb 1st   Funeral took place of Mrs Wendy Owen, CPVE tutor and member of the Home Economics Department. Her death from a heart attack came as a great shock – church filled to capacity with friends, colleagues, ex-pupils.

Feb 2nd   Mr Day – Friars Community Centre visited to discuss new building developments with Shoeburyness. Southend Council have decided to build medium to high density estates – Essential therefore, that plans are drawn up to provide additional facilities to cope with the additional children generated by these developments plus the rising birth rate in the Primary schools.

Feb 5th   Comic Relief Day – everyone wearing 'Red Noses' nationally for Famine Relief. Lower School PTA – Comic Relief Disco in evening.

Feb 10th   Memorial Service for Wendy Owen held in Baptist Church.

Feb 8th   Special Showing of Government AIDS Video to Governors and Staff.

March 13th The Rt. Hon Ray Hanrahan, Minister for Education, Northern Territories Australia, spent the morning in school talking to pupils and staff involved in a live satellite link with Alice Springs Australia. The visit went extremely well.

March 13th   Architects in school to discuss siting of 2 temporary mobile classrooms. Everyone still positive for permanent accommodation including new Sports Hall!

April 28th   Teddy Taylor MP received cheque on behalf of Shoebury Society for £756.42 which will be used to purchase and plant new trees to replace those lost in the October hurricane.

June 24th   Staffing now a major problem area in S.E. Essex Primary and Secondary Schools. This reflects high cost of living in S.E.Essex especially respect to housing. 19 staff out of 67 have left either for promotion or retirement though since Sept 1987 – three have left teaching! Have managed to replace all but four of these vacancies with good staff – although often only after one or two re-advertisements.

Oct 10th   Mr D. Lewis HMI spent two days looking at how 'Economic Awareness' was taught in the school. He was very impressed with the atmosphere in the school but very concerned about the poor upkeep & maintenance (by the Local Authority) of the buildings.

Oct 15th   Autumn Fayre took place out of doors. Weather good raised over £1000 towards school funds. Aim to buy mini-bus.

Nov 4th   Party of 28 Japanese Teachers and Administrators spent morning in school. Very interested in everything they saw including rehearsal for school production of Oliver. Also very impressed with our use of computers in the classroom. Apparently we are ahead of most Japanese secondary schools!

Nov 28th   The Mayor of Southend Councillor James Hugill spent the morning in school congratulating staff and pupils on the 50th Anniversary of the school.

Dec12th   Mayor, Councillor David Cotgrove, Mrs Day (Family Centre) in school for planting of tree in memory of Andrea Woolley who died in hospital. Mr & Mrs Woolley planted the tree and inspected the memorial plaque and bench which had been paid for by Andrea's fellow fourth year pupils.

1989

April 15th Interviews took place for Deputy Headship (Mr Douglas Hounsell retiring at end of 31 years in school.

1990

March 3rd International Womens Day. Teddy Taylor MP in school – highly successful series of workshops with Year 9 pupils.

July 16th Took my final Assembly all week – stressed main difference between now and Dec 1983 was that ownership of school belonged to pupils and parents as well as staff. Many happy memories.

July 20th School closed for the Summer Holidays. My final day before I hand over to Miss Talmadge (Acting Headteacher) and Mr Mayoh (Acting Headteacher).

Busy day with prospective parents still waiting for any available places which become vacant. Shows confidence in school!! 'The best is yet to come'

Marian Webber and Huw Williams

Steve Goodson, much loved friend, colleague and teacher.

Staff Photograph 1990

Back row from left: *Debbie Strong Bonnie Steward Christine Jan Vander Vierdof Chris Sharp Paul Mason Peter Binns Viv Butterfield Alison Heal Jane Early Kay Ager Liz Bridge Shirley Jackson Pat Thomas.*

Row 5: *Lyn Alison Driscoll Huw Williams Marian Webber Jackie Williams Malcolm Knight Steve Walsh Kirk Sheehan Jeff Goodman Charlie Cyril Steve Leftley.*

Row 4: *Derek Horne Mitch Jackson Pete Bowden Eva Junk Mark Schofield Mike Pettifer Dr Roe Veronica Boetigeg Neil Nick Mavrogodarto David Webster Ann Root Veronica Cornish Sue King*

Row 3: *Ann York Di Cater Sheila Smith Phil Stibbards Jerry Dale Marilyn Seal Anita Halpin Jane Kavendish Kilby Sian Jones Steve Goodson 10Francis Lingard.*

Row 2: *Ty Mckeown Keith Salter Sandy Clarke Jane Sandford Alan Prior Ray Thomas Julie Lenkievicz Lynn Walker Charlie Barton Dave Hill Sandra Addison.*

Row 1: *Pauline Waller Peter Rouse Hugh Malloy Glen Mayoh Kevin Arkell Liz Talmadge Malcolm Finken Tony Reynolds Mary Bright.*

Sept 9th   If the best is yet to come with trenches and pipe work surrounding the school buildings – what is the worst? Last week opening at all seemed unlikely today we are operational.

Sept 10th   Minibus problems – our simple plan to order a new one has been somewhat thwarted by long delivery periods and the offer of a second hand one for £4000. The PTA will support either.

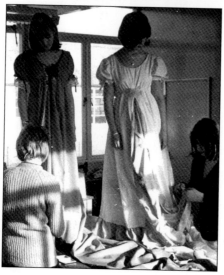 

The Language Laboratory and school productions and our boys!

Sept 14th	Headteacher Interviews – Mr J. Gardiner to take up appointment on 3rd January 1991.
Sept 19th	Minibus saga continues – inspections, advice and indecision arriving from all directions. Still no sign of a new one.
Oct 17th	Presentation of new building programme given.
Oct 29th	Have heard that the minibus is available for collection – what joy – we took delivery!
Nov 8th	11.20 Fire Drill – Minibus was presented to school – Evening Echo present.
Nov 27th	9 staff took Essex C.C. Minibus test – all passed. Dealt with problem relating to drugs – not substantive…no clear guidelines – pupils with conflicting stories. Staff have more information.
Nov 29th	Interviewed parents re: new admissions – our reputation goes from strength to strength – must avoid complacency.

Marilyn Seal.

Mr Gardiner

January 1st 1991 - 31st August 2001

1991

Jan 1st   JKW Gardiner B.Sc. (Eng). Dip. Ed. Took up his appointment as Headteacher.

Jan 7th   The school opened for pupils, 1110 on roll.

The full list of staff is:

JKW Gardiner, Headteacher, Mrs K. Ager, Mr C. Barton, Miss E. Bridge, Mrs N. Benscher, Mr P. Binns, Mr P. Bowden, Mrs M. Bright, Mrs D. Cater, Mr J. Dale, Mr S. Driscoll, Miss J. Earley, Mr M. Fincken, Mrs A. Flynn, Mrs J. Forrester, Mrs S. George, Dr J. Goodman, Mr S. Goodson, Mr D. Hallowell, MrsD. Halpin, Miss A. Healy, Mr D. Hill, Mr D. Horne, Miss S. Jones, Miss E. Junk, Miss F. Kilby, Mr M. Knight, Mr S. Leftley, Mrs J. Lenkiewicz, Mrs I Lingard, Mr P. Mason, Mr N. Mavrogordato, Mr G. Mayoh (Deputy Head) Mr T. McKeown, Mr H. Malloy, Mr N. Pankhurst, Mr A. Pattison, Mr A. Pelling, Mr M. Pettifer, Mr A. Prior, Mr A. Reynolds. Mr K. Salter, Mr M. Schofield, Miss M. Seal, Mr C. Sharpe, Mr K. Sheehan, Mrs S.Smith, Miss B. Steward, Mrs P. Stibbards, Miss D. Strong, Miss E. Talmadge (Deputy Head), Mrs C. Tancock, Mr R. Thomas, Miss A. Vartoukian, Mr J. Van de Weerhof, Miss L. Walker, Mr K. Wall, Mrs P. Waller, Mr S. Walsh, Miss M. Webber, Mr H. Williams, Mrs J. Williams, Mrs A. York, Part-time ; Mrs V. Buttigieg, MrsA. Driscoll, Mrs V. Haywood, Mrs J. Jenkins.

The Persian Gulf War 2nd August 1990 – 28th February 1991

"I was privileged to meet many of our service men and women in the Gulf last week. Their professionalism is outstanding, their confidence impressive, and their courage undoubted. You can be proud of them, very proud. Each one of them has Britain's wholehearted support, and the prayers of all of us for their safe return home. And our prayers are also for you, their families, who carry so much of the burden on Saddam Hussein's war. We are no less proud of you. Goodnight, and God bless."

John Major, Prime Minister.

Jan 25th	The war in the Gulf caused 2or 3 parents to wonder about the Year 7 visit to the Science Museum. We telephoned and Museum staff explained the checks they make. I cannot imagine that a museum full of children would be a target for terrorists.
Feb 1st	A telephoned bomb warning was received during the lunch hour. The school was cleared and the Police attended.
Feb 7th	Snow. Year 7 visit to Science Museum tomorrow postponed. Year 11 Parents Evening also postponed.

February 28th End of Gulf War.

March 19th	Ms M. Hollingworth and Mrs M.E. Jones HMI spent the first of two days examining Equal Opportunities, especially gender and disadvantage (socio economic and special needs).
March 23rd	Work started on the renovation of toilets near the Dining Room, Mr J. Clarke and Mr C. Gee being involved (and I helped for the morning). Also Year 8/9 toilets.
April 15th	Over the weekend a pane of glass was removed from Home Economics and microwave cookers were stolen.
April 17th	Bomb warning telephone at lunchtime, school cleared and Police attended.
May 2nd	A break-in: Art and Music Rooms. Art computer, disc drive and monitor broken. Key board stolen.
May 5th	Another break-in: Several key boards stolen from Music and equipment from Room 40. That room has been alarmed but the alarm is not audible to those in the room.
May 15th	French Exchange: The French Party arrived at 2am after being much delayed by a French Railway strike.
May 21st	Mr Keith Norman, currently at Highlands, Chelmsford was appointed Deputy Head. May 24th French Exchange Party left, expecting a disrupted journey because of a strike on SNCR. Police involved with theft of mail. Exams being informed although we do not believe any exam papers had been stolen. Post Office unable to advice on a suitable replacement post box!

May 27-31   Half Term holiday. A break into Home Economics between Saturday pm to
             Tuesday pm. Apparently nothing was taken.

June 3rd   PC Steward called concerning the theft of mail from post box.

June 11th   Mr Steve Leverett (Principal Area Inspector) and Mrs Janice Layton (Senior
             County Inspector) visited as part of a survey of how schools are coping with
             the demands of IT development in teaching and learning. They were very
             impressed and were able to offer suggestions for further development.

June 27th   Mr Singleton accepted a post as teacher of History.

Sept 4th   First day for School Year &: 223 pupils; Year 12: 85 and growing. The school
             looked very smart with all new pupils and the majority of established pupils in
             the standardised uniform

Sept 5th   Problem with outsiders driving recklessly on school premises. Police called.

Sept 23rd   Break-in over weekend: match footballs stolen. Police involved.

Oct 22nd   An evening meeting at Hinguar Primary. It was mainly concerned with 11+
             selection but I had the opportunity to speak informally to parents. It was again
             good to hear how highly our school is regarded.

1992

Feb 8th   Theft of mail again from post box. There should not have been a Saturday delivery.

April 23rd   Break-in. Police given names of suspects by Caretaker.

April 27th   Start of Summer Term. Another break-in was discovered: theft of Music Dept items from a practice room. The Music Room has been fitted with an alarm following other break-ins. The practice room was entered from the outside.

July 20th   Robert Duggan 10MV died yesterday from an asthma attack.

July 24th   The funeral of Robert Duggan took place today at St. George's.

Sept 11th   Interviewed and appointed Mrs E. Heath: our first non-teaching assistant.

Sept 12th   Mr David Hill, Maths Teacher, died today following a heart attack.

Sept 14th   Brief Staff Meeting at 8.30 to mark with respect David Hill's death. Assemblies for each Year in turn in the Wendy Owen Hall: except Years 12/13 which was in the Baptist Church.

Sept 25th   Afternoon school ended early for Years 8, 9 to enable many teachers and pupil representatives to attend the funeral of Mr David Hill at St. Lawrence's Church, Eastwood.

Sept 29th   School photographs, 8.50pm. Fire discovered in Hut 23. Fire Brigade attended.

Sept 30th   Re-rooming of classes resulting from fire. Visits from Evening Echo photographer, TVS cameraman. I was interviewed on the telephone by BBC Essex. Det. Inspector Frampton (a parent) visited.

Oct 1st   Meeting re sale of surplus land and re-investment of 50% of proceeds towards a plastic pitch or a very basic Sports Hall.

Oct 5th   The Caretaker discovered that an attempt had been made to start a fire in Room 26. Police attended. The room was back in use before the end of the day.

Nov 7th   Final day of the display of Art from schools at the Beecroft. Shoeburyness's extensive contribution was probably the best.

Nov 17th   Discovery of the theft of our Mod. Lang Satellite Dish.

Nov 20th	Learned that 2 pupils, Claire Moore and Angela Hall, had been accepted into the SEE Youth Orchestra.
Nov 26th	Presentation at Porters: Southend in Bloom Competition: the Caretaker's (Colin Glasscock) garden was joint first prize in the Schools section.
Nov 30th	Miss Webber and Mr Williams took Yr 12 students on day trip to Boulogne.
Dec 1st	Year 7 and Year 12 Interim Report Evenings: Many appreciative remarks from parents. Hut 23 back in use.
	Mr Karl Wall, Head of Science, took all assemblies this week in which AIDS Day occurred. His message regarding the risk of infection and how to avoid it was carefully adjusted, day to day, to suit the age and maturity of the pupils to whom he was talking. It was a masterful series of presentations.

1993

Jan 6th	Very positive meeting with Sports Council representatives, Ms Di Spinks, Mr Chris Cutforth, together with other interested parties re Sports Hall. They are considering other locations to support but so far it is very encouraging. We should hear in about two weeks.

Feb 2nd	Confirmation from Cllr. David Cotgrove that the Building Programme will go ahead though with a reduced budget. Only a rubber-stamping to be done. A change of County Council (elections this May) should not have any effect.

March 24th   Great success at the Borough Swimming Gala. Two boys won and the Sarah Hardcastle Shield was retained.

March 29th   Break-in: Music Dept. discovered.   Transport Police spoke to Years 7 and 8.

April 23rd   Headteachers Conference jointly organised by Essex Police/Essex Education re Crime Prevention and Youth Action Groups.

June 23rd   Sixth Form RE Conference, 'Conflict' Among the speakers was Bruce Kent of CND.

July 7th   Our first Awards Evening (for a very long time at least). The awards were presented by Sir Teddy Taylor MA. MP who presented the school with a House of Commons tankard. The event was very successful.

July 20th   Contractors setting up for start of building

July 21st   Borough Planning Committee rejected planning application for part of the field (re Sports Hall).

July 26th   Permission.

Sept 2nd   Site meeting re Building Programme.

Sept 7th	A good start to term despite the building work.
Sept 22nd	A tree planting ceremony was held today. Those attending included county councillor Jim Gordan (Chairman of the Education Committee) who planted the tree with help of Headteacher and Andrew Penrose (Head Boy) and Katy Newman (Head Girl), Sir Teddy Taylor MP who had given much support to the project, Mr Michael Sharpe (CEO) primary heads, friends and other associated with the School and representatives from within the School. The band performed near the CDT before and after planting of the silver birch and the speeches.
Oct 15th	We learned that Mr A.B.Reynolds, Head of Lower School and teacher of Science died in hospital. He has been suffering from motor neurone disease. He leaves a wife and three young sons.
Oct 18th	Special assemblies to tell pupils about Mr Reynolds.
Oct 19th	Termly meeting of the Governors which was preceded by a minutes silence in respect of Mr Reynold's. We had learned earlier in the day, via a site meeting, that the two class rooms and pupil entrance linking blocks on Caulfield Road were to be built.
Oct 21st	The funeral of Mr Reynold's took place today at 10am at the Southend Crematorium. With the full support of the Governors, I decided that the School should be closed for the day as a mark of respect and to allow as many staff as possible to attend. Very many staff, both teachers and non-teachers, were present to pay their respects.
Nov 11th	Weekend visit of Sixth Form Party to First World War battlefields.

Tyne Cot Cemetery. School group
led by Lee Singleton.

Remembrance 2008
Southend Cenotaph.

Nov 14th	Ceremony for Remembrance Day at the Southend Cenotaph.
Dec 13/14	A much acclaimed Carol Service at the Baptist Church. A tape of carols written by Mr Colin Waller, husband of our Head of Music and sung by members of the school choir, went on sale, the profits to go to the Motor Neurone Association in memory of Mr Tony Reynolds who died earlier this term.. His widow, Mrs Zoe Reynolds was at both services.

1994

Jan 20th	Meeting re the management of the Recording Studio.
Jan 28th	Meeting regarding proposed changes to our Admission Arrangements with respect to 'music'.
April 20th	Launch of Computerised Library System.
Dec 14th	Interviewed by Tracey Williams BBC Essex about my concerns for Education if Southend becomes a Unitary Authority.
Dec 15th	The recommendation that Southend becomes a Unitary Authority was announced.

1995

Mr Gardiner and staff 1995

April 27th   The school did well at the Borough Swimming Gala, winning the Sarah Hardcastle Shield for the mixed relay for the 4th consecutive year.

April 28th   Visit to the Alec Hunter School about EARS, Electronic Attendance Register System.

Sept 5th   First day of term for new pupils. Work continues on the installation of a new Admin computer system

The death of Mr Douglas Hounsell, former Deputy Head of the school occurred yesterday. The news caused great sadness in the staffroom.

Doug Hounsell and Mary Bright, Bath.

Sept 11th   Mr Douglas Hounsell's funeral; many staff attended either the Salvation Army Citadel or the Crematorium.

Oct 6th   Many staff and pupils attended the funeral of Kevin Collyer who died of meningitis on 29th September. Kevin, who was extremely popular left school in the summer of 1994. Holy Trinity Church, Southchurch was packed with mourners.

Mrs J. Wolstenholme, Shoeburyness Schools Liaison Social Worker, (a newly created post) visited as did the new Shoeburyness Police Inspector Trevor Chaplin – an old boy of the School.

Oct 20th   Interview for our new Head of Year, Mrs Alison Dominey appointed.

1996

Feb 9th   I R A bomb kills two civilians at Canary Wharf, London.

Feb 28th   Mrs Susan Murphy, Senior Teacher at St Peter's High School, Burnham on Crouch appointed Deputy Head Teacher to replace Mr Glenn Mayoh.

Sue Murphy, Jim Gardiner and Keith Norman

March 5th   Discussion with Inspector Chaplin re 'Drug Policy'.

April 2nd   Informed that the National Lottery bid for Sports Hall funding has been successful: £648,680 the highest award made in Essex to date – according to the Evening Echo which reported it on page 7.

Oct 24th   Prospective Parents Evening: well received by the parents who attended. Regrettably two areas were undermanned because of NAS/UWT members had been instructed not to volunteer. (Only two members responded and one regretted it afterwards).

Nov 11th   A silence was observed by the School at 11am.

1997

Jan 9th   School closed at lunch time because of snowy conditions.

April 7th   A group of Governors and others met to consider a Technical College Initiative Bid. Mr Paul Burton, School Development Adviser made a presentation.

July 3rd   Mrs Bright, Senior Teacher, (Pastoral Manager) was interviewed and promoted to Deputy Headteacher.

Sept 6th   Reunion of 1948 cohort. We went ahead even though it was the day of Princess Diana's funeral.

Sept 7th   Memorial Service at Cliffs Pavilion for Diana, Princess of Wales.

Sept 30th   Meeting of Governors' Curriculum, Staffing and Pupil Welfare, Mrs Sheila Taylor co-opted.

Oct 9th   The TCI (Technology College Initiative) Bid was launched to all pupils/students in the morning and to parents in the evening. The slide presentation which was so effective at the launch at KeyMed was repeated and we are grateful to KeyMed for their support.

Mark Schofield.

Nov 18th   Accepted as affiliated members of the Technology College Trust.

Nov 20th   Drug Education Evening presented by Health Education and Police. Only 20 parents attended a good event.

Nov 26th   PTA Ladies Night. A great success. It will be repeated.

Nov 30th   (Sunday) 5 mile race organised by our Miss Bridge in aid of TCI. 76 men and women took part including 8 teachers including the Headteacher who finished ahead of 3 of his staff! An excellent event which may be repeated.

Dec 20th   Meeting with Mr Philip Miller, Peter Pan's Adventure Island, re TCI sponsorship.

1998

Jan 14th   Headteacher and Governors Stuart Greengrass and Ashley Reynolds to TCI HQ in Whitehall. As a result TCI will allocate £20,000 from unspecified donations if our bid is accepted by the DFEE.

Jan 25th   (Sunday) Visited ASDA to talk to the Store Manager , Mr David Prescott (TCI).

Jan26th   TCI fund raising meal in Hadleigh.

Feb 5th   TCI Public Auction, over £2000 raised.

Feb 9th   TCI Fund Raising Meal at Polash (Bangledeshi) Restaurant in Shoeburyness. Donation and Raffle raised £600 & £130.

Feb 10th   Visit (am) of Mr Roger Walters, Managing Director of the Shoeburyness Company EGL. Mr Walters agreed that the £5000 already offered for TCI could be 'Gift Aided' to give us the tax advantage.

Feb 27th   Official Opening of the Leisure Centre by Sarah Hardcastle.

SPORTS HALL BOOST FOR SHOEBURY

New £1m facility is major asset for school and community

March 2nd   Model of Custer's Last Stand made by Mr Colin Glasscock (Caretaker) in the Library (MRC).

April 1st   Vesting Day for the Unitary Authority.

Sept 4th   First day of term for pupils. 245 in Year 7.

1999

May 12th   A whole school photograph was taken, partly to commemorate 60 years at Caulfield Road.

May 26th   This is a very special day for Shoeburyness County High School and for me (Jim Gardiner, Headteacher) personally. 60 years ago on Friday 26th May 1939, pupils and staff, who until then had been in premises at Hinguar Street, used 'soap boxes on wheels' and other means to move books and equipment to Caulfield Road. It is probable that the constant reference then to the Caulfield Road site gave rise to the unofficial name of the school (still sometimes used) of 'Caulfield School'. It is an interesting coincidence that I was born on the day of the move and so celebrate my 60th birthday today.

For me the day started very well with the morning staff briefing (normally held on Tuesdays and Fridays) being taken over by staff. On my arrival in the Staff Room I was greeted with a fanfare played by members of the staff which turned into 'Happy Birthday' to you! Party poppers popped and so did the corks of bottles of 'Blaquette de Limoux' which I had bought several weeks ago in France and which had been taken by my wife Francoise to school. Francoise and my daughter Rebecca (who had been in our Sixth Form 1993-95) were present and saw me cut the cake that had been made by a Governor Mrs Phyllis Dibden. I was presented with two fine Waterford Crystal 'Toasting Flutes' from their Millennium Collection and other gifts.

Celebration from School archive.

273

The School Walk took place today. Sixth Formers walked from Leigh, Years 8,9,and 10 from Chalkwell and most of Year 7 walked from Chalkwell along the sea front to Gunners Park and then to Hinguar Primary School. Mr Len Stibbards (husband of our former Head of Humanities and father of Mrs K. Phillips, present Head of R.E.) who had helped with the move in 1939 was there. We then walked back to School 're-enacting' the journey made 60 years ago. The Union Flag was flying from the very recently renewed flag pole.

Members of staff Mr Huw Williams, Mr Steve Goodson and Mr Nigel Brunt, together with Governor Mr Graham Davis had worked very hard to transform the Sports Hall ready for the evening concert. They had worked until midnight and then from 5am because we only had one evening's use of it. The Concert was magnificent with past and present pupils taking part as did future pupils from Richmond Avenue, Hinguar and Bournes Green. Among the guests were Mrs Sellicks who had helped in 1939 and Miss Dale, the daughter of Mr Dale the Headteacher whose entry in the log in May 1939 had, in effect, inspired the day. She had made the journey in 1939 though was only a little girl and not a member of the School.

It had been a truly memorable day. In thanking all those who had made the Concert possible I said that Shoeburyness was special, special people making it so. I thanked Huw Williams especially for his work in masterminding the School Walk, Concert, the whole school photograph and other aspects of the 'Sixty Years Here!' celebrations. Mr Williams in an Acting Senior Teacher.

May 28th   Our Year 7 High Achievers group of 20/22 pupils have been doing extension work over and above the normal curriculum in the lunch and other times. Three girls had prepared a time capsule to be unearthed in 60 years time in 2059. They invited the Mayor of Southend, Cllr Tony North of Shoeburyness, to bury it. this was done with due ceremony in Colin's garden (Colin Glasscock, Caretaker) which is to the East of the Library (known as the Mills Resource Centre (Mr Mills, former Headteacher) which was the Hall when the school was opened in 1939. Mr Len Stibbards who had participated on Wednesday 26th May, also helped.

June 11th   Received a telephone call from DFEE that our Technology College Initiative bid had been successful. However, I was told that I should tell no-one until it had been made public on Tuesday 15th June 15th

I was able to tell the staff of our TCI success! After our first bid we had been unsuccessful. I quoted Kipling about Triumph and Disaster and treating these two imposters just the same. This time we did not need to be stoical. We had been successful! Once again corks were popped – at my expense, not the school's.

June 16th   Southend Times took photographs and I was interviewed on BBC Essex Radio.

Nov 10th   After an interview today we shall have as a pupil a girl refugee from Kosovo. (We enrolled an Iranian earlier this term.)

2000

Jan 4th   The School opened on time, repairs and refilling of the hot water system being completed the evening before. More work has to be done before heat can be restored to Science and Technology and T 7 – 10. No Millennium Bug problems

Jan 13th	Sir Teddy Taylor MP visited the School to answer questions put to him by members of the School Council. This event was inspired by UNICEF and was part of 'Put it to your MP' campaign. A very successful occasion.
March 9th	Staff and Governors farewell to Sarah Devereux, Governor since 1988.
May 3rd	School Council's visit to Houses of Parliament, Sir Teddy Taylor being the Host.
Oct 5th	Official Opening of the Technology College by Mr Michael Woodford, Managing Director of Key Med.

2001

Jan 1st	I wrote to the Chairman of Governors, Mr Stuart Greengrass, to inform him of my intention to retire at the end of the academic year i.e. 31st August 2001. (I took up my post at Shoeburyness High School on 1st January 1991).
March 20th	Meeting of the Independent Appeal Panel to consider the case of a Year 11 boy, I had, in line with the Governors' Policy, excluded permanently for possessing and smoking cannabis at break on the School premises. The parents' appeal was not upheld, that being in contrast to the case heard last week concerning a boy from another school.
March 22nd	Discussed with four Year 11 Librarians (Sarah Little, Linzi Tegerdine, Daniella Tullio and Claire Paine) and Mrs Poppy Byford, CDAC Manager, their wish to redecorate the CDAC Office as a leaving present to Mrs Byford. A very fine gesture to which I readily agreed.
	The School and its four feeder schools working together won a Gold Metal at the SE Essex Technology and Arts Competition. The project was based on video conferencing and the making of plastic bookmarks. ICT Technician Dean Curtis was very much involved.
May 10th	Year 11 Football v. FitzWimarc, SE Essex Cup Final. Our Year 11 were not given any chance but drew 3-3. They scored first and were leading with one minute to go. Cup shared; 6 months each. Year 10 Football Team won the Southend Cup, beating St Thomas More 3-0.

July 5th   Awards Evening in the Leisure Centre.

Two new Awards.

- **The Stuart Bright Award** for the Outstanding Sports Person. This was initiated by Mary Bright (Dep.Head) and Tony Bright (Asst Caretaker) in memory of their son, Stuart, a former pupil of this school, who died suddenly last October at the age of 36. The Cup, a clock and a plaque were purchased from a fund set up by Stuart's friends.
- **The Francoise Gardiner Award** for Languages.

Stuart Bright who died suddenly from Cardiomyopathy on 2nd October 2000 shown here on a family holiday in Cuba.

July 12th   Music For A Summer's Evening ' was held in the Sports Hall. Francoise (my wife) and I were taken via the empty Wendy Owen Hall to the concert where the audience were waiting in the dark. As we entered fireworks were let off and the Band started to play. It was a fine concert, the items being interspersed with 'This Is Your Life, Jim Gardiner' and then with items illustrating the School's progress. I was very moved by comments made by my Deputies and the Assistant Headteachers. The pupils presented me with a magnificent watch and a painting. It was a most memorable occasion.

July 13th   A very special INSET breakfast and fizzy wine (which I supplied); some of my presents from staff given.
             The evening reception at Chalkwell was most enjoyable and moving. After being collected by a chauffeur driver Key Med Jaguar we arrived after the guests including my parents and sisters had assembled. We were greeted with a fanfare and 'Congratulations'. The Reception was wonderful, the kindness of people very touching and appreciated and the presents were generous beyond belief. A truly wonderful send off, except school next week!

Aug 31st   My last day as Headteacher. I have found the last 10 and two thirds terms the most satisfying of my professional life. We have achieved a great deal and the School is justifiably highly regarded and in a good position to make further big advances. I wish the staff, pupils and students, and all associated with Shoeburyness High School, including of course the Governors, well, knowing that they will continue to be 'Striving for Excellence'.   *Jim Gardiner.*

Pupils celebrating with Headteacher Jim Gardiner his achievement in gaining Technology College Status and new buildings for the school.

Our boys, School Photography Group.

Appendix 1

Kelly's Directory for South Shoebury 1900 – 1

SOUTH SHOEBURY.

SOUTH SHOEBURY is a parish at the mouth of the Thames, and is the terminal station of the London, Tilbury and Southend railway, 7 miles south-east from Rochford, 5 east from Southend and 45 from London; it is in the South Eastern division of the county, hundred and union of Rochford, Southend petty sessional division and county court district, and in the rural deanery of Canewdon, archdeaconry of Essex and diocese of St. Albans: the parish contains Shoeburyness. A road runs across the Maplin Sand at low water to Foulness Island, and nearly opposite is the Nore light, in about the centre of the estuary of the Thames, which is here 6 miles broad to the Kentish shore. The parish is governed by an Urban District Council of nine members, formed in Dec. 1894, under the provisions of the "Local Government Act, 1894" (56 and 57 Vict. c. 73). The town is lighted by gas and supplied with water from works the property of the Urban Council. The church of St. Andrew, a small and ancient building of stone, formerly a chapel attached to the Cluniac priory of Prittlewell, consists of chancel, nave, south porch and an embattled western tower containing one bell: originally Norman in style, subsequent restorations, including that of the tower, have left it almost wholly Perpendicular: the chancel arch is a well preserved example of 12th century work: there is a leper window and a hagioscope now built up: most of the windows are stained: in the nave is a brass to Dale-Knapping esq. d. 1878: there are 120 sittings. The register dates from the year 1704. The living is a rectory, net yearly value £240, with residence and 5 acres of glebe, in the gift of the Rev. E. A. Causton M.A. rector of Fairstead, Essex, and held since 1900 by the Rev. B. G. Popham M.A. of Corpus Christi college, Cambridge. A Church of England service is also conducted at the National school every Sunday evening. The Wesleyan chapel here, erected in 1893 at the cost of £1,000, is of brick with stone dressings, and will seat 250 persons. In the parish are remains of a camp: there are extensive brick works, where malm bricks of the finest quality are manufactured. The Misses Dale-Knapping, of Blackheath Park, Kent, are ladies of the manor and principal landowners. The soil is sandy loam; subsoil, sand and gravel. The chief crops are barley, potatoes and beans. The area is 1,037 acres of land, 2 of water and 3,424 of foreshore; rateable value, £15,796; the population in 1891 was 2,990, including 988 in the School of Gunnery, Artillery Barracks.

Sexton, John Page.

SHOEBURYNESS is a point of land in this parish to which the London, Tilbury and Southend railway is now extended: here is Her Majesty's School of Gunnery, at which officers and non-commissioned

Gooch Albert George, hair dresser & cycle agent, High street

Gosling R. F. & J. A. drapers, West road, Cambridge town

Green William, grocer, High street

Gregory William, boot maker, Cambridge road

HARRIS & ROWE LIMITED, builders & road contractors, Rampart st. Shoeburyness

Higgleton James, house decorator. 2 Arch cottages, Smith street. Shoeburyness

Hill James, boot maker, High street

Hills Thomas, fruiterer, West road, Cambridge town

Jackson Alfred, shopkeeper, 4 Rampart street, Shoeburyness

Johnstone S. L. (Mrs.), grocer, High street

Kirby Henry, shopkeeper, West rd. Cambridge town

Lancaster Samuel, shopkeeper, Cambridge road

Law James, wardrobe dealer, Cambridge road

Lay William, carman & contractor. High street

Lee Moses, painter, West road

Lewin William, shopkeeper, 8 Rampart street, Shoeburyness

Mann Henry, farmer, Ness road

Moggridge Frank, hair dresser. Cambridge road

Mott George, farmer, Friar's farm, High street

Mulard Auguste, hair dresser, Smith street, Shoeburyness

Murphy Edward, tailor, Smith st. Shoeburyness

Murray William, jun. shopkeeper. Smith street, Shoeburyness

New Eagle Working Men's Club (Joseph Boosey, sec.), Sea View road, Cambridge town

Notley Benjamin, cabinet maker, Sea View road. Cambridge town

Offord George. shopkeeper, 1 Stafford place. High street

Ogden William, shopkeeper, Sea View road, Cambridge town

Pallant George, cab proprietor. 5 Sea View road, Cambridge town

Parkins Ernest, grocer, 6 & 7 Rampart street, Shoeburyness

Pelling George Marshall, grocer. High street

Ponton Wm. Shoeburyness tavern. High street

Prictor Samuel, insurance agent. Ness road

Raper Matthew Henry M.D. registrar of births & deaths for Wakering district, Rochford union; office, Dane street

Read E. J. grocer, Cambridge road

Robinson William, baker, Cambridge road

Rose Albert, draper, High street

Rose Charles, barge builder, Acorn villa, Wakering avenue, Shoeburyness

Self William. butcher, 10 Otthouhu terrace, West road, Cambridge town

Shoeburyness Gas Consumers' Co. Lim. (Jas. Glasscock, manager). Smith street, Shoeburyness

Short James Edward, pork butcher. High street

Small Isaac, grocer, Grove road

Soldiers' Home (Miss M. Shubrick. matron), High street

Spalding Charles, coal merchant, Friars house, High street

Sweeney Jeremiah, shopkeeper, Sea View road, Cambridge town

Talmage Christopher Henry James. plumber & decorator, 2 St. Andrew's road

Tattershall John, draper, Cambridge road

Topsfield Henry, shopkeeper, Cambridge road

Urban District Council WaterWorks (Thomas Gilbert, engineer), Elm road

Walter Ernest William M.R.C.S. Eng., L.R.C.P.Edin. physician & surgeon, & medical officer of health to urban district council & medical officer & public vaccinator. Shoebury district, Rochford union, 1 Roxburgh terrace, High street

Watts Louisa (Mrs.), shopkeeper, 2 Rampart street, Shoeburyness

Webb Frederick Charles, draper, High street

Whent George. cycle agent. grocer. & post office, Sea View road. Cambridge town

Appendix 2

A farmer from an Essex farming family, Dale Knapping accumulated his large fortune from the development of brickworks in South Shoebury, serving the rapid growth of Southend in the middle of the 19th century.

His great-grandfather farmed Shopland, his grandfather (an attorney) farmed Suttons (South Shoebury), and his father farmed South Shoebury Hall. Dale's wife was Margaret (or Mary) Asplin, of Wakering Hall and they had three daughters, Margaret, Edith and Gertrude: all died unmarried. Of them, it was Margaret who became Lady of the Manor at South Shoebury, living for many years at Suttons, the family home overlooking Maplin Sands.

He inherited a lot of land from his ancestors, (although his brother William took on South Shoebury Hall) but sold part of the land known as The Ness to the Government for the development of Shoebury Garrison in 1848.

Dale established a small brickfield as early as 1840 and brought experienced brick makers over from Kent. The arrival of the army increased demand in the area so that by 1862 the number of brick makers had grown substantially. In 1858, Dale bought a section of land from the government to provide access to East Beach. Production of the bricks was located below the coastguard station and thence along Elm Road. Sailing barges carried bricks away not destined for local construction, but many were used in the district. A larger brickfield was opened nearby ten years after Knapping's death, using new chain driven machinery.

Not only a Justice of the Peace, he also took on the responsibility for the first formal education in the parish in 1863. He built the first local school in Dane Street, although by 1886 a further school was needed and built in Hinguar Street. The school meant that local children no longer had to travel to Wakering, and gave instruction to 200 children with its Sunday Evening service.

The range of facilities he offered to his employees was much later offered by the state, and he was renowned as a benevolent employer. For example, he organised a working men's club for his employees in Dane Street, one of several streets established during his lifetime, along with the High Street and others.

More quirkily, Dale provided a long term home for a local character, Mr Cundy (known as Mr Punch) and his dog – an upturned ketch on East Beach that Dale had bought in originally to store boat tackle and equipment. Mr Punch once swam in chains from Gravesend to Tilbury for a bet.

Photograph of the ketch.

Dale Knapping died in Paris following a heart attack.

The body was brought back to St. Andrew's Church, South Shoebury, and a plaque was affixed to the North wall in his memory. Mary, his wife and her unmarried daughters inherited his fortune and his property.

*Mr Cundy or
Mr Punch.*

Appendix 3

Danish and Viking Invasions

Information provided by Andrew Cook former Hinguar pupil.

Vikings began arriving on the Essex coast from 790 AD. The Danes attacked Sheppey across the Thames Estuary from Shoebury in 835 AD and continued to raid the south and east coasts of England.

Danish camps were built at Shoeburyness, Benfleet and Foulness. In AD 884 the Danish warlord Haesten fought against Alfred the Great's Saxon forces at the Battle of Benfleet. This event is recorded in the Anglo-Saxon Chronicle. Defeated by Alfred the Danes fled to their camp at Shoebury and built defensive ditches and re-fortified the Iron Age rampart. Legend states that Ingvar one of the Danish leaders, on hearing the news that his father had died at Shoebury, sat down and gnawed his fingers to the bone with grief. That site is named after him: Hinguar Street. Dane Street and Rampart Street also recall the Viking presence in the area.

Stenton's Anglo-Saxon England refers to Ingware. Ivar the Boneless is also called Yngvarr and Ynguaar in other texts and in the Ulster Annals. These variations are mainly due to linguistic differences between chroniclers, or mistakes from copied manuscripts. If this is a link to Ingvar, which seems likely, then Hinguar Street was named after one of the most ruthless and bloodthirsty Vikings in history. The two leaders who martyred St Edmund are named as Ingware and Ubba. Ingware had the 'blood eagle' carved on the back of King Aelle of Northumbria before subjugating most of Britain and Ireland.

Appendix 4

Roll of Honour – Essex – Great Wakering
Lest We Forget - *Sidney Morris Smith*

Private 14100 11th Battalion, Essex Regiment. Killed in action 26th September 1915 in France and Flanders. Born and resident in Great Wakering, enlisted Southend-on-Sea.

Private Smith was the son of Mr and Mrs Smith of 5, Shoebury Road, Great Wakering and he enlisted at Southend in August 1914. He was reported missing after Loos, and was subsequently presumed to have been killed at Hulloch on the 26th or 27th September 1915 aged 24. He had the following poem published in the Southend Standard three days after he was killed.

Twas early in September
I saw it, by the way
"Your King and Country need you,
Enlist my lad today"
I thought the matter over
A soldier I would be
And help across the water
To keep old England free.

So off I went to Southend
A pleasant town nearby,
I saw the colour sergeant
And told him I would try,
I went before the doctor,
And – Well you know the rest
He put me on the scales mate,
And measured round my chest.

Ah well! A year's gone by,
Things are changed with you and me,
But still I am busy fighting
Somewhere far across the sea.
So "Land of Hope and Glory",
For ever we will sing
May God give England Victory?
And save our gracious King.

The following letter was sent to the Southend Standard by Private W.F.Letton, H.Q.Section, 11th Essex Regiment, and was withheld by the paper until Private Smith's family had been officially notified that he was missing.

"I have read with interest the few verses in your issue of the Standard of September 30th, by Private S.M.Smith, of the Essex Regiment. Being one of our signallers, and knowing him so well as I do, I think it is only fair to tell you that we have had the misfortune to lose him. We went into action on Saturday evening last, and on Saturday had a share in one of the greatest battles in the war. When the roll was called on Tuesday he was found to be missing, and, therefore we cannot really say what happened. He may have been wounded and taken to hospital, and if this is so it will be a little consolation to us. He is missed very much by the signallers of the 11th Essex Regiment."

His brother Daniel was killed at Gallipoli on 10th June 1915 and his mother had two other sons on active, one in France and one in Salonika and three sons in law as well.

Information kindly received from Andy Pay and Martin Edwards, Essex Great Wakering Roll of Honour.

286

Appendix 5

June 13th Raid over Shoeburyness and 13 June 1917 Daylight Raid.

Target: London
Enemy forces: 20 German Gothas, 18 attacked
Results: 162 killed, 432 injured, £129,498 damage.
Defence sorties: 94.

Of the 20 Goths that took off, two turned back with engine failure. As they continued on course to London, two unloaded their bombs over Shoeburyness. One plane went on to bomb Victoria docks in London, the remaining fourteen, flew on in a diamond formation to bomb Liverpool Street Station, the East End docks and warehouses. 128 bombs were dropped; one hitting a school in Poplar killed 16 children.

The Royal Flying Corp home defence squadrons had made several attempts to intercept and stop the attack and British pilots met groups of 7, 4 and 2 aircraft over Essex. There were sightings at Southend and Rochford but only 3 pilots got anywhere near the formation before the bombing started.

Two Sopwith Pups operating independently were closest to achieving success. Frederick Fox from RNAS Grain saw the Gothas over Southend and dived on one of the rear aircraft firing a drum Lewis at close quarters. Three aircraft returned fire, he was forced to descend and after his gun jammed when he gave chase. He broke off 25 miles from Foulness.

The other 'Pup' was flown by James McCudden, who was one of the greatest air aces of the First World War. McCudden was able to achieve sufficient altitude to to engage the enemy as when he had reached 15,000

Mc Cudden's SE5a.

James McCudden in Royal Flying Corp Uniform.

feet he saw the Gothas over Shoeburyness. It took him 15 minutes to position 500 feet below the enemy aircraft and he then fired off three drums. Having insufficient ammunition, he was unable to make any significant impact.

James McCudden was awarded: The Victoria Cross

Distinguished Service Order and Bar

Military Cross and Bar

Military Medal

Croix de Guerre (France)

The citation on his Victoria Cross stated:

For most conspicuous bravery, exceptional perseverance, and a very high devotion to duty. Captain McCudden has at the present time accounted for 54 enemy aeroplanes. Of these 42 have been destroyed....

McCudden's story is all the more remarkable because he rose through the RFC ranks from Air Mechanic to Major and at his death had amased 57 victories. He died on the 9 July 1918, aged 23, en route to take up the command of No.60 Squadron in Northern France. His brothers who were both pilots also died during the First World War, Willie was killed in 1915 and Jack in 1918.

His grave has the line "Fly into the sun dear boy.."

Select Bibliography

Benton, P. The History of the Rochford Hundred, updated by Jerram-Burrows, L.

South Shoebury (1978) North Shoebury (1981)

Cole C. & E.F Cheasman The Air Defence of Britain 1914 – 1918 (1984)

Crowe K. Zeppelins over Southend (2008)

Education Committee Essex (1914-1974)

Echo Newspapers The Way we were 111 (1992)

Gordon D. People Who Mattered in Southend and Beyond (2006)

Hey D. (Editor) The Oxford Companion to Family and Local History (2008)

Hill. T. Guns and Gunners at Shoeburyness (1999)

Hinguar and Shoeburyness Log Books (1898 -2000)

Kelly's Directory South Shoebury (1900-1901)

King T. & Furbank K. The Southend Story 1892 -1992 (1991)

Orford, M. The Shoebury Story (2000)

Stibbards,P. The Listed Buildings of the Shoebury Area (1988)

The Tideway Shoeburyness High School Journal

Williams J. Shoeburyness A History (2006)

Willmott F.G. Bricks and Brickies (1972)

Wiseman G. History of the Wakering and Barling Barges (2005)

Index

References that relate to illustrations only are given in **bold.**